My My!

My My!

ABBA Through the Ages

Giles Smith

GALLERY BOOKS UK

First published in Great Britain by Gallery Books,
an imprint of Simon & Schuster UK Ltd, 2024

1 3 5 7 9 10 8 6 4 2

Simon & Schuster UK Ltd
1st Floor
222 Gray's Inn Road
London WC1X 8HB

Simon & Schuster: Celebrating 100 Years of Publishing in 2024

www.simonandschuster.co.uk
www.simonandschuster.com.au
www.simonandschuster.co.in

Simon & Schuster Australia, Sydney
Simon & Schuster India, New Delhi

A CIP catalogue record for this book is available from the British Library

Hardback ISBN: 978-1-3985-2970-0
Trade Paperback ISBN: 978-1-3985-2971-7
eBook ISBN: 978-1-3985-2972-4

Typeset in Bembo Std by
Palimpsest Book Production Limited, Falkirk, Stirlingshire

Printed and Bound in the UK
using 100% Renewable Electricity at CPI Group (UK) Ltd

For Simon and Jem

'I would still like to know why we had the success we did with ABBA. But I have no idea. I mean, we wrote good songs, we made good recordings and the girls are great singers. That's not the reason for it. There is something else which can't be defined which has nothing to do with us in a way.'

Benny Andersson of ABBA

INTRODUCTION

These days we are (very many of us) entirely comfortable with ABBA's ubiquity, their presence in the air we breathe. I pluck this randomly from my own experience: in the summer of 2023, wandering around a market in France, I heard a stallholder break briefly into song while looking for change for a customer. 'Money, money, money!' he sang. Then I went along the road and had coffee in a café where 'Knowing Me, Knowing You' came on. Driving back to where we were staying, I stopped in at a supermarket and dropped food into a trolley to a backdrop of 'Take a Chance on Me'.

Three casual encounters with the music of ABBA in the space of about ninety minutes, then. Just occasionally, as you move around Europe at this point in history, you can be forgiven for concluding that it's ABBA's world and we only live in it.

What gets harder to remember is that it hasn't always been this way. It would possibly surprise many of the people happily thronging the ABBA Voyage show in London, unselfconsciously browsing among the ABBA sweatshirts and ABBA key fobs and ABBA tea trays in the arena's store, to hear that a love for ABBA was ever a love that dared not speak its name, or certainly not among thirteen-year-olds in a school playground. But as we'll see, this author – with his carefully concealed copy of the 1975 album, *ABBA*, on pre-recorded cassette – can personally attest to that.

The fact is, for a long time it seemed that where ABBA had come from – both in the sense of Sweden and of the 1974 Eurovision Song Contest, where they first came to prominence – had placed a tight restriction on what the band and their music could ever be or mean to people. Almost three years after they sang 'Waterloo' in Brighton, a review in the *Guardian* of a rare ABBA live performance in London could describe them wanly as 'four Euro-persons' who made 'elegant Eurorock pop', and could remark by way of conclusion that it was 'nice to be able to put four faces to a pleasant sound'. There is, of course, no term in the critical lexicon more damning than 'pleasant'. As for the term 'Euro' – as in 'Euro-persons' and 'Eurorock' – it too comes up again and again in writing about ABBA in this period and is rarely meant positively either.

Two years after that, in 1979, the American rock critic Robert Christgau, writing in the *Village Voice*, didn't even try to gild it: 'We have met the enemy,' he wrote, after experiencing ABBA in concert, 'and they are them.' That same year, back in Britain, a reviewer in the *Guardian* would dismiss ABBA as the manufacturers of 'disposable pop songs', another frequent accusation. And one sees why the claim arises, although (with the benefit of hindsight) it's a funny kind of disposable that sticks around for half a century and lands its creators with a museum dedicated to them in their home city.

As ABBA tried to make their way in the world, it rapidly emerged that the Eurovision Song Contest was a unique kind of springboard that could also function as a trap. Blasted high off that Brighton stage, ABBA would look around for months and years afterwards and discover that somehow all the scenery had tiresomely come with them and was threatening to drag them down again.

So: a Swedish act, a Eurovision act . . . ABBA and their defenders would be a long time struggling to answer the band's repeated arraignment on these twin charges, both of which, of course, had the disadvantage from the defence's point of view of being completely undeniable.

'Personally, I hate what they stand for,' a critic wrote in 1979, 'and think they are brilliant.' Here at least was evidence of a thaw. But it was also evidence that even defenders of ABBA would for a while have to tie themselves in knots of equivocation. *So great . . . and yet so cheesy. This ought not to be working for me . . . and yet it so clearly is.* Even their most fervent admirers would find themselves acknowledging sometimes that there was something confounding about ABBA, something that was just beyond the grasp.

And then there was their manifest success, which was a whole other problem for critics to deal with. 'Calculatingly commercial' was the frequent accusation here, and it was made with a special vigour and persistence by critics in Sweden where the 'biggest export after Volvo' line could often seem to contain traces of high-minded disgust. But 'commercial' is, of course, a complaint that can only be attached with the benefit of hindsight, because you can't make this claim of a commercially *un*successful band. And it ignores the fact that ABBA's success – the shape of it, the scale of it, the duration of it – was frequently a surprise for ABBA, too; that, with pop success, calculations are not as readily possible as people like to think;

that, ultimately, even ABBA could only do what they did and then wait and see what happened to it. And what happened to it was down to us, the listening public. This means the band subsequently knew the sensation – exhilarating, no doubt, but also, surely, at times alarming – of unleashing forces that they could not completely control.

And prime among those uncontrollable forces? Well, that was us, too. We'll have a lot to answer for, in relation to ABBA, in the following pages.

At the same time, as deeply part of our lives as the band can be, their presence has often seemed to come with a certain amount of detachment as part of the package – with something remote, something even possibly a little chilly. And people who are not Swedish are apt to attribute that remoteness to ABBA's 'Swedishness' – by which they tend to mean that they detect something undemonstrative and dispassionate about the band and their music, which they then assume to be present by dint of the national character. But that all sounds suspiciously swift and simple, as well as presumptuous, and maybe that whole area might merit a slightly harder look. Like so much about ABBA, in fact.

ABBA are (the chances of this are, I suspect, very high) the band you know best that you barely know. Of course, there are ABBA fans and superfans whose commitment to the study of Agnetha, Björn, Benny and Frida in all their manifestations is both clarifying and humbling – and, indeed, I spent a very nice weekend with some of them in Stockholm not long ago, which I'll be writing about later in these pages. But in the slightly less specialised and more ad hoc place where ABBA intersect with the general listener (the place where I consider the main action to be, ABBA-wise, and certainly the place I'm most interested in for the purposes of this book), it's clear that a certain amount of cloudiness about the band can frequently persist.

Somewhat distant even at the blazing height of their fame, the band were only fully and openly embraced by the world some years after they had, to all intents and purposes, ceased to exist. Consequently, today, familiarity with ABBA's music outstrips familiarity with anything else about them. The band's members are, by any definition of the term, superstars, yet in 2024, even in circles where ABBA are prized and adored, a confident and unerring ability to know your Benny from your Björn – or even, in some cases, your Agnetha from your Anni-Frid – betokens ABBA-knowledge at practically PhD levels. We know, perhaps, that they were two couples (Björn and Agnetha, was it? Benny and Anni-Frid?) whose marriages came apart yet who somehow (is this right?) kept the band on the road even after that, heroically channelling the pain of separation in timeless songs such as 'The Winner Takes It All' and 'Knowing Me, Knowing You'. But Björn wrote the lyric for the second of those songs two years before he separated from Agnetha and when they were together, seemingly happy and enjoying the arrival of their second child. And Benny and Frida didn't get married until after Björn and Agnetha had decided to split up, so . . .

The truth is, we don't know much, and most of what we do know is wrong or improvised or conjecture or (most frequently of all) projection. Glory in its fullest form came to ABBA posthumously, when they had stepped down from the stage and out of the studio, and so, with a purity which is rare in the history of pop – and practically impossible in the social media age – Agnetha, Björn, Benny and Frida burn most brightly in our minds as a set of seemingly bombproof songs which a very large number of us appear tirelessly happy to hear. The songs, we do know.

But *how* do we know them? To all intents and purposes, ABBA finished being a band in 1982 – forty-two years ago. They had more or less eight years of creative life together as recording and performing artists – about the same as The Beatles. Then, albeit without ever making an official announcement that they were done, they withdrew, apparently exhausted or wrung out to some extent, and tired of each other's company, and moved on to other things – solo albums in the case of Agnetha and Frida, the composition of musicals in the case of Björn and Benny. At that point, ABBA were widely felt to have outlived their purpose and, more than that, were regarded in many quarters as irredeemably naff. There is no image of the members of the band on the front of the sleeve of *ABBA Gold* – the nineteen-song compilation album put together by the Polydor label in 1992, eleven years after the band's last set of studio recordings – because the album was carefully market-researched in advance of its release, and the feedback from the focus groups was that although people were potentially interested in buying a record of ABBA's hits, and more than happy and able to nominate the songs they wouldn't mind hearing on it – 'Take a Chance on Me', 'The Name of the Game', 'Super Trouper' – they didn't especially want to own something with the band's faces prominently displayed on it. So the record company went with simple gold lettering on a black background. Such were the feelings around ABBA in 1992.

Yet it was *ABBA Gold* which began to change the climate around the band, ushering in what we can now regard as ABBA's renaissance period, helped along, somewhat randomly, by two Australian movies which featured their songs – *The Adventures of Priscilla, Queen of the Desert* and *Muriel's Wedding*, both released in 1994 – and in due course by the 1999 jukebox musical *Mamma Mia!* and, in 2008, the first of the two films that arose from it. At that juncture, a decade into the twenty-first century, ABBA, once presumed dead and buried, were arguably more alive than they had ever been. *ABBA Gold* has now sold more than 32 million copies worldwide and is behind only Queen's *Greatest Hits* as the UK's best-selling record of all time.

And then, as 2021 ended, almost out of nowhere, the band re-emerged among us – not just with one final, completely unexpected and time-defying burst of new music, but in the form of the magnetically engaging and mysteriously moving *Voyage* stage show, which was nothing less than a complete re-imagining of the live concert experience and which revealed the band as a set of idealised, computer-generated versions of themselves which were somehow at once entirely them and not them at all.

At this point, approaching forty-two years since their last formally ticketed concert and with the band now well into their seventies and apparently entirely indifferent to the idea of performing together in the flesh, ABBA had probably never been more prominent – and had arguably never been more ABBA.

'I've been reading you all my life,' a gushing fan once told the author Samuel Beckett.

'You must be very tired,' Beckett replied.

Well, here I am, a full half-century after 'Waterloo', and in a position to say much the same to the members of ABBA, were I ever to meet them, which (I should probably mention at this point) I never have.

'I've been hearing you all my life,' I could say, 'or for nearly all of it that I can remember. And no, actually, before you ask, I'm not tired. Or not of ABBA, anyway.'

Because what would it even mean, in 2024, to say you were tired of ABBA, except by way of admitting that you had run out of patience with pop music altogether, or that pop music had run out of patience with you?

And I could hardly be said to be alone in feeling this way. The critical tide turned and even Clive James in the end recanted. James, as we shall see, was one of the first to dismiss ABBA, labelling them 'incurably negligible' on the dynamic but slim evidence of that Eurovision appearance in 1974. In 2013, however, he reviewed a documentary about the band and expressed regret about having been quite so quick off the blocks. Apparently, having a daughter who had listened to their music ceaselessly in the meantime had altered James's view.

'The intensity with which millions of people enjoyed ABBA's music was hard to argue with,' James wrote, and whatever ABBA had or hadn't worn while delivering it was, he had realised with the passing of time, irrelevant.

'What mattered was the four voices, and how they blended, generating melodies and harmonies which, on the records, filled every hole in the mix. You could dance to them forever,' James concluded.

I don't think that's right, about the voices filling 'every hole in the mix'. I'm not sure what a record in which the voices filled every hole would sound like, in fact. And it makes me wonder how closely James had actually listened to ABBA in the process of reaching his change of heart. But, then, why would he have felt he needed to? It's surely one of the magical qualities of pop music that many of its most fervent adopters don't listen to it terribly closely nor feel they have to. Pop frequently communicates with the heart before it talks to the head, and sometimes it doesn't get round to talking to the head at all. Writing about pop music doesn't mention this nearly often enough.

What's certainly true is that, over the fifty years since 'Waterloo', ABBA have been liked by pretty much every kind of person and in pretty much every way that it's possible to like a pop group. They've been screamed at by lovesick teenagers and smiled upon fondly by Clive James at seventy-four. They have been consumed in a hurry as sugary pop stars and appreciated soberly as abiding musical craftspeople of exceptional talent. They have been enjoyed ironically and enjoyed entirely sincerely. They have been a guilty pleasure and an utterly unashamed one. Their records have managed to define whole periods and to slip free of history altogether, with the result that, in 2024, their songs are warmly familiar to both '70s *nostalgistes*, hungry to revisit their childhoods, and people who weren't even born when the twentieth century ended. They have been feted alike as exuberant gay icons and as the reliable providers of pan-generational dance music for heterosexual wedding receptions. Their music knows the unequivocal love of the very best among us, and yet has also been used to soundtrack lockdown-busting piss-ups in Downing Street (the notorious 'ABBA party' of 13 November 2020, about which Benny Andersson said, with an understandable instinct for dissociation, 'You can't call it an ABBA party. It's a Johnson party').

They have been paid heartfelt homage by acts as diverse as U2, Dionne Warwick and the Foo Fighters, and strip-mined for comedy purposes by French and Saunders ('C'est La Vie'), Rowan Atkinson's *Not the Nine O'Clock News* team ('Super Dupa') and

Alan Partridge (a-ha!), who loves ABBA so much he named his only son Fernando. ABBA's music is one of very few bonds directly connecting the late Sid Vicious of the Sex Pistols, who once rushed across an airport to meet the band, with the late Queen Elizabeth II, who apparently told someone that she especially liked 'Dancing Queen' because 'I am the Queen and I like to dance'. And they are the only winners of the Eurovision Song Contest who have ever been inducted into the Rock & Roll Hall of Fame, which happened in 2010 and would have been unthinkable – directly contradictory, in fact – during the time that ABBA were actually making the records that earned them that accolade. In this wildly elastic range, they outperform even The Beatles. Certainly, it is given to vanishingly few groups to have been so many things to so many people at so many different times. It is given to even fewer to have been so many things to so many people while the group's members simply sat in their various houses for four decades doing nothing (or, at least, nothing ABBA-related).

And that, surely, is the most delicious detail in the deeply satisfying narrative of ABBA's eventual widespread vindication. All of the things for which they were routinely teased and dismissed along the way (their dress sense, their dancing, their accents, their seemingly unavoidable *Swedishness*) eventually turned into things for which they could be uncomplicatedly celebrated and loved, if you were of a mind to. Yet this complete transformation of their cultural standing happened through no effort of their own, in the long years of their absence when only the recorded music was out there to speak for them and agitate on their behalf. All Björn, Benny, Agnetha and Frida had to do in order to be fully and resoundingly appreciated was . . . nothing. They just had to stand by until the rest of us came around.

It occurs to me, then, that the story of ABBA and their abiding hold on the world is a unique place from which to try to answer questions about the nature of hit pop songs and the nature of pop stardom as time goes by. Maybe if we take a good look at our interactions with ABBA through the ages – at how they variously came in and out of our lives, how our relationship began and grew, waxed and waned, blew hot and cold and finally hot again – and all in the spirit of honestly trying to work out *just what the hell was going on there*, we may reasonably arrive at some truths that hold good for our inter-actions with all of pop music, and not just ABBA's.

And as an obvious extension of that, it also occurs to me that if you want to approach the mysteries of the universal pop song – what it's made of, how it gets built, how it works its magic and, perhaps above all, why we clasp such songs to ourselves as hard as we do – then the ABBA catalogue is not just a good point to set out from. It may actually be the best one that we have.

Only one way to find out, though. I bought a vinyl copy of *ABBA Gold* (gold-coloured vinyl, natch). I rummaged in various boxes for old ABBA singles and cassettes. I scanned the horizon for potentially enlightening ABBA-related events. I took some history books from the shelf and opened YouTube.

And then I drew a deep breath and journeyed out into the ABBAsphere.

1

The history book on the shelf

It's Britain at the dawn of 1974, and things aren't looking that great. Energy prices are through the roof. Strikes abound. Production is in decline and people are getting battered by galloping inflation and a soaring cost of living. The governing Conservative Party is badly split over trading arrangements with our closest neighbours in Europe, politicians on the far right are enjoying disproportionate levels of media attention, and the country will be asked to vote in two general elections in this single year – a level of political instability unknown in this country since 1910.

Yeah, I know – just imagine.

Plus, the forecast is for extreme weather events: storms and floods, tornadoes even – twenty-one of them are set to twirl across southern England on the night of 10–11 March alone. With the Labour Shadow Chancellor of the Exchequer Denis Healey predicting 'an economic apocalypse', and the *Spectator* magazine going so far as to wonder whether a military coup might be on the cards (and even, perhaps, desirable), embattled Prime Minister Edward Heath declares a fuel-saving 'Three-Day Work Order' from New Year's Day, restricting industry to three days per week – kind of 'working from home', but without the work. The Order will stay in place until 7 March.

Meanwhile, on billboards and in leaflets, an 'SOS' campaign is urging people to 'Switch Off Something', there are time-tabled power cuts, and the national speed limit has been lowered from 70mph to 50mph to conserve petrol.

Amid this general slide backwards, a feeling is spreading that Britain in general, and England in particular, can't do anything properly any more – apart, possibly, from football hooliganism, which is about to enter a particularly busy period. So is the Irish Republican Army, whose mainland bombing campaign will, in the coming months, produce explosions at Westminster Hall, the Tower of London, pubs in Guildford, Woolwich and Birmingham, and on a coach on the M62. In spring's London council elections, the National Front will have its strongest-ever showing, winning more than 10 per cent of the vote in some especially disaffected areas, and in March, a mentally unstable man driving a white Ford Escort will narrowly fail to snatch Princess Anne from her chauffeur-driven limousine at gunpoint after, somehow symbolically, the royal protection officer's auto-matic weapon jams.

If the fabric of society holds, the coming summer will at least offer the potential diversion of a football World Cup in West Germany – but not for England, who have failed to qualify. Meanwhile, as winter turns to spring, Terry Jacks, from Winnipeg in Canada, will have a number one hit record with 'Seasons in the Sun', a song about someone dying, knocking off the top spot Nottingham's Paper Lace and 'Billy Don't be a Hero', a song about someone else dying.

It's not all doom and gloom, though. In May, Manchester

United will be relegated from English football's First Division for the first time since 1938.

And on Saturday 6 April, in Brighton and live on television throughout Europe, the United Kingdom will host the 19th Eurovision Song Contest.

2

Atkinson's Folly

The four members of ABBA fly from Stockholm to London on the Monday before the competition, landing at Heathrow Airport entirely unremarked by the British public – the last time in their lives they will be able to do this. They are met by a chaperone from the publicity department of Epic Records, who accompanies them into the city for a short round of press interviews. The previous autumn, ABBA had signed a contract with Epic for the exclusive release of their records in the UK – a deal struck by Paul Atkinson, formerly a guitarist with The Zombies but latterly an executive in Epic's A&R department. Ignoring the raised eyebrows of his colleagues, Atkinson decided to back ABBA to the tune of £1,000 (roughly £10,500 in 2024 terms) on the strength of a brightly burnished pop song called 'Ring Ring', which had been a number one hit in Sweden. But the single had flopped in Britain, selling only around 5,000 copies and coming nowhere near the charts. Consequently, as they arrive in London on this overcast and drizzly Monday, ABBA are mockingly known around the Epic offices as 'Atkinson's Folly'.

Atkinson's Folly spend that night in London and, the following day, travel south by car, checking into the Grand

Hotel on the seafront in Brighton. Then they begin to get ready for Saturday night's competition, which will be broadcast from the Brighton Dome. There, appearing eighth on a roster of seventeen, they will represent Sweden with a song called 'Waterloo' and, in precisely two minutes and forty-six seconds, change pretty much everything about their lives forever.

If the sense of four people on an imminent date with musical and cultural destiny didn't noticeably linger over the members of ABBA that week in Brighton, it should hardly be surprising. For one thing, the band was Swedish – or, to be more precise, three-quarters Swedish and one-quarter Norwegian/German/ raised in Sweden – and up to that point, not a lot had emerged from Sweden in the way of vital, era-defining, international pop music, unless you count The Spotnicks, which the chances are you don't.

A kind of electric skiffle outfit, The Spotnicks performed instrumentals, partly in the style of the British band The Shadows, but while wearing spacesuits, which was their own idea. The band had had a couple of breakout hits in the early '60s, outgrew the spacesuits and continued to exist in various line-ups until 2019, by which time they had released the impres- sively persistent total of forty-three albums. Yet, despite these accomplishments – and possibly even to some extent because of them – it's fair to say the world in 1974 was not anxiously scanning the horizon for the next Spotnicks.

And even if the world *was* looking for the next Spotnicks, it was highly unlikely to be looking for them at the Eurovision Song Contest. What was ever really felt to be stake for posterity on this night of a thousand rings and dings and bongs and bing-a-bangs? Though it had found a place as the reliable annual provider of around two hours of frequently eye-opening musical entertainment, and even as the source of the occasional pan-European hit single, after nearly two decades in business, Eurovision could lay no claim to a reputation for breaking unknown global talent and ensuring that it remained broken.

True, already established names of international renown – Nana Mouskouri, Sandie Shaw, Cliff Richard – had dutifully done shifts on the contest's stages down the years, but they'd not always done so successfully, and often seemingly at the risk of everything they'd established. And even the successful ones didn't always seem lastingly proud of their association with the competition. Sandie Shaw, for instance, had, in 1967, become the UK's first Eurovision winner, with the ineffably and perhaps exhaustingly bouncy 'Puppet on a String', a record which went on to sell four million copies around the world. But she later spoke to broader reservations about the contest when she said of the song: 'I hated it from the very first "oompah" to the final "bang" on the big bass drum. I was instinctively repelled by its sexist drivel and cuckoo-clock tune.' (Phil Coulter, who co-wrote the song, responded semi-philosophically: 'As they say in the music industry, if you're expecting loyalty, buy yourself a dog.')

Essentially, most years it appeared to be the prime function of Eurovision to propose the discovery of a song the whole of Europe might enjoy – and then to demonstrate with painful clarity how almost impossibly problematic the discovery of such a song is. For UK audiences, certainly, Eurovision had long since settled into the niche which it still to a large extent occupies: as a barn-door target for satire and a yearly opportunity to adopt a position of slightly sniggering superiority in relation to things from other countries, a hobby which British people seem to have enjoyed indulging in since time immemorial.

In addition to that, the UK was home to an unhelpful suspicion, harboured with varying degrees of intensity, that the contest's multi-country jury system was in any case rigged firmly against British interests. This dark conspiracy theory had as its source the allegedly inexplicable experience of Cliff Richard at Eurovision in 1968. At that time, Cliff was arguably Britain's most brightly shining pop star after The Beatles, and he reported for duty on Eurovision's frontline that year in a state of high confidence, with home advantage (at the Royal Albert Hall in London, indeed) and packing a seemingly surefire continental unifier ('Congratulations'). He nevertheless lost out by a solitary point to Spain's Mariella and 'La La La'.

Even by the Eurovision Song Contest's notable standards in this area, a song called 'La La La' seemed daringly on-the-nose, and its narrow exaltation was certainly a punch in the gut for Cliff and his backers. The UK actually won the following year, Lulu expertly targeting the 'La La La' demographic with 'Boom-Bang-A-Bang'. But subsequent failures by ostensibly well-positioned yet more conventionally syntactical contenders (Mary Hopkin with 'Knock Knock Who's There?' in 1970, Clodagh Rodgers with 'Jack in the Box' in 1971, The New Seekers with 'Beg, Steal or Borrow' in 1972) had allowed a feeling to persist that the Eurovision Song Contest was engineered against the UK out of . . . well, what exactly? Was it spite? It could only be, couldn't it? It had to be spite.

This theory struggled for coherence, clearly – even taking into account the aforementioned superior sniggering. But its undeniable advantage was that it enabled thwarted British

Eurovision artists and audiences to nurture a feeling of having been cheated, rather than merely defeated, a consolatory narrative which has also served the nation well over the years as an explanation for various – and actually perfectly inevitable – sporting disappointments, most frequently in football.

In 1974, with the contest again on home turf, the smoke of the UK's suspicion hung as thickly as ever over Eurovision. Indeed, it hung even more thickly, if anything, since the previous year's competition in Luxembourg, when Cliff (nothing if not indomitable) returned into battle, looking to purge the traumas of 1968 once and for all, and wielding an olive branch in the shape of a song entitled 'Power to All Our Friends'. Unfortunately, he ended up doing slightly worse and finished third. Now, as ABBA and their fellow contenders readied themselves for action in Brighton, Cliff could be found on the cover of the TV listings magazine *Radio Times*. The studio-shot photograph depicted him, as so often, bristlingly dressed in a jacket of humbug stripes as if on his way to some interminable Buckingham Palace garden party, and standing solidly shoulder-to-shoulder with Olivia Newton-John, the latest combatant to take her risks at Eurovision under the UK's flag. Above them both ran the trenchantly loaded headline: 'Congratulations?'

Still, even allowing for these various layers of contempt, Eurovision remained a significant British crowd-magnet. Around 21.5 million UK viewers had tuned in to see Cliff get robbed of his destiny for a second time in 1973, a giant television audience even allowing for the fact that there wasn't much else on (three channels only, remember, in these content-light days). And similar or even better numbers could be expected this year, when the contest was merely up against Julie Andrews and Max von Sydow in an eight-year-old movie called *Hawaii* on ITV, and *War and Peace* on BBC2 – a repeat of two episodes, first shown in 1973, from the expensive twenty-part TV adaptation of Tolstoy's very long novel.

It's a rare choice, then, for viewers of the national broadcaster this evening: Napoleon's retreat from Moscow as re-imagined at great expense by the BBC's drama department? Or Napoleon's later defeat by allied forces near a village in what is now Belgium as re-imagined by an unknown Swedish pop group in pantaloons and glitter paint?

And it's no choice at all in the sitting room of the suburban house in Colchester, Essex, where, having recently turned twelve, I am spending this particular Saturday night – like pretty much every other night, actually – watching television in the company, more or less, of my parents.

I say 'more or less' because it's fairly obvious that the only one of the three of us who will be fully concentrated on the screen throughout tonight's protracted spectacular (subsequent programmes may overrun, cautions our Cliff-fronted copy of *Radio Times*) is going to be me. My mother, typically, with an anglepoise lamp ablaze beside her armchair, will be devoting the better part of her energies to the creation of one of the patchwork quilts that she seems to be producing in industrial quantities in this period. My father, equally typically, will be dividing his attention between the screen, a newspaper, and the backs of his eyelids.

I alone in this room will be achieving the state of trance-like engrossment which Eurovision no doubt merits – though not, I should admit, because I am helplessly in thrall to the contest's allure, but because I learned a long time ago in this sitting room that any discernible lapse in concentration on my part will automatically invite an instruction to go to bed. And at this point in my life, the avoidance of bed is essentially the mission of any and every evening, outstripping all consideration of what you might be doing while you are avoiding it, which probably isn't very much apart from watching television. (The Song Contest, incidentally, is starting enticingly late for the semi-professional bed-avoider: 9.30 p.m.)

Anyway, whether I make it to the end or not, Tolstoy is off and Eurovision is on, which means that I am about to have my first meeting with Born, Anna, Frida and Benny.

Well, that's what David Vine told me they were called.

We were just over half an hour and seven songs into the show, and I think it's fair to say that the evening had not yet prepared us for anything that was going to tilt our worldview lastingly, nor even, in my father's case, cause us to open our eyes for very long. Olivia Newton-John – *our* Olivia Newton-John – had come and gone, with an unhelpfully syllable-packed number called 'Long Live Love', gamely bouncing on her heels and swinging the floor-length sleeves of her baby blue maxi-dress, an outfit which seemed designed to put her exactly at the point where a Disney princess begins to morph into a tablecloth.

She took with her, I'm sure, the reflexive patriotic support of our living room – wakeful or otherwise – but I suspect that our hopes were tempered by the realisation that the song's chances of cutting through in this setting depended precariously on a lot of people, for whom English was at best a second language, knowing what 'the Sally Annie band' was, while also being up for a song with an overt Christian ministry message. Not that there's anything wrong with one of those, of course, but 'Long Live Love' – it seemed obvious – was no 'Boom-Bang-A-Bang' in the directness of its appeal.

And anyway, they all hate us over there, don't they?

Beyond Olivia, the night's songs have been weighted heavily, as ever, towards emotionally fraught ballads, each one delivered with an expression of grim thoughtfulness of the kind you might see more commonly on the face of someone struggling to process a worrying medical diagnosis. We were used to this dichotomy from Eurovision: the outfits suggested a lairy wedding reception, but the demeanours indicated some difficult months ahead for all concerned. Utterly typical were ABBA's direct precursors on the roster, song number seven, the Yugoslavian entry, a heavily coiffed but thoroughly combed all-male group named (this was daring) Korni. The collars of their metallic green and purple shirts were staging a riotous party on the shoulders of their white tuxedos, yet the band themselves seemed, to a man, unreachably anxious.

In other words, so far, so Eurovision.

But all this was about to change.

'And we move now across into Sweden,' says David Vine, the BBC's voice, more famously, of skiing and snooker, but whose gently enthusiastic Devonian burr is on secondment to the Brighton Dome for the night and is providing the voice-over for a short preliminary film package which has opened on some footage of city rooftops under a wintry sun.

Sweden is 'the largest of the Scandinavian countries,' Vine knowledgeably confides. 'And although we're looking at streets,' he continues, 'it's a country full of mountains, lakes and forests.'

Even before one can reflect on this suspiciously broad-brushed picture of the Scandinavian peninsula, Vine charges on.

'And, of course, it's also full of blonde Vikings,' he adds, 'and this is one of the reasons why it's good for pictures.'

The second part of that sentence is offered with a low laugh. Does my twelve-year-old self pick up on this winking association of blonde Swedes with 'photography'? I'm not sure it does, but Vine now generously develops the theme to the point where, even for a relatively sheltered twelve-year-old, his larger point is unmistakeable.

'If all the judges were men, which they're not, I think this group would get a lot of votes,' Vine says, again with a practically audible wink. 'You'll see what I mean in a minute.'

The introductory film has now departed Stockholm and for the first time we see the actual band, standing together. Atkinson's Folly, in person. They are compliantly holding a pose at what seems to be a general press photo-call, and as the camera pans along the line and pauses on each of their faces in turn, Vine carefully identifies them for us.

'These are the ABBA group,' he explains. 'Born . . . Frida . . . that's Anna beside her with the blonde hair . . . and Benny.'

It will be a little while before I discover that Anna generally prefers to go by the name Agnetha (or 'Agneta Faeltskog-Ulvaeus', as it appears in the official programme), and that Born actually has a 'j' in his name (and also, in the programme, an 'e' – 'Bjoern' – translating the presence in other printed sources of an umlaut over the 'o'), and that, accordingly, with apologies to Vine, his name includes a shadowy second syllable. Or maybe not, depending how quickly you can say it.

It will also be some time before I know for certain that the one Vine confidently told me was Born – but who is really Bjoern or Björn – was, in fact, Benny, and the one Vine

23

authoritatively labelled as Benny was, in fact, Born/Bjoern/
Björn.

Still, as Vine usefully explains, if you put all four of these
peoples' initials together, it spells ABBA, although only if you
restore to Frida her full name, Anni-Frid (or, as it appeared in
the programme, 'Annifrid').

Getting to know ABBA is already proving to be quite complicated. In a lot of ways, it would continue to be.

No time to worry about that now, though, because there's
one further small indignity to be visited on the band in the
form of a short concluding sequence in which they take it in
turns to part, and peer semi-smilingly through, the leaves of
what seems to be a giant potted yucca plant. These images have
been jump-cut to create a 'now you see them, now you don't'
effect and, compounding the powerful sense of cheapness, the
whole set-up has been filmed conveniently close to the stage door
at the Dome, possibly by the bins – or so it would appear from
the backstage passes dangling from lanyards around the group's
necks and from the metal air-conditioning vents which are this
scene's less-than-arresting backdrop, containing not even a hint
of Sweden's famously abundant mountains, lakes and forests.

And, with that, the film ends and we're back, live, in the
arena and witnessing the arrival at the podium, to ritual applause,
of the Swedish delegation's conductor.

'The song is called . . .' Vine begins, but then he has to pull
himself up short.

'Oh! And it's Napoleon!' he cries, his voice breaking over
what sounds like a genuine bark of delight.

Indeed, Sven Olof-Walldoff ('Olaf-Waldorf' in Vine's again
slightly chaotic pronunciation) has just marched to the head of

the orchestra in full nineteenth-century military regalia, including tailcoat and tricorn hat, and with one hand tucked away beneath his jacket, just like in the portraits.

So far, still so Eurovision.

But here they come, as promised by Vine – the ABBA group. There's a couple of bars of galloping guitar, bundled together with a brightly chiming piano, and as it plays, Anna/Agnetha and Frida/Anni-Frid/Annifrid come barrelling down the catwalk from the back of the stage and into our lives, microphone cables paying out behind them.

'My my!' they sing, and it's as if the show has suddenly shifted a gear and somebody somewhere has stepped on the accelerator.

Frida/Annifrid is in some kind of slashed peasant skirt in rust and ivory, and a white blouse strung with chains that glint like fairy lights. Anna/Agnetha is in an electric-blue bomber-jacket-and-pantaloons combo, with a matching knitted cap and stack-heeled silver boots, and is obliged to remove a stray wisp of hair from her face before she can properly get down to business. They are both rocking their shoulders and singing in unison, their voices clear and hard.

'Oh yeah!'

Then they're into the chorus and swinging their hips, twisting as much as the vertiginous heels on their respective footwear will allow. They smile a lot – down the camera and into our living room, which is, of course, smart showbusiness, but also at each other, at which point they seem to be smiling because singing the song is making them smile. At one point, Frida gathers her skirt in one hand and swishes it backwards and forwards a couple of times. Something about this unpretentious and slightly self-mocking gesture, alive to the absurdity of the moment, reminds you of something which the evening has not much offered until this point: unforced fun.

'A-wo wo wo wo Waterloo . . .'

This song, you are obliged to concede, is catchy as hell. It doesn't just build to a hook; it glistens with hooks, all the way along its length – in the vocal lines, between the vocal lines, around all the edges, at every transition: piano crashes, guitar splashes, a tooted saxophone. It doesn't seem to be wasting a second or leaving a moment to chance.

It also sounds an awful lot like *now*, which in this context is the most startling thing. The music of the Eurovision Song Contest in these years tends to dabble with contemporary ingredients much in the way my Aunt Eileen might add a sightly risky brooch to a sober Sunday church outfit. But this song from Sweden is wholeheartedly and persuasively a piece of pop music as the world beyond Eurovision currently understands it. It's Wizzard's 'See My Baby Jive' meets The Sweet's 'Blockbuster' meets The Foundations' 'Build Me Up Buttercup' meets The Supremes' 'Baby Love' meets The Beach Boys' 'Help Me Rhonda'. And it seems to have been made in a studio where Phil Spector and Tony Visconti were, at the very least, popping in and out to keep an eye on things production-wise. Not that I'm in a position to put my finger on much of that right now, of course. But it doesn't matter because the song is also performing one of the great magic tricks of pop piracy when it's done well: it's reminding you pleasingly of what you know and love, while coming at you as something convincingly and wholly new, which you also love.

Meanwhile, the director of the television pictures is acquainting us very thoroughly with Agnetha and Frida as they sing and bop and smile. But what of Born and Benny? Whither those two? If he doesn't already know it, this is the night Björn Ulvaeus learns a harsh lesson about showbusiness, and it's this. You can zip yourself into a black boilersuit hung with chains, lower your legs into a pair of knee-high silver boots with heels like house bricks, and hang around your neck a novelty electric guitar in the shape of a squashed satellite, but in the force-field generated by the mutual operation of Agnetha Fältskog and Anni-Frid Lyngstad, no television producer on earth is going to offer you more than a few grudging flashes of screen time for your efforts.

And it's worse still for the one we think is Born but who is actually Benny. There's occasionally a long shot of the stage which includes him, seated out to the right. But otherwise his hands, glimpsed briefly on the piano keys, are the only bit of him that we are invited to contemplate in detail for quite a while. Indeed, by the time the producers finally get around to showing him in close-up, we are into the song's last chorus.

In fact, the two session musicians on the stage get more exposure than Born and Benny, particularly the bassist, Rutger Gunnarsson, whose position puts him behind Agnetha's left shoulder and who holds his electric bass in an unfashionably upright position, its neck practically pointing to the ceiling, as if he's trying to squeeze through a narrow gap. Meanwhile Ola Brunkert is as stationary as a person can be while playing a drum kit. It's almost as though the pair of them – these members of ABBA who are not ABBA – have been carefully briefed not to create a distraction. Frankly, though, in this circumstance, with Agnetha and Frida doing their thing, they could set fire to each other and perform a flaming tango together, and Camera 2 would still only come to them fleetingly and in the smouldering aftermath.

Still, in as much as we see him, Born who is actually Benny has got my attention. He's at the piano, and that's my instrument. There's an ancient and poorly tuned upright taking up (my mother will eagerly tell you) too much space in the adjacent room – technically my father's office – but on which, while it survives, I am doing quite a lot of untutored thumping during this period, to my own pleasure, if no one else's. Yet, to my chagrin, the piano is not an instrument you frequently see in the pop arena. OK, Elton John is doing some sterling work in this area, but mostly the piano seems to be cropping up in marginal and frequently even undesirable roles, such as being played by Gilbert O'Sullivan in his chosen persona as a hollowed-out Victorian chimney sweep's assistant, or by Hilda Woodward, who is literally the *mum* of one of the blokes in Lieutenant Pigeon of 'Mouldy Old Dough' fame, and what a low blow *that* moment in history was for the self-esteem of apprentice pianists everywhere.

This is how the world is arranged, as far as I can tell: playing the piano is an accomplishment, but playing the guitar is a *statement* – especially the electric guitar, but actually any guitar. I am overdue an acoustic pianist whom I can properly revere at the frontline of up-tempo pop, and certainly at the frontline of glam rock, where the instrument has been foregrounded just about never.

Still, here's this guy Born, who is really Benny. Is this my redeemer? OK, the frilly cuffs protruding from his glossy lilac jacket seem a bit ornate, and possibly even a little obstructive – but there's the glimmer of something, from my point of view.

His eyes aren't locked on his fingers, the way mine have to be. He doesn't seem noticeably trapped by the instrument, nor awkwardly cornered by it. He doesn't seem to be at all embarrassed to be playing the piano. On the contrary, he looks as if there is nothing he would rather be doing.

It's fleeting, obviously, because the cameras pass back to Agnetha and Frida as soon as is politely possible, but there's an example there, maybe. A potential way forward.

Each of the singers takes a little stepped turn through 360 degrees as the saxophone plays its chorus-sealing riff for the last time and the song ends.

At this moment I know, as well as I know anything, who I want to win this thing.

3

Numbers game

David Vine is definitely impressed. 'How about that for an on-stage performance? Sweden have never won it, but they've surely got to be up among the reckoning with that one.'

Well, I only hope he's right. And when has he ever been wrong?

This much I know: if ABBA win, they will have to come back out and repeat the song. And that's an outcome very much to be desired because I'm not sure when I'll get to hear it again otherwise. There's a long way to go, though. Another nine countries still stand between us and an encore at this stage, including, most dangerous of all, the act which David Vine will remind us has come into this evening as the bookies' favourite – the Netherlands' entry, Mouth & MacNeal. (ABBA, you may care to know, were somewhere out at 20/1 by the time betting closed.) Up twelfth, these two are offering a wave-along duet called 'I See a Star', which does indeed seem to have a poten-tially Eurovision-clinching aura about it, not least in sounding like the kind of tune that might reasonably accompany the gentle rotations of a children's fairground ride – and when have the Eurovision juries ever been able to resist one of those?

This could be tight.

Known in other circumstances as Big Mouth, and on his passport as Willem Duyn, Mouth presents as a kind of Dutch Meat Loaf – a *gehaktbrood*, if you will – in knee-length boots and a giant leathery jerkin fastened across his big chest with chains, and staring out at us hot and wide-eyed from beneath unruly hair. He is clearly devoting some serious energy to not appearing to take this Eurovision lark seriously. In the preliminary film package, he has been shown capering in circles on a piece of Brighton greensward while holding some balloons on a string and towing his unbelievably complaisant singing partner behind him in a handcart. Crazy guy, clearly. Now, as they sing together, he playfully nudges and cuffs MacNeal, and at one point ruffles her carefully arranged blonde hair. MacNeal – who is more fully Maggie MacNeal, but was born Sjoukje van't Spijker; fortunately, David Vine doesn't go anywhere near any of this – does a magnificent job of not looking remotely irritated by any of these surely amazingly infuriating antics, but continues to bop gamely in a blouse and trousers.

In a further worrying development, Mouth & MacNeal have come with additional help in the form of a prop. Standing just to one side, their band's keyboard player is burdened not only by surely the largest pair of loon pants flown in an indoor setting in 1974, but also by a bulky carnival-barker's music box, hung by a strap around his neck and topped with foot-high puppets representing . . . well, hang on. Now we're in close on them, that's Mouth and MacNeal, isn't it? Mouth and MacNeal in cloth form.

Come the first chorus, where the arrangement breaks down to a jaunty pipe-organ theme, the full-size Mouth approaches the keyboard player, kneels beside him and cranks the music box's handle, causing the miniature MacNeal on top to spin beside the floppy miniature Mouth while the real Mouth looks out into the audience and gapes in exaggerated delight.

Talk about a *coup de théâtre*. OK, these days, when Eurovision entrants routinely perform while being menaced by dancers in gorilla suits (Italy, 2017), setting fire to the ornate staircases on which their pianos are resting (Ukraine, 2018), or depicting themselves naked in hologram form beside howling wolves (Belarus, 2016), this piece of craft-class puppeteering would barely merit a stifled yawn. However, on the largely bare and entirely static pastel-coloured stage of the Brighton Dome in 1974, it feels like the circus has suddenly come to town. And bringing puppets.

These are troubling scenes. But will it be enough to swing the judging against ABBA? That's the big question. And I find I am surprisingly keen that it shouldn't be. It would be a musical travesty, for one thing. And I really do want to hear that ABBA song again.

The rest of the contest passes without much further ado, and certainly without further scene-stealing puppetry. While the judges finalise their various decisions prior to the voting phase, we get a moment to gather ourselves with the interval enter-tainment, which is supplied by The Wombles. This is probably the moment when my father stirs himself to depart for the kitchen and make the two cups of instant coffee with boiled milk that is my parents' habitual mid-to-late-evening drink. But I'm not going anywhere. As a poster-owning fan of long standing who will shortly be taking delivery of The Wombles' next commitment to wax, the single 'Banana Rock', I am very happy to see Orinoco and company on board, and perfectly content that this is what the producers of the show should be offering up to the rest of Europe as an exhibition of contemporary British excellence in this window of opportunity for what we would now call UK plc.

OK, I suppose it's not quite as strong as the moment in Stockholm in 2016 when Justin Timberlake turned up halfway through and blew the place apart by performing 'Can't Stop the Feeling' (written and produced by Sweden's Max Martin, hence the connection). That's just unfair, you thought – like Novak Djokovic randomly attaching himself to some weekend foursome on a public court somewhere, and not even having the grace to go easy. But as The Wombles, with the able assistance of Ronnie Hazlehurst and his orchestra, casually bolt together their two (so far) Top 10 smashes – 'The Wombling Song' and 'Remember You're a Womble' – and meld them to a film in which Orinoco, Great Uncle Bulgaria and the others spin about on Brighton Pier and thrash up and down the seafront in a dune buggy, I'm proud enough. In 1974, this was showing them how it's done.

After that, it's time for the reckoning. This is the UK's chance to marvel once again at the work of Katie Boyle, the onstage presenter, who has not underestimated the evening's formality and is wrapped from head to toe in peach with a matching froth of feathers at the neck. And in particular it's our chance to marvel at both her cut-glass English and her, if anything, even more cut-glass French, which is surely as English as French has ever been made to sound. Katie gracefully glides to her place beside the scoreboard, which is a steeply towering construction, earnestly black and white, and with a rudimentary articulated number display. Quite closely resembling a train departures board, it gives the set something of the feel of an Eastern European terminus between the wars. On this cumbersome apparatus will ABBA's fate be drawn.

This is all happening before the miracle of satellite imagery can bring the representatives of the various far-flung juries to the screen. So what we are treated to for the next twenty minutes or so is the less than visually compelling spectacle of somebody in an evening gown answering a series of long-distance phone calls. Nevertheless, let nobody underestimate the high drama of this phase of the show, nor its lastingly eerie continental 'otherness'. Frankly, when it comes to disembodied voices evoking whole worlds out there of which we know frighteningly little, *Star Trek*'s regular opening monologue – 'Space, the final frontier' – has absolutely nothing on 'Good evening, Brighton – Helsinki calling. These are the results of the Finnish jury.'

The calls come in from Finland, from Luxembourg, from Israel, and the numbers clatter onto Katie's bleak departures board, and very quickly it starts to look quite encouraging. 'Sweden still very much in the lead,' says Katie. We flash backstage where the four members of ABBA stand stock-still, looking incredibly tense – until they notice the camera is on them, at which point they all dutifully drop their shoulders a bit and smile. It's just a bit of fun, after all . . .

Except, obviously, it isn't. The tension is clearly excruciating – for them and for those of us rooting for them. Monaco comes out strongly for near-neighbours Italy, in the form of Gigliola Cinquetti and a truly horrible power ballad called 'Si', and the gap narrows agonisingly to just two points. The Netherlands are showing quite strongly, but Italy is showing stronger. How? *How?* Because Eurovision, of course. But even so . . .

But then Switzerland – rigorously neutral, no doubt – bangs in five votes for Sweden and *none at all* for Italy and it's all looking good again.

Only Belgium can screw it now. That nation's votes are phoned in faintly by a man apparently speaking from a cupboard in Brussels, and possibly from somewhere inside a roll of carpet. Still, thanks to Katie, his drift is clear: no votes for ABBA, but only one, thankfully, for Gigliola, which means there's still six points in it, with only the Italian jury remaining to vote.

At this moment, then, there are no further points possible for Italy (you can't vote for your own entrant, obviously), and unless, in an unprecedented move, this woman in Rome who we're about to hear from heaps all the Italian votes on Mouth & MacNeal, currently nine points back, Sweden are home and hosed.

Don't let us down, Rome.

'Buona sera, Roma,' says Katie.

'Hello, Brighton. Good evening, Ketty,' says the woman in Rome.

'Good evening!' replies Ketty.

Get on with it, a waiting audience screams.

'These are the votes of the Italian jury. United Kingdom . . . three votes . . .'

That's it! As soon as Italy drops the first of its points on our Olivia, it's over. The lightbulb behind Sweden's name on the scoreboard is blinking and Katie is wreathed in smiles almost to the same degree that she is wreathed in orange feathers.

'There's no doubt about it,' says Katie. 'The winning song

of the 1974 Eurovision Song Contest, la chanson gagnante du Concours de . . .'

She then makes a rare hash of translating '1974' into French, laughs and recovers elegantly.

'C'est "Vaataloo", c'est Sverige at "Vaataloo", chante par ABBA!'

Italy, with Gigliola Cinquetti, are second. Mouth and MacNeal, in both real and cloth form, are beaten back to third. Olivia finishes fourth and nobody even has the energy to cry 'fix'.

It's ABBA's prize. It's ABBA's night. And also, completely implausibly, it's ABBA's future.

4

Repeat performance

Stig Anderson, a large, thickly mustachioed man looking over-dressed and hot in a vast bow tie and sleek dress shirt, comes, humbly stooping, to the stage to accept the Grand Prix from the Director-General of the BBC, Sir Charles Curran. Known (and in some quarters gravely feared) as Stikkan, Anderson is ABBA's manager, but he is also the lyricist whose idea it was to substitute 'Waterloo' for the song's original working title, 'Honey Pie'.

Benny and Björn, who are the song's other composers, have attempted to join him and receive their own medals, but have been repelled by security staff minding the stage. The winning musicians aren't due back in front of the cameras until after the medal ceremony, so the assumption is presumably that they are misguidedly jumping their cue and need to be prevented from doing so. In later interviews, Björn will not entirely seri-ously advance the theory that the staff took one look at the pair of them, in their silks and boots and chains, and decided that they couldn't possibly be songwriters dressed like that – a considerable category error with hindsight. In the staff's defence, though, only ABBA, Peret from Spain and the aforementioned and notably glum Korni of Yugoslavia competed at Eurovision 1974 with a song that members of the performing act had played a part in writing. Eurovision just wasn't a big *auteur* zone, and even the bouncers knew it.

Benny eventually makes it through, but by that time Stig has completed his no-nonsense acceptance speech (a simple 'thank you' in a number of languages) and Katie Boyle is now wrapping things up, also in a number of languages. Meanwhile, behind her (shades here of some kind of Morecambe & Wise sketch), Anderson, Benny and the Director-General turn their backs and point, and have an animated conversation, presumably about the detainment of Björn at the border.

And now we get to hear the song again. There's a brief glimpse behind the scenes of a grinning Frida picking up her microphone and heading for the stage. This time there's no run down the catwalk – just straight in.

'My my!'

Björn lets out a couple of random whoops, which might be in celebration of his liberty, except that he did that right at the start of the first performance, too. On the piano beside Benny Andersson sits his winner's medal in its navy-blue presentation box. Once more, Agnetha and Frida sing, bop and smile, and, in the great tradition of Eurovision-winner reprises, the song sounds the way it did the first time, but with a few extra degrees of elation.

'Oh yeah!'

Frida and Agnetha do their 360-degree turn again, and the song ends again. Stig Anderson joins them and everybody stands in a line and waves during the lengthy final fanfare while the credits roll up the screen and my parents send me to bed.

Nearly 11.30. Pretty good work. But I had help.

There's a fair amount on my mind as I head up the stairs. I've fallen for musicians off the telly before. That was how Marc Bolan of T. Rex and I got our thing going, way back in 1970, a thing which has only relatively recently run its course. (No blame necessary. The spark eventually just went out of it for both of us. It happens.) So I recognise these feelings. But it's definitely the first time I've developed a crush on two people off the telly simultaneously, which is bit disorientating and, in fact, quite overwhelming.

Actually, three people, if you count Born, who is really Benny.

Those two performances of 'Waterloo' set off an itch which will only be partially scratched by rapid acquisition of the 7-inch single, in a plain white paper sleeve, at the cost of 45p from Harper's Music on the corner of Colchester High Street (instruments downstairs, records upstairs). And that single, played repeatedly, sets off vibrations which will continue to be felt for the next fifty years. Or, to put it another way, for the rest of my life up to now.

5

Gaudy pleasures

It's tempting from this distance to argue that ABBA prevailed in Brighton that night by offering things in short supply in Britain at the time: things like electricity, energy and good teeth.

In this version of the story, they came on us like a shaft of sunshine and glitter paint through a brown fug of depression and boarded-up petrol stations. The people who had walked in darkness saw a great light, and it was Agnetha's electric-blue pantaloons.

But that's not quite right, of course, because it depicts ABBA, in their brightness, as outliers, which might have been true in Eurovision terms, but was hardly the case in the wider world beyond Eurovision. Consider: in the week of the contest, the band that featured on the cover of music newspaper *Sounds* was Slade, Noddy Holder's gleeful stomp-rock outfit, never knowingly outdone in the wearing of tartan pant-suits, teetering heels and top hats restyled as mirror balls.

Also much in evidence on the singles charts and in the pop papers at this time: Mud, a glam-pop dance band whose singer, Les Gray, bestrode the world – or certainly *Top of the Pops* on Thursday nights – in sateen drapes, and whose guitarist, Rob

Davis, modelled a fabulous wardrobe of floor-length evening gowns and dangly earrings.

And then there were the solo singers Suzi Quatro and Alvin Stardust, both of whom favoured skin-tight leather in various cuts, and the now unmentionable Gary Glitter, who routinely went out wrapped in Bacofoil like some kind of oven-ready Elvis, wore an almost permanent expression of cartoon outrage, and was quite funny before he wasn't. Pop music in the '70s, one quickly realises, was almost always overdressed – and rarely not in some way strange.

In order to stand out in this crowd of clashing checks, thunderous gloss-painted boots and absurdly repurposed Victoriana, it was not enough to perform a merely casual raid on your aunt's linen basket. Rising above the fashionable tide at this moment in history took a trained eye for underutilised accessories, acute bravery with face-paints and some serious energy for the extra mile. ABBA seem to have entirely understood this, and from the very beginning; here, and repeatedly over the ensuing few years, Agnetha, Frida, Björn and Benny would concertedly put in those hard yards. But they were hardly alone.

And then what about the notion that we leapt on ABBA for what they offered us by way of relief in a time of unrelenting misery and decay? This, too, depends on a highly selective view of what the '70s felt like to live through – a view of the era which has rather come to dominate in discussions of it: the fabled 'decade that taste forgot'. Most of us who have seen a few of the television documentaries can run you without too much effort through the checklist of shame: platform soles, Watneys Red Barrel, nylon sheets, faux-velvet wallpaper, butterscotch-flavoured Angel Delight, home-brew . . .

Again, though, is this quite enough? If you can remember the '60s, it has frequently been alleged, you weren't there. By the same token, if you remember the '70s as one long Vesta chow mein eaten miserably in a polyester tank top by candlelight in the vicinity of an underwatered spider plant, maybe you weren't there either. Or maybe you were there, but memory and competing documentary series have pulled the polyester over your eyes. As the pre-eminent historian of that period, Dominic Sandbrook, has pointed out, in three indispensable volumes on the subject, the '70s are easily painted as brown and violent, but it takes a selective artist to do so, and an equally selective artist to forget that, for those of us living through them, those days were in many respects the promised future to which time had finally delivered us.

'For most people,' Sandbrook writes sagely, 'daily life never approached the extremes often commemorated in histories of the 1970s. Even though the language of British politics was becoming increasingly aggressive, most voters were much more interested in the new series of *On the Buses*, the supermarket opening down the road and their forthcoming holiday on the Costa del Sol.'

Well, no foreign holidays for us, sadly, but most of the rest of that sentence rings cleanly true to me. Consider the perspective of my parents on the economic crisis of early 1974. By then in their forties, these people had lived through an actual world war. What would seem difficult or even surprising about the recent spate of timetabled power cuts and the threat of rationed petrol to these two Blitz veterans, one of whom, from the playing field by her childhood home, had watched bombs drop on Colchester in broad daylight from a passing German plane, while the other had spent nights during his teacher training course in west London on voluntary fire patrol?

And now look at these people, with their own new-built house in an Essex suburb; these people who both grew up in council houses but who now have their own garage – and what's more, a garage with a very recently acquired deep freezer at the back of it containing a large stock of Findus Crispy Pancakes.

OK, that particular bounty is not unconnected to the fact that one of my brothers is currently on nightshift at the Findus warehouse in Gosbecks Road where boxes do, it seems, sometimes get dropped between the shelf and the lorry . . . But nevertheless, a freezer! A *chest* freezer!

These people have spent the last two decades raising four children on a schoolteacher's salary. But three of those children are out of the door and working now (and will very shortly be out of the door entirely) and the fourth (me) no longer needs minding anything like as much as he once did, which means my mother has taken a job in a department store. Suddenly there seems to be evidence of disposable income, as there never used to be.

And to illustrate, I only need to point out to you a couple of new additions to the aforementioned sitting room that hosted the 1974 Eurovision Song Contest. The wooden radiogram cabinet which, for as long as I could remember, had stood like a waiting coffin under the front window has just been replaced by a far less spirit-sapping Garrard stereo: a fancy boxed record player on an aluminium stalk, linked by wire to a separate speaker on the other side of the room, both these pieces of furniture being thematically linked by their matching white leatherette trim.

And that thing in between those two items that my father is adrift on? That's a freshly delivered Parker Knoll reclining armchair (my mum's employee discount activated).

Look, no one's trying to pretend it was the best of times, but under the right light, and for some of us lucky ones, some of those '70s browns start to look more orange – golden, even. And it's certainly true that Sandbrook points up a vital paradox when he describes 'the grim calamities and the gaudy pleasures of life in Britain at the dawn of the 1970s'. ABBA were a gaudy pleasure that came upon us in a time when, for quite a lot of us, gaudy pleasures seemed unusually available.

Did we actually leap on ABBA back then, in any case? Did the nation swoon in unison on that Saturday night in April and open its arms out wide to our new sparkly Swedish over-lords? True, a couple of weeks later, following their first appearance on *Top of the Pops* (for which the band wore the same outfits they had worn in Brighton, effectively pinning them in my mind as a uniform), 'Waterloo' had sold enough copies that it could complete a symbolic journey of sorts and replace Terry Jacks' 'Seasons in the Sun' at number one in the UK chart – those minor turns and doomy ruminations on how good it was to die, blown out of the door in a blast of glam-rock riffing and a gale of saxophone.

However, let's not forget that, on the night of the contest itself, the ten-person UK jury, sequestered in a BBC studio in London, watched, along with the rest of us, Agnetha and Frida arrive at speed down that catwalk, calmly absorbed the following two minutes and forty-six seconds of life-enhancing and poten-tially culture-altering exuberance, and responded by awarding ABBA no votes whatsoever.

Looking back, part of you now thinks, *Well, OK: history can be hard to read when it's happening under your nose.*

But another part of you thinks: *No votes? For that? Hello?*

Afterwards, too, the critics were hardly unanimous in praising ABBA and warmly endorsing what they had to offer. Clive James, whose television reviews for the *Observer* were often life-endangeringly funny, chose to focus on Eurovision for the following weekend's newspaper. Describing ABBA as 'a two-girl and two-man outfit', he picked out Agnetha as 'the girl with the blue knickerbockers, the silver boots and the clinically interesting lordosis'.

What was he getting at there? Lordosis (an online medical dictionary informs me) is 'abnormal inward curvature of the lumbar spine just above the buttocks'. Was this James's way of letting us know that he'd noticed Agnetha's bum without (he was writing for a broadsheet newspaper, after all) mentioning Agnetha's bum?

And was it really not felt to be even remotely unsound for a male TV critic in the '70s to get a gag out of posing as a doctor on the topic of a woman's body? Obviously not.

Whatever, on the basis of a handful of moments in Agnetha's televised company, James confidently asserts: 'There could be no doubt that in real life she was squarer than your mother.'

And the song? James interpreted 'Waterloo' thus: 'a T. Rex riff and a Supremes phrase . . . delivered in a Pickettywitch style that pointed up the cretinous lyric with ruthless precision'.

Ruthlessly precise the delivery of the lyric may have been, but James nevertheless misheard it, believing that when the band sang about how they couldn't escape if they wanted to, they were actually singing the opposite: 'could've escaped if I wanted to'.

Does this matter? Of course not – except that, if you're going to go after someone for being cretinous, I guess you'd better be sure you've understood them. Let's be fair, though: assuming he stayed tuned for the victorious encore at the end of the night (and, in fact, he seems strongly to imply in the review that, much like my father, he fell asleep before then), James had probably heard the song twice at most, and didn't have the internet – or even, at this point in history, a video recorder with a rewind button – with which to check back. He's due some slack.

In any case, when it comes to precise comprehension of the lyric of ABBA's 'Waterloo', I'm not really in a position to be throwing stones. In my own muddled hearing of the song that night in 1974, the chorus appeared to contain the question, 'How would you feel if you won the war?'. This illusion would endure for me, not just as the ensuing weeks came and went, with my copy of the record on repeat in my bedroom, but through year after year of exposure to the song.

Indeed, that false impression would travel unchallenged through numberless encounters with 'Waterloo', both planned and random, and through countless singalongs, both private and public, all the way up until . . . well, until just a couple of minutes ago, actually, when I thought I had better go online and check that I was right about Clive James being wrong.

At which point, with the click of an overhead light going on in a dim and curtained sitting room, I learned the truth. It's not a question, it's a statement. No 'How would you feel if . . . ?' The singer was *defeated*.

So, it turns out that for half a century, I have carried around in my head what is pretty much a nonsense version of the chorus of 'Waterloo', yet with no noticeable consequences for my unshakeable sense that it's a really strong chorus, albeit a mere foreshadowing of the still-stronger choruses ABBA would go on to produce.

Clive James, it seems, agreed that the chorus had staying power, but was less persuaded that this longevity was unreservedly a good thing.

'The hook of their song lasted a long time in the mind,' he wrote, 'like a kick in the knee.'

Ah well. At least ABBA could rely on proud and well-disposed critics at home in Sweden for some straightforwardly warm appreciation and encouragement. Or maybe not, actually. There's a video clip from the archives which now plays on rotation – somewhat exultantly, it must be said – among the exhibits in the ABBA Museum in Stockholm.

At a late-night after-show party in the wake of their Eurovision victory, Frida, who has enjoyed a celebratory cigar, and Stig Anderson are cornered by a reporter and a cameraman from a Swedish current affairs show called *Rapport* (in English, 'Report'). Invited, with no apparent spin on the question, to ruminate on the writing of 'Waterloo', Anderson talks good-naturedly about how a Eurovision entry needs to communicate across languages if it's going to get anywhere. ABBA had tried that and failed the previous year, 1973, he explains, with 'Ring Ring', which had finished third in Sweden's national trials. (That year, by the way, having dismissed ABBA, Sweden ended up sending to Eurovision a pop duo called The Nova and a set of backing singers called The Dolls to sing a song entitled 'You Are Summer (You Never Tell Me No)', the chorus of which compared a lover's breasts to 'swallows a-nestling'.

Incredibly, it finished fifth.) But this time, with 'Waterloo', Stig explains, the members of ABBA and himself had got the multi-lingual trick right and gone the whole way.

Here the reporter spots a window of opportunity. 'Last year was a song about calling each other,' he says flatly. 'This year, you've got a song about 40,000 people dying, to put it cynically.'

Well, he'd done his research, clearly, this reporter. In fact, he'd probably gone in on the low side. Reliable estimates put the allied losses at Waterloo at around 24,000, and Napoleon's losses at between 24,000 and 26,000, so a total of 48,000 or even 50,000 for the battle as a whole, would not have been unreasonable. No matter. His point was the same: how could ABBA and Anderson be so heartless and so disrespectful in the face of this manifest human tragedy?

Perhaps understandably, Anderson seems both baffled and piqued at the same time by this turn in the conversation. (Off-camera, at the conclusion of the interview, allegedly he lets the reporter know more clearly how he feels.)

Also, has this reporter not heard 1973's The Nova and their 'breasts like swallows a-nestling'? Because if there was ever a time to go earnestly after a Swedish Eurovision entrant for lyrical opportunism, it was surely twelve months prior to all this.

But no. In their moment of triumph, when ABBA might reasonably be expecting at least grudging congratulations for efforts on behalf of their nation, they instead become surely the first and only pop band to ever be upbraided publicly for insensitive use of Napoleonic history.

Though in many ways, no doubt, they would seem to shoot past, it was already clear that the next eight years were going to be, in some respects, very long for ABBA.

6

Puppet state

Move forward seven months from the Eurovision Song Contest in Brighton to a Wednesday evening in November. Same sitting room as before, same television set, same more or less engaged audience. A picture of St Paul's Cathedral and its reflection in a surprisingly blue river divides and resolves itself and the Thames Television horn fanfare plays. It's 8.00 p.m. and time for *The Tommy Cooper Hour*.

'. . . with his guests tonight, Kristine Sparkle, Topo Gigio, ABBA . . .'

Kristine Sparkle? She's a singer who does a sideline in impressions. (She's also a songwriter who will later, with Terry Britten, write 'Devil Woman' for Cliff Richard.) Earlier this year, Sparkle (real name, Christine Holmes) has released a glam-rock version of 'The Hokey Cokey', which was every bit as unlikely as it sounds and every bit as unsuccessful as you might imagine. She has also attempted to sprinkle glam's magic dust – stomping drums with a slap-back echo, crunchy electric guitar – over a cover of The Beatles' 'Eight Days a Week', which, it could be argued, didn't much need it. But tonight she's promoting a cover of 'The Shoop Shoop Song (It's in His Kiss)', which is entirely without stomping drums and crunchy guitars and is altogether, it turns out, un-glam in flavour – though Sparkle will be performing it with a dusting of glitter on her cheeks, in keeping with her name.

And Topo Gigio? Well, he's a mouse. Specifically, a model of a mouse, three feet tall or so and operated from behind with rods and strings. This means that, a little more than seven months after 'Waterloo', and in an eerie premonition of Spinal Tap's experience on tour at the Themeland Amusement Park in the 1984 rockumentary *This is Spinal Tap*, ABBA find themselves billed below a puppet show.

To quote Jeanine Pettibone at that precise moment in the movie: 'If I told them once, I told them a hundred times to put Spinal Tap first, Puppet Show last.'

Also on the show, the ventriloquist act Ray Alan and Lord Charles. And, of course, Tommy Cooper himself.

'I went window shopping today. I bought four windows.'

Just one line, there, from the magician's almost fifteen-minute-long opening monologue, in which he also juggles badly with a ping-pong ball, fluffs a card trick that appears to have been an awfully long time in the making ('that's fifteen years wasted'), pauses to observe that his teeth itch, and does a one-man Dr Jekyll and Mr Hyde play performance in which he keeps forgetting which character he's meant to be.

ABBA eventually appear on a set hung with day-glo rhomboids. It's quite a squeezed space. Frida wears what appears to be a snakeskin onesie and a matching choker. Agnetha is in some kind of fishnet bodystocking, overlaid with a pink and black striped halter-top and pink hot pants with silver sparkles, and with matching sparkly pink fold-overs on her knee-length white boots. Benny, at a piano, wears the pink jacket worn by Björn during the Eurovision preambles – the garment, indeed, in which Björn first peered out at us through the fronds of that Brighton yucca plant near the air-conditioning units – and a ruched ivory silk shirt, the collar of which extends to the tips of his shoulders on both sides. (Flared trousers get so much of the attention in retrospective appraisals of '70s fashion, but my surveys remind me that we should never fail to credit the unbelievable amounts of ground covered by shirt collars in that era. You could make a whole other shirt from the collar on this one of Benny's and still have enough material for a bedspread.)

As for Björn, exactly as in Brighton, he again draws an almost unimaginably short straw, appearing in a sparkly black vest, a blue and silver amulet, tight blue pants and blue boots, all accessorised (and this really is a killer touch) with a red Superman-style cape attached to him round the neck by a thick silver band which seems to be placing his windpipe in jeopardy.

They're here to perform 'Ring Ring', which, in the UK, is the follow-up single to 'Waterloo'. Elsewhere in Europe, record labels are going with a newer ABBA song called 'Honey, Honey' – and making headway with it. But Paul Atkinson at Epic Records still seems to hold out hope for the song that attracted him to ABBA in the first place, and has proposed a re-release. Epic have asked the band to remix the track, adding thicker guitars and some parping saxophone to the rhythm section, in the hope of establishing a stronger connection with 'Waterloo'. The band have obliged, but to no real end. The single will fail to reach the Top 30.

Under the rhomboids, Agnetha and Frida attempt to muster

some magic. They clap their hands over their heads in the song's bridge and gamely shuffle and turn when the chorus comes around, but there's a detectable lack of enthusiasm in the delivery, even some extremely rare misalignment in the vocal blend. There is none of the fire of the Eurovision performance, none of the effervescence, no way that they seem to be saying (as they did in Brighton), 'We've got this song, and we think it's pretty great, and now you're damn well going to hear it.'

Well, why would there be? This song is old hat as far as they're concerned. Also, they've had months of this kind of thing since 'Waterloo' – endless semi-mimed promo appearances on the spangled sets of mid-evening television shows all over Europe, trying to generate the momentum that will make their career take off and fly. And now here they are back in Britain, where the resistance to their charms feels almost tangible, and where the record company in control of their destiny doesn't actually seem to have a clue what to do with them.

They have haunted eyes.

7

Preserved fish products and bubblegum cards

It's late November 2023 and I'm at Waterloo in southern Belgium where, as ABBA indelibly taught us, Napoleon did surrender. Here, at the preserved site of the battle, visitors can look over the battlefield from the Lion's Mound monument, survey the Hougemont Farmhouse where some of the most intense fighting took place that summer all those 200-plus years ago, and scrutinise a giant, 360-degree painting of the battle in the circular Panorama building.

But that's for another day maybe. Today, I have come to the fabled scene of the great French reversal of 1815 to examine a display of historic artefacts pertaining to the life and times of ABBA.

'From Waterloo to the World: ABBA Expo 1974–2024' reads the giant hoarding on the glass-fronted visitor centre, emphatically announcing what is the centrepiece of the Domaine de la Battaille de Waterloo's celebrations of the 50th anniversary of the Eurovision Song Contest in Brighton and the historic part played by ABBA that night in putting Waterloo on the map. I mean, obviously Napoleon, Wellington, the Prince of Orange and assorted others had done a fair bit in that regard already. But credit where it's due. And frankly, yes, the French emperor had his moments, both in what is now Belgium and elsewhere. But if we're weighing CVs, how many songs by Napoleon can *you* still sing?

This exhibition is not the only gesture the Domaine is making in the run-up to this anniversary year. The site has already opened during the summer for a 'Candlelight ABBA Vigil', a programme of ABBA music arranged for a string quartet and performed by candlelight beneath the floodlit lion statue, and which I'm quietly disappointed to have missed. But 'From Waterloo to the World' is running for eight months in total, making it a much bigger target, and I'm visiting relatives in the area, so it would be foolish not to, wouldn't it? Especially when the general exhibition curator, Jean-Marie Potiez, is on the Domaine's website promising us access to 'the sparkling, wonderful world of Swedish stars'.

So I've made the fifteen-minute train journey from Brussels to Braine-l'Alleud and then jumped in a taxi which has dropped me at the site's main gate, where I have taken a moment to look out across this storied, grassy terrain, now permanently battered by the roar of traffic from the nearby motorway. Then I have descended the steps to the quiet and warmth of the site's newly built, partially underground museum and expo arena.

On this cold and rainy morning, at arguably the lowest point of the low season, other visitors are few. A small scattering of middle-aged men in anoraks, museum audio-guides clamped to their ears, are carefully studying the detailed models of the battlefield which stand in the reception area. But I turn away from them and follow the signs through the gift shop to the special exhibition area.

I've got to admit, I'm feeling slightly sheepish about this and experiencing some flickers of guilt at the idea of travelling quite a long way to visit a major European site of historic interest in order to look at painstakingly restored ABBA costumes. But on top of that there's my strong and, I think, well-founded suspicion that nobody is likely to be able to curate the ABBA story as well as the ABBA Museum in Stockholm, which I've already visited. At the ABBA Museum, you get life-size reconstructions of the band's writing hut on the island of Viggso, Stig Anderson's office at the Polar Music record label, the recording studio where they constructed their later albums, and even the kitchen from whose window Björn stared and felt moved to write the lyric for 'Slipping Through My Fingers'. My fear is that this offering from the Belgian guardians of the Domaine de la Bataille, however pluckily inventive it may turn out to be, will have the same relation to the 'walk in, dance out' experience available in Stockholm as the Brading Waxworks on the Isle of Wight used to have to Madame Tussauds, until the former's sad closure in 2010.

Still, I'm here now, so I hold my ticket's barcode against the scanner, click through the turnstile and enter. A little later, a group of three middle-aged women will make their way past me and I'll hear them at one of the display stands up ahead of me, singing along to the 'a-ha' bits of 'Voulez-Vous' (not to be confused, of course, with the 'a-ha' bits of 'Knowing Me, Knowing You'). But apart from that, for the rest of the morning it's just me and what turns out to be, indeed, a pluckily inventive display of photographs, record sleeves and carefully housed collectibles, telling the ABBA story – which, I suppose, would have its unlikely elements however, and wherever, you told it.

So, over here on the wall to start things off is Björn Kristian Ulvaeus in his late teens – goofy smile, close-cropped hair, the instantly trustworthy acoustic guitarist in a folk-and-skiffle trio who wear matching red shirts, matching black slacks and (nice touch) matching red socks inside their matching black shoes. These are the Hootenanny Singers, who were the Westervik Singers, or 'West Bay Singers', until Stig Anderson got hold of them and changed their name to . . . well, arguably one of the worst names a band has ever had. Then again, let's allow some credence to the Engelbert Humperdinck principle. Never mind whether it's cool; choose a name that people won't forget. In the mid-'60s, the Hootenanny Singers are all over the Swedish charts and Swedish television, and all over the Swedish outdoor festival circuit – the folkparks.

And here, nearby, is Agnetha Åse Fältskog against blazing autumnal foliage on the cover of her hit 1968 debut album: Agnetha, who has grown up obsessively playing the piano and listening to heart-tugging Connie Francis records like 'Who's Sorry Now' and 'You're Gonna Miss Me'; who was performing in a three-part vocal harmony group at thirteen; who hit the road as vocalist for the dance band Bernt Enghardt's Orchestra at sixteen; who has had a number one at seventeen with her first single, a song she wrote called 'Jag Var Sa Kar' ('I Was So In Love') and who, soon after that, was bombing around Stockholm in a sports car and a mini-dress.

The first time Björn sets eyes on Agnetha, she's on television; the first time they set eyes on each other is when their respective bands collide at a folkpark; and the first time they get to talk to each other properly is on the set of a television special in 1968. When they marry, in 1971, in the village of Verum, it's a Swedish news story and the path to the church is mobbed with photographers.

And here's the organist at that wedding: Göran Bror Benny Andersson, beardless and polo-necked in his mid-'60s role as keyboard player and songwriter with The Hep Stars, a five-piece, corduroy-heavy and determinedly English-singing pop act – the Stones, you might say, to the Hootenanny Singers' Beatles. That long hair, though, is scrupulously clean and shiny – not just in Benny's case, but band-wide – and the repertoire leans more to the Stones of, say, 'Ruby Tuesday' than the Stones of, say, 'Satisfaction'. Nonetheless, it's as a Hep Star that Benny – nearly always standing at the keyboard – evolves his onstage performance style: abrupt bursts of head-tossing, over as quickly as they start, and which, only slightly tamed, will filter into his seated onstage performances with ABBA.

Benny and Björn collide on the folkpark circuit and, despite the differences in hair length and stage clothing, hit it off, allegedly sitting up through one of those very short Stockholm summer nights playing Beatles songs together. They quickly form a cross-group musical alliance and songwriting partnership. The first number they write together is called 'Isn't It Easy to Say', a piece of lovelorn pop whimsy in 3/4 time which feels significantly indebted to The Beatles' 'Norwegian Wood' from the previous year, but which, when The Hep Stars record it in 1966, features an ornate spinet accompaniment and some piano overdubs that sound very Benny Andersson in the light of what we now know.

The pair write a handful of other songs which The Hep Stars record, but they have their first major hit as a writing team in the spring of 1969 when a Swedish singer called Brita Borg records 'Ljuva Sextital', a title which seems to contain multitudes but in fact simply means 'The Good Old Sixties'. All rinky-dink pub piano and parping brass, this number strips right down for the verse and then winds up into a blaring oompah chorus that seems almost to oblige an outbreak of communal singing from beneath a sea of raised and foaming beer glasses. It's a classic piece of schlager music, then – the sentimental, frequently Germanic, singalong pop form that goes down a bomb in northern Europe. Indeed, specifically it seems to be a Swedish take on the Austrian schlager singer Willy Hagara's 'Du spielst 'ne tolle Rolle' – or, as it became in the Nat King Cole version with which you might be more familiar, 'Those Lazy-Crazy-Hazy Days of Summer'. The schlager side of Benny and Björn will certainly subside a little in the years to come, but it will never entirely go away. This stuff is in their blood.

Meantime, here's Anni-Frid Synni Lyngstad, somewhere in the mid-'60s, on the poster for a cabaret night, wearing a glittery silver sheath dress and wedged between two goofing male comedians in fright wigs and false ears. And here she is at twenty-two, hair tied up high, on the cover of her first Swedish single. She has had her first gig as a singer with a dance band at the age of just thirteen, has diverted to jazz combos by the age of eighteen, has married a jazz singer at nineteen (they would have two children) and has won a national talent contest in 1967. First prize: a record deal with EMI Sweden and a slot that night on national television.

This just happens to be the day that Sweden switches from driving on the left to driving on the right, meaning that a larger than normal portion of the population is at home, sheltering from any drivers who didn't get the memo. Frida sings 'En ledid dag' ('A Day Off') to this inflated audience and becomes a celebrity. Two years later, she competes at Melodifestivalen, the Swedish national heats for the Eurovision Song Contest. She finishes fourth, but backstage she meets Benny Andersson, who also has a song in that contest. In 1970, Frida and her husband divorce and, by 1971, she and Benny are engaged and living together. They will eventually marry in 1978.

At this point, then, the ingredients are all in place. Here are two couples, all four of them big talents in the music business, who socialise with each other and go on holidays together. Yet it doesn't seem to occur to any of them very quickly that they constitute the material for a globally successful pop group. Björn and Benny step away from their bands in order to write, produce and record together. Sometimes they write and produce for Agnetha and Frida, who continue to release records. In 1970, they're all together at one point on Agnetha's third solo album – but still nobody twigs. It's only later that year, when Agnetha and Frida end up singing on two tracks on a Björn and Benny album, including one called 'Hej Gamla Man' ('Hey Old Man'), that they start to wonder whether something about the blend might work. Even then, though, they directly kibosh the idea by going out on tour as a cabaret foursome, calling themselves Festfolket ('engaged couples'), and pretty much bombing on a nightly basis.

Eventually, though, they recover and regroup, recording the song 'People Need Love', an arms-aloft hymn to universal brotherhood which contains unashamed yodelling. Two passages of it. This they release in the summer of 1972 under the name Björn & Benny, Agnetha & Anni-Frid. But that's a mouthful, so Stig Anderson proposes ABBA. It's easy to say, works in any language and means nothing in any of them: perfect. The only problem is that Abba is already the name of a well-known Swedish fish-canning concern. (Here, the curators of the Waterloo Expo play a blinder by producing, in a glass case, a small set of samples of Abba's preserved fish products, including red and black cod roe, and a toy articulated lorry bearing the Abba logo.) Anderson applies to Abba for clearance, and the company declares that it has no problem with ABBA, as long as the band do nothing to bring the fish-canning industry into disrepute. ABBA, I think it's accurate to say, go on to hold up their end of this deal for the entirety of their career.

So this is roughly how things stand in 1974. These are the four people whom, when the music starts in Brighton, we in the UK know nothing about, beyond what David Vine has mostly wrongly told us from the commentary box, but whom Sweden already knows well. From our point of view, they are four obscure artists who are, in fact, a supergroup – albeit a Swedish supergroup, which is a significant qualifier. Agnetha has just had her twenty-fourth birthday, the night before the show. Anni-Frid and Björn are twenty-eight, and Benny is twenty-seven. They have all toured the folkpark circuit to the point, certainly, of familiarity, and possibly even to the point of exhaustion with its charms. Agnetha and Björn now have a daughter, Linda, who is not yet two. (They will have a son, Peter, in 1977.) All four of them know, more or less, what it is to be big in Sweden, and also to chafe at the restraints of that and to wonder if there might be, somewhere out there, a slightly bigger world for what they do.

This is, of course, where the Eurovision Song Contest comes in. Frida and Benny, we already saw, have already tried their luck individually at the Swedish national heats in 1969 (Benny's song finished joint first, in fact, but came out second in the tie-breaking vote-off). Agnetha had submitted a song a year before that, in 1968, but it had been rejected by the panel. Björn and Benny had two entries turned down in 1971, managed to get selected with a song for a singer called Lena Andersson in 1972 ('Sag det med en sang', or 'Say It With a Song'), but saw it finish third, and then fell short again as ABBA in 1973 with 'Ring Ring'. (The Waterloo exhibition offers a big red plastic phone that you can pick up and hear 'Ring Ring' sung in four different languages. Out of curiosity, I get as far as the chorus of the German version, but when it turns out that the German for 'ring, ring' is 'ring, ring', I feel a bit under-rewarded and hang up.)

Undeterred by those cumulative setbacks, the members of ABBA are back for more in 1974. But it's not hard to see why. Eurovision is the escape route. It's the only way the four of them can tunnel out and reach beyond the boundaries that geography and language have arbitrarily placed around their talent.

Naturally some people in Sweden feel affronted that they should even want to do this, finding it somehow treacherous that these stalwarts of the Swedish music scene should need to put on silver boots and English accents and go batting their eyelids at the world beyond Sweden's borders. Ironic, really, the claims of cultural betrayal that would be levelled at ABBA for years after they broke big, given how stolidly the three Swedish-born members of the band remained domiciled in Sweden. Much later, after ABBA had stopped recording, Frida would find homes in other places – England, Switzerland, Spain. But there was no Californian exile for the other three showbiz millionaires; no permanent residence in tax-light Monte Carlo, as tempting as that may have been. They all stayed put in Stockholm or thereabouts. These people weren't too big for their Swedish boots after all.

But they did think it would be a shame if only Sweden knew their songs.

'Waterloo' changes all that, of course, and sets a whole new train in motion. And now, here at Waterloo, the Expo remembers how. Here, in a glass box, is Benny's star-shaped silver guitar from that night . . . although, on closer inspection, it's a replica. The original sits in the ABBA Museum in Stockholm and is presumably, like the *Mona Lisa*, never loaned out except in the rarest of circumstances.

But here are Inger Svenneke's boldly attention-seeking costumes for Brighton, run up at a frugal cost of just €50 per ensemble, allegedly, in today's money, and still crisp and bright, from the silver toes of their boots to Agnetha's blue knitted cap.

Although these, too, turn out to be replicas because the originals are . . . well, guess where.

But no matter, because these replicas have been painstakingly put together, down to the exact positioning of the oh-so-'70s black and white button badges that were fastened to their chests and arms, featuring photographs of Stan Laurel, Buster Keaton, Marlene Dietrich, and Fred Astaire, plus . . .

Hang on a moment . . . what's this?

On Agnetha's blouson, there's a bigger, white badge I've not noticed before.

And there's another one, identical, on the shoulder of Björn's outfit.

Two large white badges, reading . . . can it be?

Yes, it can. The badges read, 'Remember You're a Womble', around a drawing of Orinoco.

How? What?

Well, this is what research is for, I guess. Apparently, Mike

Batt, the composer and singer behind The Wombles' musical incarnation, went around the backstage area that night in 1974, distributing these badges among the contestants, including to Agnetha and possibly also to Frida. (At the time, Batt confessed, he assumed Agnetha and Frida were competing as a duo.) Come showtime, one of those badges had ended up pinned to Björn, where it was mostly concealed by his guitar strap. And Agnetha's ended up in full view on the right-hand side of the front of her bright-blue blouse, though the television cameras were never close enough to pick it out precisely. Which is probably just as well, from my point of view, because the knowledge that this newly arisen pop goddess was wearing a 'Remember You're a Womble' badge would probably have melted my childish synapses to a point beyond repair.

Anyway, by the time the band came to put the costumes back on to pose for the cover of the 'Waterloo' album, Stan Laurel and the others remained, but the Wombles badges were gone, swept into history's dustbin (about which the Wombles would no doubt have had something to say). Accordingly, there are no badges on what are allegedly the actual, as-worn costumes in the ABBA Museum, either.

One obvious conclusion here: if it's fully detailed historic accuracy that you're after, then clearly you have to go to the proper source – an academically curated battle site.

With my heart rate just about restored after this revelation, I move on to the stand dedicated to Brighton's aftermath, which in the first instance seems to have involved the rapid under-taking of Waterloo-related photo opportunities. First up, I'm gratified to see, was Waterloo Station in London, where the band posed on a luggage trolley under a platform sign and in front of a poster reading 'Wherever you are, wherever you're going, Inter City's got just the ticket for you.'

And second up, the site of the Battle of Waterloo itself. Here's a photograph of ABBA sweeping into town, waving from the windows of a vast black limo, flanked by police outriders. Evidently they climbed the 226 steps to the monument at the top of the Lion's Mound, surveying the battlefield and the many further miles of Belgian countryside which are visible from up there, but, oddly, the exhibition has no photographs of them doing so. But here they most certainly are, meeting the mayor of Waterloo, Andre Caussin, and signing the town hall's visitors' book before each of them departs with that most '70s of leaving gifts – a souvenir ashtray.

The consequence of all this is, of course, a life measured out in magazine covers – or so this exhibition now strongly implies: *Det Nye, VeckoRevyn, Tiffany, Bravo, apo, Das Freizert, Youpi, Hitkraut, Veronica, Vi Unge, Story, Musik Joker* . . . My mind went back to the four naively beaming people in those early photographs and the surely unforeseeable life that lay ahead of them as faces on newsstands, and as faces on bubblegum cards and soaps, on fridge magnets and calendars, on annuals, jeans patches, jigsaws, purses, branded clogs and colognes and all the other myriad ways we were offered back then to own a piece of ABBA in plastic or card and bring them closer to us, while actually bringing them nowhere nearer us at all.

And on it goes. In the final glass case, which is devoted to the ABBA Voyage show, I recognise the hat, programme, ABBA tea tray and sundry other pieces of merchandising currently on sale to ticket-holders at the ABBA Arena in London and wonder if, strictly speaking, it's a little soon to be regarding these items as museum-ready relics. Then again, that's surely one of the most imposing lessons that this exhibition teaches, and that the story of ABBA in general teaches: that history creeps up on you fast.

I'm leaving when I notice a curtained-off area to one side, with music coming from behind it. I part the curtain. It's a small dance space, hung with mirror balls, swept by disco lights. 'Gimme! Gimme! Gimme! (A Man After Midnight)' plays and the lyrics scroll down on a giant screen on the wall. The room is deserted and there's nobody whatsoever in sight.

Tempting . . .

It's time to go.

Back in the gift shop, in another arresting contrast on a day for such things, ornamental Napoleon-era weaponry (a rifle at €195, or a cheaper pistol option, at €105, or the sword and sheath in between, at €145) is on offer directly alongside a stack of ABBA picture books. Walking through, I check my phone and realise that, despite my initial scepticism, more than ninety minutes have passed since I went in. This means – I calculate, with a slight wince – that I have spent longer dwelling on those displays of ABBA memorabilia than I spent going round the David Hockney exhibition at the National Portrait Gallery in London earlier in the month, and possibly twice as long as I spent looking at the Frans Hals retrospective at the National Gallery a few weeks before that.

Which feels kind of wrong.

On the other hand . . . well, show us your platinum discs, Hockney.

And you, Hals.

8

'Kill me afterwards'

They nearly didn't enter 'Waterloo' for Eurovision at all. The song was recorded and ready to go by mid-December 1973, when Björn and Benny showed Stig Anderson the outline for another contender with a finished melody but only sketchy lyrics. They had given this new song the working title 'Who's Going to Love You?'. It seemed to have something.

It was a bit late in the day, though: the deadline for entries in the Swedish heats was just around the corner, in January, and Stig was about to head off to the Canary Islands for a Christmas holiday.

But a good lyricist, like a good comedian – and also like a good music business impresario – is never off duty. At his hotel, Anderson played a cassette of the demo over and over and tried to come up with something. And eventually, drawing inspiration from the Spanish being spoken around him, he found a title that scanned and wrote some verses to go with it, in which a lover laments the end of their relationship but looks ahead to the reconciliation they believe to be inevitable. Then he phoned the words back to Stockholm very loudly down a bad phone line – an act of agitated dictation one would very much have liked to have witnessed from Anderson's end.

'Darling our love . . . was much too strong . . . to die . . . yes, die . . . Got that? . . . OK, new line: We'll find a way . . . are you still there? . . . We'll find a way to face a new tomorrow . . . no, *tomorrow* . . . *TOMORROW!* . . . Hello?'

'Who's Going to Love You?' had become 'Hasta Manana'. It was a mid-tempo ballad, with a hooky pan-European title and a singalong chorus. It had Eurovision written all over it. A safer option than 'Waterloo', definitely.

But why play it safe? Was this about simply winning the competition? Or was it about making a lasting impression?

Anderson seems to have been the most adamant of the three that they should enter 'Waterloo'. And Anderson – not unusually – prevailed. Carl Magnus Palm, in the ABBA biography *Bright Lights, Dark Shadows*, quotes Anderson telling Benny and Björn, 'If it all goes wrong, you can kill me afterwards.'

Out and about in Brighton on Friday morning, the day before the main contest, Benny and Stig found a bookie. Up with the favourites in the early running, and available at 6/1 at one point, ABBA had by now drifted out to 20/1 as the money came in for Mouth & MacNeal and their naggingly obvious 'I See a Star'.

Benny placed a £10 bet on himself. Stig put £20 on, suggesting, perhaps, that he was twice as confident as Benny was that they were about to find the exit.

9

Gorilla outfits and custard pies

It was like nothing you had heard before, while sounding like a number of other things you already loved. Pop music may be at its very best when it pulls that combination off, ticking the boxes you need ticked while also ticking some further boxes that you hadn't realised you had about your person. There's a lot to be said for the absolutely bracing shock of the new, of course, and let's never write that off. But the shock of the new combined with the comfort of the old is a special pleasure. And 'Waterloo' managed that.

We've mentioned some of the other records this song is patently enamoured of. 'Baby Love' by The Supremes and 'Build Me Up Buttercup' by The Foundations are both in the genes of its chorus line and at the source of its effervescence. And with its muscular gallop and the chorus's happy, major ascents and descents to and from the fifth, via the fourth, the song is also clearly in awe of The Beach Boys' 'Help Me Rhonda'. But perhaps most of all you hear the debt to Wizzard's 'See My Baby Jive'.

Roy Wood, that song's composer and the maverick pop genius behind Wizzard, was a former member of The Move and Electric Light Orchestra who, in the early 1970s, embraced the possibilities of glam rock with perhaps unmatched enthusiasm. He wore large quantities of face paint – so large that he frequently seemed to be sharing his face with an exotic parrot – and draped himself in floor-length harlequin robes. A TV appearance in support of 'See My Baby Jive', which came out in 1973, found a robed and painted Wood holding a French horn, for no apparent reason, while members of his backing band, in gorilla outfits and angel costumes, staged a custard pie fight behind him. It was not clear, exactly, which planet Wizzard were on, but nobody seemed to be taking themselves terribly seriously there. And the song – as Benny and Björn had clearly noticed – was a stormer (as was its predecessor, 'Ball Park Incident', and as was its successor, 'Angel Fingers', before 'I Wish It Could Be Christmas Every Day' put Wood in with two members of Slade, Paul McCartney and Mariah Carey as the composer of a seasonal song that will not go away).

Wood also went about his business below an enormous quantity of hair, in which he was by no means unique at the time. But Wood had a super-abundance of the stuff – hair to spare. There was a lastingly memorable moment during a *Top of the Pops* appearance one Thursday evening when, mid-song, Wood raised his hands from his electric guitar, reached up to his ears, took hold of two fistfuls of his mane, yanked them out and flung them across the studio.

'Drugs,' my friend Nick confidently told me when we discussed this moment earnestly on the bus to school the next day. Nick's dad had said so. He had been looking on disapprovingly from an armchair in the classic manner of so many '70s parents during *Top of the Pops* (they couldn't bear to watch, but somehow they also couldn't bear not to) and, at the wretched sight of this unflinching depilation, had issued an instant diagnosis: that bloke must be on something.

I digested this information, which felt almost sickeningly disorientating to me, opening up a hinterland, the scenery parting to reveal something that went back so much further than I had realised. Your teenage years were a succession of these awakenings. There was always so much more going on than you had been aware of, and not all of it made you feel entirely comfortable. You thought you knew these people who flashed before you so colourfully on *Top of the Pops*, introduced to you with a comedy yodel by a satin-jacketed Jimmy Savile. But the truth behind the surface was so often so much darker.

Wood's hair-removal stayed with me, a cautionary tale of the follicle-weakening properties of hard drugs. Indeed, I reckon I was well into my twenties before it dawned on me what had actually been going on: that Wood's great bundles of hair were not entirely his own; that he was fixing extensions to his naturally luxuriant shoulder-length locks; and that those extensions brilliantly loaned themselves to acts of hair-tearing for show-business purposes.

Not drugs, then. Wigs.

Now, of course, I wonder: did Nick's dad – a physics teacher – seriously believe his own diagnosis? Or was this just a parental wind-up? Alas, too late to ask him now. But either way, it worked.

Anyway, connections are important, and if you liked Wizzard, the chances were you would also like this new band, ABBA. Except the Wizzard link turned out to be an unhelpful one. Wizzard went on being Wizzard – at least for a few more singles. But ABBA didn't go on being Wizzard at all. 'Waterloo', one would eventually realise, was a false steer. It was the first and only time ABBA came at us in that particular mode, and the first and only time they would offer us this kind of uninflected joy. This was ABBA's glam-rock period – and it lasted fewer than three minutes.

Indeed, as I soon discovered, it didn't even extend as far as the B-side of 'Waterloo'. Now, as a newly fledged investor in singles in the mid-'70s, you learned very quickly that B-sides were not somewhere that artists were particularly concerned to show the best of themselves. In most cases, the flip-side of any seven-inch single was a dumping ground, a contractual obligation, a space to be filled. Because radio stations never played them, except by accident, they were the vinyl equivalent of the desert air, and any old offcut would do. So, you knew the risks, and the chances were you would be wincing in anticipation even as you lowered the needle towards the groove. I'd been let down relatively recently in this area by The Sweet ('Hell Raiser' good; 'Burning', on the B-side, not good at all) and at other times by artists as diverse as Gary Glitter, Linda Lewis and Chelsea Football Club. ('Blue is the Colour' unquestionably set the gold standard for records sung by football teams, and it's not just prejudice that leads me to say that. But 'All Sing Together', its flip-side, is as bad as any recording made by anyone, in any studio, at any time, anywhere.) And furthermore, very shortly after this, I would be flipping over my copy of The Wombles' 'Banana Rock' and forlornly concluding that 'The Womble Square Dance' was really not their finest work.

But at least in each of those cases the B-side was, however underpowered, recognisably the work of the act on the A-side. The same could by no means be said of ABBA's 'Watch Out', which, as I now found out, represented a change of approach from 'Waterloo' so radical you wondered whether some unfortunate confusion had occurred at the pressing plant.

'Watch Out' started with the chunter of a heavy metal guitar over a thrashed snare drum and some squirty synthesiser. Then in came the vocal in the form of a tight-throated rock melodrama, delivered, not by Agnetha and Frida, but by Björn. Even at that early stage in our relationship, I think I concluded that having Agnetha and Frida in your band and delegating vocals to Björn was like having access to a packet of matches but choosing to rub sticks together. The song ploughed its way through a fist-shaking minor-key verse and chorus, modulated a little uneasily to major in its bridge section, repeated the routine a couple of times and then ended with a grungy skitter down the fretboard and a literal explosion – ka-boom!

Was this some kind of parody? I really didn't know, and I really still don't. But my hunch (and it's only a hunch) is that Christopher Guest, Harry Shearer, Michael McKean and Rob Reiner may have had ABBA's 'Watch Out' in mind when they wrote the admittedly slightly slower 'Sex Farm' for Spinal Tap.

So, as the reverberations from that terminal ka-boom eventually died away and the room fell silent, I had questions. What *was* this band? Who *were* these people? We would be puzzling over that for some time – and perhaps they would, too. 'Waterloo' went to number one in the UK, but it would be eighteen months before ABBA reassumed that pinnacle – long enough in those days for an act that was fresh off the blocks to slip through the cracks and disappear entirely.

Still, whatever now happened, they had at least rewritten the rules of Eurovision, hadn't they? They had banished the format's tired cliches and, with a fresh blast of contemporary pop, blown open the doors and windows for good. The competition could never be the same, surely.

Or maybe it could, in fact. The following spring, the contest was, in keeping with tradition, held in the country of the reigning champions. The winners in Stockholm in 1975 were Teach-In from the Netherlands. And, true, their guitarist, bassist and (yes) vibraphone player might have felt less inclined to perform in tight baby-blue metallic jumpsuits without ABBA's cue from twelve months earlier. But their song was called 'Dinge-Dong' – a title which would have felt too on-the-nose, surely, as an entry in a satirical 'guess the title of next year's Eurovision winner' competition. Sweden's reward for hosting the contest was to finish eighth out of nineteen, Lars Berghagen & the Dolls with 'Jennie, Jennie' attracting for the most part mild indifference from the international juries.

And ABBA? They weren't even invited. There was reckoned to be no room in the show for a lap of honour by the previous year's winner.

So, no, ABBA didn't change Eurovision at all. Eurovision, temporarily squashed into a new form by their impact, duly popped back out like a perforated plastic ball resuming its shape.

Over that year's 15th-placed entry, Finland's unfortunately titled 'Old Man Fiddle' . . . well, let's just quietly draw a veil. ABBA, at least, would survive.

10

The virtue of virtual

May 2022. I'm on a crowded train heading to east London for the opening night of the ABBA Voyage show. With each stop, the space in the carriage occupied by exuberantly dressed people expands, until the final change, at Stratford, when the whole platform becomes an undulating sea of brightly coloured evening finery. And hang on – is that Sophie Ellis-Bextor in the lavender jump suit and gold slippers? Why, yes it is. Not often you see her on the Docklands Light Railway, or maybe I don't look carefully enough.

As the general flutter attests, we are a gathering of people united by our excitement and sense of privilege at being a part of this hot-ticket occasion. We are also united by having not even the foggiest idea what we're about to see. We are headed, we know, for an ABBA concert – the first such thing in London for forty-three years: since November 1979, indeed, when the band appeared for six consecutive nights at Wembley Arena.

But we also know that, very much unlike then, this will be an ABBA concert in which none of the members of ABBA will be actively performing.

Which, in itself, is no surprise, of course. This is ABBA, after all, who, having toured for the last time in 1980, set themselves so firmly against the notion of a reunion show that they once turned down a billion-dollar offer to perform again. True, by that point – the Noughties – nobody in ABBA really needed any more money than they already had. But history is not exactly littered with already very rich people who have declined the opportunity to make another billion dollars when it was on the table.

Not the members of ABBA, though. 'They were talking about one hundred and twenty gigs or something,' Benny Andersson told an interviewer. 'It would have taken ten years out of my life – just the stress and leaving people disappointed all the time.'

Our disappointment? That was a rare scruple on Andersson's part. How many pop musicians, offered a lucrative opportunity to join the comeback trail, have made our likely disappointment a deciding factor in their decision-making? For at least a quarter of a century now, the concert schedules have overflown with veteran performers who have studied the marketplace, reviewed the numbers and somehow managed to get over our disappointment.

Remember how The Eagles, irreconcilably ruptured and thoroughly fed up with it all, vowed they would never tour again before hell froze over – and then eventually hit the road for what they unashamedly called the 'Hell Freezes Over' tour? In the rock arenas and enormodomes of the twenty-first century, history now routinely repeats itself – not necessarily as tragedy or farce, but in the shape of a sort of heritage battle re-enactment, which may contain traces of both. Or in other words, hell now essentially freezes over on repeat, and what went around is nearly always persuaded to come around again eventually – a little older, a little more tired, a little more disappointing.

But ABBA – different in this as in so many things – were unusually adamant that we should be left un-disappointed, left with that unfashionable thing, our memories. And also, for that matter, left with our money. *It could never be the same* was the essential and unpopular principle the band upheld. They weren't the people they once were, *we* weren't the people we once were . . . Why would any of us even think about pretending otherwise?

Yet, in a major reversal, here are ABBA in 2022, all set finally to rematerialise on a stage in front of us. Except not. Here they won't be, in fact. Yes, there will be real musicians somewhere on the stage for ABBA Voyage, ten of them, and yes, there will be ABBA's voices (but recorded), and yes, there will even be ABBA themselves – but not *actually* them. Tonight, and on every night the show is staged (length of run to be determined by demand, of course), the part of ABBA will be played by computer-regenerated projections of ABBA. A virtual ABBA.

What is that going to look like, though? In advance of actually seeing the show, precedents are neither many nor encouraging. I've found myself recalling that moment in the mid-'90s, when a decision was taken to revive by electronic means Nat King Cole, who died in 1965, and send him out on the road again, resulting in a spectacle in which his daughter Natalie was briefly joined on stage by a patch of television interference. Will ABBA Voyage be anything like that?

Or how about the Whitney Houston touring hologram show, which reached the UK just before the pandemic descended in 2020 and was described in one review as a 'jerky simulacrum', a 'ghoulish cash-in' and 'a flickering chasm where a huge talent and vulnerable person used to be'. Will it be anything like that?

Or will it be more like that time in 2012 when Tupac Shakur, in direct defiance of his death in a shooting in Las Vegas sixteen years earlier, rapped again for five minutes in a trick of the light at the Coachella festival in California?

'What up, Snoop?' said the reanimated Shakur that night. 'What the fuck is up, Coachella?'

'Ayo, Pac, let these muthafuckers know what kind of party they at right now,' responded a genuinely onstage and forty-one-year-old Snoop Dogg.

The illusion, produced with screens and mirrors, does not seem to have photographed particularly well, but was quite convincing, according to witnesses, albeit that this was day three of the festival and presumably a significant portion of the audience had been seeing reincarnated rap stars for many hours by that point, and other visions too. However, the *Guardian* was unimpressed, declaring with a weary sigh that 'what was a revelation this week will doubtless become a tired gimmick rather swiftly'.

So, something like that?

Of course, the term we are being strongly encouraged *not* to use in connection with ABBA Voyage is 'hologram'. That doesn't stop the *Daily Mail*, who will still be referring to the spectacle as a hologram show the day after it opens and people have seen it. But this is despite the fact that the producers have spent the weeks leading up to the opening patiently explaining to anyone who will listen that this is *emphatically not a hologram show*. Rather, ABBA will appear before us as avatars or, better,

'ABBA-tars'. And those ABBA-tars will take the shape of apparently fully modelled, uncannily realistic, idealised versions of the band members' younger selves.

How have these ABBA-tars been created? 'Digitally' is, of course, the helpfully broad term to be wielding here, although those of us who have read a little further into the articles have also become confident enough to drop the expression 'motion capture' into our conversations, albeit without really knowing in any useful detail what that means either.

Meanwhile an official photograph has been widely circulated of the four members of ABBA standing in a studio in Stockholm and wearing what appear to be black pyjamas with coloured sticky patches attached to their bodies at various points, as if undergoing some kind of skin-firming treatment at a particularly boundary-pushing health clinic. Again, intriguing. But none of this has really helped us get our heads around what this production actually is − what we're actually going to see, let alone what we're actually going to feel, if anything.

At this point, with merely half an hour or so to showtime, the only thing we can say for sure about ABBA Voyage is that it has cost a lot of money. Bloomberg have quoted £140 million as the price of developing this production through to launch, which would make it the priciest theatrical music spectacle ever staged, and certainly the priciest at which the stars − the evening's main and entire attraction − will not be appearing.

And perhaps the most tantalising thing is that, when you examine the options in the light of your limited understanding of how this thing is meant to work, there doesn't really seem to be any middle ground for ABBA Voyage to land in. It's either going to produce one of the greatest hey prestos in the history of modern entertainment, in which ABBA rise out of retirement, shake off the wearying chains of time and stand before us re-made; or it's going to be a colossal error of taste and judgement, evocative of a rainy Tuesday afternoon in . . . well, I'm reluctant to return to it, but the now-defunct Brading Waxworks on the Isle of Wight comes to mind again.

Either way, I'm really keen to see it.

The train disgorges its shimmering load one stop down the line from Stratford at the somehow, in the circumstances, ominously named Pudding Mill Lane station, and we all sashay across the road in the cloudy, early-summer evening light. Directly in front of us rises the black-slatted polyhedron that is the ABBA Arena, this show's purpose-built 3,000-seat home. (Early reports have enjoyed mentioning that this mostly timber construction can be disassembled and transported to future locations. A flat-pack stadium! So IKEA. So *Swedish*.) The atmosphere outside the venue is very strongly 'film premiere': a throng of enthusiastic onlookers craning behind metal crush-barriers; a prowling parade of people-carriers with tinted windows; a watchful corps of security guards who are as discreet as twenty-two-stone men in black suits can be; the periodic burst of screams marking the latest arrival of a recognisable attendee.

Predictably, the evening will indeed be dignitary-rich – and not just Sophie Ellis-Bextor. Not just Zara Larsson, Myleene Klass and Jarvis Cocker, either. Tonight, we will be in the presence of Swedish royalty: King Karl Gustav and Queen Silvia, who probably didn't come by DLR. To be honest, though, I'm more awed to be in the presence of Australian royalty: Kylie Minogue, who probably didn't come by DLR either. A little later, in the general drift into the auditorium, I will be eased aside – gently but also in a way that brooks no resistance – by a large man in a dark suit, one of (I think) a quartet of such large men, operating in unison to ensure Kylie's untrammelled passage to her seat. I am probably more thrilled by this inter- action than I ought to be. But I am someone who was once forcibly flattened against a wall in a corridor behind an awards event in New York so that Barbra Streisand could come through, and I am collecting these moments.

A tall white marquee with plastic windows has been erected along the front of the arena and we are fed into it at one end along, excitingly, a red carpet. Very shortly afterwards, however, the red carpet divides, a bit like the DLR at Stratford. At the junction, busy assistants in stretchy black gear, wearing earpieces and holding iPads, carefully filter the prominent guests onto the outward-facing side of a long hoarding, for their moment in front of the cameras of the media, and the rest of us are gently shunted down a branch-line on the hoarding's other side, where we are hidden from view and can do nothing to diminish the night's glamour.

My companion and I have completed our journey along the corridor of obscurity and are lingering on the edge of the entrance to the arena, surveying the scene, including the crowd packed behind the barrier, some holding ABBA pictures and albums and signs, many waving agitatedly. And that's when I notice the four backs standing together nearby, and realise with a lurch that I am about ten feet from ABBA.

There they are. They they *actually are*. Not projections – ABBA themselves. There's Agnetha Fältskog, aged seventy-two, in a floor-length white silk dress and a matching jacket, her blonde hair loosely swept back. There's Frida Lyngstad, now Frida Reuss, or Princess Reuss, or the Countess of Plauen if you wish to employ one of the courtesy titles she married into in 1992, and which are still in operation in her widowhood; Frida at seventy-seven, in a white silk trouser suit and very comfortable-looking white loafers and sunglasses and holding a walking stick. There's Benny Andersson, seventy-six, slightly owlish behind tinted circular spectacles, with a mop of grey hair and in a shin-length cotton coat of many colours, covered in prints of flowers. And there's Björn Ulvaeus, seventy-seven, trim and tidy and crisply bearded, in sharp eyewear and a navy suit over a white t-shirt, the evening wear of the tech entrepreneur.

They have paused to be interviewed while the cameras of the press clatter at them from a short distance, and it's a lesson in the growth of a legend to reflect that these four people who first agitated for the world's attention on the stage of the Brighton Dome in satins and silks and button badges now only have to stand next to each other somewhere to create an international news story.

It also sharpens the senses to reflect how infrequently this act of standing next to each other happens for ABBA. The last time these four people were together like this in public was eight years ago, in 2016, at the opening of a *Mamma Mia!*-themed restaurant in Stockholm. The time before that was eight years previously, in 2008, at the Stockholm premiere of the *Mamma Mia!* movie. And the time before that was in 2005 at the opening night of the *Mamma Mia!* musical, again in Stockholm, although on that occasion they sat in different parts of the theatre and did not pose together for photographs.

And before that? Well, since they ceased to be a functioning band in 1982, maybe just a handful of private occasions that we know about, including a party for Stig Anderson in 1986, and an event in Stockholm in 2016 marking fifty years of Benny and Björn's writing partnership, where Agnetha and Frida sang to their ex-husbands 'The Way Old Friends Do' from 1980's *Super Trouper* album, which must have been quite the moment.

So, that's three public assemblies and a tiny smattering of private ones in forty years before their collaborations on this Voyage show and the surprise album of new music that accompanied it. However you divide it, a sighting of a complete ABBA in the wild, from any distance, is, by modern standards, an event of practically comet-like rarity. But a sighting of a complete ABBA in the wild from ten feet, and quite suddenly, and after fifty years of intimacy with them, which has in fact involved no intimacy at all . . . well, I can further attest from my own point of view that this feels particularly agitating.

Or let me put it another way. I don't personally do screaming at celebrities, and especially not from ten feet away. This is partly because I worked as a journalist for a number of years and it was frowned upon. But I can definitely understand why screaming is going on at this juncture, over there at the barrier, and also some light weeping.

What's further clear is that this sighting of ABBA would be nowhere near as discombobulating if these four people hadn't so carefully removed themselves from our lives in those intervening years – if they hadn't so strictly rationed our chances to get discombobulated by them. ABBA's absence from the ABBA story turns out, as so frequently, to be a crucial engine in the ABBA story.

'Could we imagine,' the writer David Hepworth once asked, 'even for a moment, being tired of The Beatles the way we get tired of most things?' No, we could not, is the answer – and the reason we don't have to is because, Hepworth shrewdly and unsentimentally argues, The Beatles did us all the immeasurable favour of breaking up in 1970 and never getting back together.

'The group's story remains the best in pop,' Hepworth wrote, 'because it has a trajectory we retain in our heads. Their catalogue is perfect because they didn't hang around to sully it. ABBA,' he adds, 'who enjoy comparable affection, are one of the few acts about whom you could say the same.'

Indeed. As with The Beatles, ABBA's artistic career is blessedly free of a typical protracted late period. They got out and stayed out, with a full forty years of no returns leading up to these Voyage activities. And it's probably impossible to overestimate how much we all benefited from that, both those of us who love them and those of us who couldn't care less. They painstakingly refused to give any of us – attached to them or otherwise – the chance to grow weary of them in the way that, as Hepworth points out, invariably happens.

There was, for example, no opportunity through the 1990s to watch ABBA become increasingly depleted and less fond of each other while smiling their way through a series of greatest hits tours and periodically lowering the keys a semi-tone to be able to continue reaching the high notes. And thus were they spared one of the prime curses of pop stardom in longevity, we now well understand, which is to become your own tribute act. (See the history of The Rolling Stones since about 1976.)

For ABBA, there was no TV-advertised turn-of-the-century album on which, in the absence of new material, they revisited their best songs – but this time with an orchestra. They were never four starkly older faces in the multi-starred choir gathered earnestly around the studio mics for a post-hurricane charity single, and nor was there the opportunity to feel in any way uneasy about them taking up a Las Vegas 'residency', which was in fact only twelve shows per year. We never saw them in the early 2010s release a Christmas collection with vocal contributions from, say, Norah Jones and Gregory Porter, or make an awkwardly second-fiddle appearance behind the professional dancers on the *Strictly Come Dancing* results show, or turn up to perform two under-rehearsed numbers between Andrea Bocelli and Craig David at the King's pre-coronation bash at Buckingham Palace, or do any of the various spirit-sapping things that ageing pop acts must do to keep themselves in our thoughts while at the same time incrementally diminishing themselves in our memories every time. And for all of these reasons – every one a cause to rejoice – they have been able to remain most vitally in our minds as the ABBA we knew.

Which is what makes seeing the four of them now, in the flesh, finishing up their interview and turning to make their way slowly and a little stiffly into the arena, so very moving.

Now, it's perfectly possible that forty years of ever-gathering goodwill towards all the things these people stand for could be entirely spent at some point in the next couple of hours, and in high style, in the digital shark-jump of this ABBA Voyage show. But, given that these are the stakes, you would have to say they seem supremely relaxed about it. Nonchalant, even.

On Benny's face plays his familiar expression of slightly distant bemusement. Björn seems more tightly focused, as if possibly running the evening's agreed timetable through his head even as he deals systematically with the current item on the agenda. Agnetha, wreathed in smiles which flicker between warmth and mild hesitancy, appears to be both gratified by this high-watt attention and also to be slightly shrinking from it, something in her eyes suggesting that the desire to be doing this is only narrowly winning a battle with the desire not to be doing it. Frida, probably the most comfortable of the four in the circumstance, seems to be someone in whom the attention spontaneously brings something to life, and also someone to whom a laugh and a joke with a complete stranger on a night like this comes perfectly naturally.

And all of that paragraph is, of course, pure conjecture and projection, based on half a century of observing ABBA as they present themselves in public, which they very rarely do.

The four band members are guided through to some kind of inner sanctum, out of my sight, and, still somewhat over-wrought about having seen them, I make my way around the arena's bar and restaurant areas, in a heady cocktail of perfume, new woodwork and freshly applied varnish, and eventually take my spanking new seat in the spanking new auditorium.

While we wait for the show to start, I look through the programme and discover that Agnetha, Frida, Björn and Benny have put their signatures to a short letter at the front of it which ends: 'Again, welcome to a little strange, but hopefully enjoyable concert experience.' And I find myself wondering whether I have ever read anything so perfectly ABBA as that eleven-word statement, whoever wrote it. To devote your creative energies (and, incidentally, six years, on and off, and £140 million, and the best part of your reputation) to something which, even as the first audience is crowding into the arena, you yourself calmly acknowledge to be 'a little strange' – well, it seems to me that there is something quintessentially ABBA about that.

Meanwhile, an animation on the vast screen that arcs across the space in front of us shows snow falling gently and rather entrancingly through a dark pine forest, rendered realistically enough to make you feel ever so slightly cold in your spanking new seat. But it's OK, because heat and light are on their way. Along with an impeccable simulation of a total eclipse of the sun, as it happens. But more of that later.

For now, the four real members of ABBA take their seats in the arena to cheers and screams and reciprocated waves. And then the lights go down and the snowy forest vanishes and the music begins, and out of the darkness, searingly backlit, the four members of ABBA in virtual form, as they were in the '70s, rise up through the floor – to the right, the figure of Benny at an electric piano, to the left, the figure of Björn and his guitar, the figures of Agnetha and Frida in the middle. And even in advance of trying to compute how lifelike and solid those figures appear, I am suddenly powerfully aware of how much this band, which hasn't played for forty-two years, has imprinted itself in the deepest recesses of my memory as a *shape*.

For me, the next few minutes pass in a state of some bewilderment. The set opens with two songs from the more obscure end of the ABBA catalogue, in as much as it has one: 'The Visitors', the title track from the band's final album, and 'Hole in Your Soul' from 1977's *ABBA: The Album*. During these, I'm scrambling a little for a toehold, looking at the stage (which isn't a stage), looking at the big-screen projections of the action on the stage (which isn't a stage), wondering what, exactly, I'm watching here, and how, exactly, it's appropriate to react to it.

But then there's a pause and the next thing I hear is the descending piano notes which are the introduction to 'SOS'.

It is, I think, the moment the show starts to work its magic properly, or certainly for me – the point where the tiresome questions you've had in your mind about holograms and avatars and motion capture technology and how this illusion has been created and just *what the hell this even is*, suddenly stop nagging at you and float away.

Because it's obvious what this is, isn't it? It's *ABBA*. And here to prove it is that simple descending piano figure, that moment in ABBA's career at which something perceptibly clicked, and the moment at which something perceptibly clicks in the ABBA Voyage show, too.

That simple descending piano figure plays, and at that point there's nothing really that I can do. We're used to old pop songs pulling this stunt on us – the way they can suddenly, in the reverse of ABBA's arrival through the stage, dissolve the floor under your feet and drop you with a clump into a pile of cardboard boxes in the basement where your past is kept: a basement which turns out to be holding items of clothing you had completely forgotten about, and pieces of long-abandoned furniture, and scents that certain girls wore, and rooms where parties took place, and whole streets, in fact, and passages of weather and entire holidays, actually, and, blimey, even the rolled-up carpet from your bedroom.

It's pretty much a cliché to talk about it, and it's certainly a cliché to describe the effect as 'Proustian' – the pop user's substitute for the cracked paving stones and cakes dipped in tea that caused Marcel Proust to ponder the past's eerie persistence before the invention of archived *Top of the Pops* repeats on BBC2 made that whole business so much easier.

But just because it's a cliché doesn't make it any less true.

And so here, in this specially constructed arena, during this pioneering and ostensibly future-altering piece of digital entertainment, that descending piano figure plays – the sound of ABBA suddenly becoming ABBA – and the floor disappears and my stomach drops and, entirely despite myself, I go plummeting from a seat in Block J, Row N all the way down to 1975.

11

Notes on paper

Because the piano in our house was ancient and equipped with an inadequate and possibly even rotting wooden frame, it could only be persuaded to stay in tune for about ten minutes before the central heating came on and the fug in the room caused the strings to wilt and sag like over-boiled spaghetti. This mostly caused me, at thirteen, to resent that piano bitterly and regard it as the thing that was holding me back – the cruelly inadequate piece of equipment that would eventually, unless someone intervened, stand between me and my manifest destiny as an international pop performer of substance.

But what do you know? The treated sound of Benny Andersson's piano on ABBA's 'SOS' – which seems to have been fed through both an electronic chorus effect and a phaser so that it swings around in the air – and the entirely untreated noise made by this knackered instrument that had once belonged to my grandfather seemed to have quite a lot in common, all in all. I was delighted. I had found the purpose for which our piano was born: playing the intro to 'SOS'.

I bought the sheet music. It would be three years before I watched Dennis Potter's TV drama series *Pennies From Heaven*, with Bob Hoskins as a travelling sheet music salesman whose business is under terminal threat from the arrival in the culture of shellac records. And therefore it would be three years before I fully understood that sheet music for individual songs had been on its way out as long ago as the 1930s, which might explain why acquiring the sheet music for 'SOS' didn't feel like an especially fashion-forward thing to be doing in 1975.

It was, of course (the clue was in the name), only a sheet of paper. The man at Mann's Music in Colchester High Street, who didn't seem to be beating back customers for individual pieces of sheet music with a stick at this point in the business's history, kindly put it in a bag for me, but there was something faintly irrelevant about the gesture; it sort of already *was* a bag. It had a disappointingly drab brown front, featuring a low-grade sepia reproduction of the image from the sleeve of the 1975 *ABBA* album – a photograph of the band in evening wear, drinking champagne in the back of a chauffeured car and looking rather pleased with life while members of the public press their curious faces to the window. (The significance of that image – a calculated nose-thumb at the hard-line Swedish critics who accused ABBA of being treacherous, English-adopting sell-outs – completely eluded me.)

And the sheet music cost 20p at a time when the single itself – surely a more satisfying investment in both the short and longer terms – would only have cost 45p. Nevertheless, I felt it would contain the key to mysteries I needed to solve, and it had to be owned. I took it home and propped it behind the brass clips on the wilting piano's somehow still-functioning music stand.

Now at this point, I suppose, it would have been helpful if I had been able to read music. But I couldn't. At least five years prior to this, I had been the beneficiary of a handful of lessons from a home-visiting piano teacher called Mrs Galley. But those lessons had, of necessity, very abruptly stopped when Mrs Galley died. (Just to be clear, my playing was not actively implicated in the death of Mrs Galley, though I can't imagine it helped. She was, as my family concluded in our sober review of the situation, already elderly – by which, I realise now with a wince, we probably meant somewhere in her mid-sixties.)

I carried on playing the piano, though, although now purely by ear, on an auto-didactic and definitely non-music-reading basis, which, of course, as I was reassured to think, put me among many, if not most, of pop's greatest practitioners, from Paul McCartney down.

Fact: Benny Andersson cannot read music.

Still, the faint residue of my formal musical education meant I could at least pick some of the notes off a stave to get myself started and then hope that my ears would do the rest. And, as it happened, the introduction to 'SOS' was gloriously easy to play, once you knew where to start – just two fingers moving, consistently spaced, down the white keys, with just the one black note thrown in around halfway to keep you concentrating. This seemed extremely straightforward. Indeed, it was a bit like one of the late Mrs Galley's less vindictive starter-pieces.

In due course, I would work out that a sixteen-year-old Todd Rundgren had moved his consistently spaced fingers up and down the white notes and written the practically perfect pop song 'Hello It's Me'. And these twin realisations – about Todd's 'Hello It's Me' and about Benny and Björn's 'SOS' – would play their part in enabling me to form the idea that writing perfect pop songs was simple. Literally, kids' stuff.

Then I would spend a decade and more trying to write a pop song that hundreds of thousands of people wanted to listen to and discover that it wasn't simple at all – that it was actually next to impossible and dependent on forces that could remain stubbornly beyond a person's power to summon, no matter how much they longed to do it and no matter how hard they jabbed away at a keyboard.

But there was another lesson, more immediately absorbed, from these studies of the sheet music for 'SOS' and it was this: sheet music for pop songs is useless. I mean, utterly useless. OK, so this 'SOS' score could show me the intro's descending figure, and also the bouncing bass notes that come in beneath it (though not the accenting that Benny gives those notes which is deftly sprung in the way that . . . well, in the way that a proper pianist would play them; run the track on Spotify and check out the extra heavy ones in the gaps at 0.09 and 0.11).

But the achingly pretty classical étude-style counter-melody, echoing the first guitar hook, which the piano plays to accompany the first verse (0.16–0.40)? No sign of it anywhere on the paper. Some kind of direction regarding the boldly prominent ninth note (I now know) in that counter-melody that sits against the root note of the vocal on the last syllable of the line at 0.32, in which Agnetha says she wishes she understood? Nope, not a jot. And that upwardly swirly synth line like an excited intake of breath that flies you from the verse into the chorus (0.40–0.44)? Forget it, mate.

And as for some clues about the flute-like synthesiser part that harmonises with the piano in the second verse (1.16–1.38) . . . well, you're having a laugh, aren't you? Sheet music, you quickly realised, bore only the broadest of relations to the arrangement on the record which had made you reach for the sheet music in the first place. It was like wanting to find your way around the streets of London and being handed a Tube map.

Moreover, as it belatedly dawned on me, no member of ABBA had had anything to do with this piece of writing. It was the work of some time-impoverished transcriber, blending the top line of the sung melody with a vague representation of the overall arrangement so that people like me could sit at home and delight our families and friends by playing 'the song'.

But I didn't want to play the *song*. And, frankly, I wasn't all that interested in delighting my family and friends either. I wanted to play what Benny Andersson was playing. I wanted to play the *record*. And, clearly, sheet music was going to be zero help to me here.

No wonder they turned against it in the 1930s.

Still, amid the exertions and the extensive finger-prodding that were the prelude to this important disillusioning, there were two mini-revelations for which I would be lastingly grateful. The first involved that aforementioned jangly guitar hook that starts to answer the descending piano riff at 0.06. It gets played over a minor chord in the introduction (D minor, to be specific), and is then repeated in the chorus, exactly the same, but this time over a major chord, an F (0.48).

And when you do this, something magical happens. Set against that altered context, the repeated figure changes entirely, without changing at all. The same trick gets played in Rodgers and Hammerstein's 'My Favourite Things', from *The Sound of Music*, where the verse melody unfolds over a minor chord the first time around and then over a major chord the second. And so transformative is the effect of that shift that you can stare at your own fingers in disbelief that the melody hasn't moved, that it's still the same notes in the same place. It's one of music's most confounding illusions, and it's gratifyingly present in 'SOS'.

Mini-revelation two: that there was a density to this song that was unlike anything ABBA had thus far shown us, certainly, but was also unlike anything anybody else in pop music seemed to be up to at the time. Agnetha's fleetingly vibrato solo lament in minor at the top of 'SOS' is many miles across sad terrain from the sung-on-a-smile, hip-swinging, belt-it-out sass of 'Waterloo', so that was quite a surprise in itself. Indeed, she seems in this vocal performance to be narrowing the gap between singing and crying until there's only a breath between them.

Yet it's by no means the song's only tone, nor its whole story. Within seconds of that aching verse finishing, 'SOS' has bubbled up into a naggingly affirmative toe-tapping chorus in a major key.

It's a trick, once again, I would suggest, from schlager music – the verse sung by a mournful solo voice, minimally accompanied, before the song sweeps upwards into its chorus, taking the audience with it, and everyone dives in and the sentiment becomes somehow redemptively communal. And that transition would probably be enough for most pop composers to hang a song on, assuming they could pull it off without it sounding jarring.

But Björn and Benny don't leave it there. 'SOS' carries on into a third phase, heading out to another patch of ground beyond the chorus, populated unexpectedly by a rock guitar playing (from 0.59) a rising surge of four power-chords, by which point the song has taken on a new kind of energy again and started sounding positively grungy. Then it all gets stripped out and the journey upwards starts again from the bottom.

There is also what is, for pop, an unusually forensic attention to detail in the arrangement, particularly as the song wears on and the risks of repetition grow. For instance, that bubbly synth line that takes us infectiously into the chorus each time is halved the last time we hear it. Similarly, the descending piano intro figure is cut back to half its length when it gets repurposed as an outro at the finish. The instinct always seems to be to tighten the arrangement against the possibility of our impatience. Having found these catchy devices, and made themselves comfortable to be around, the band are seemingly on high alert to ensure that they don't outstay their welcome.

Nineteen seventy-five is the summer of 'I'm Not in Love' by 10cc, as much a sound collage as a pop record: tape-loops of 256 choral voices, wafting in and out over an electric piano and a bass-drum heartbeat, which is actually someone plugging away on some new-fangled thing called a Moog synthesiser. So I'm listening hard and wonderingly to that – egging it on, indeed, on its climb to the top of the charts like it's some kind of football team and I'm *supporting* it as much as listening to it.

But I'm equally mesmerised by 'SOS': by its rolling cluster of successively unfolding hooks; by the three tiers of vocal in the chorus, with Agnetha and Frida accounting for the upper two and with Björn supplying the lower; by the insertion of that rhythmically quickening 'and' into the final repeat of the penultimate line of the chorus, which adds an extra flourish at the last. (When Stig Anderson rewrites the song in Swedish for the version which appears on Agnetha's solo album *Elva kvinnor i ett hus* – 'Eleven Women in One House' – which is released that December, either he or Agnetha will ensure that he retains that final extra-syllable kick, even in translation.)

And I'm mesmerised, too, by the song's video – for, yes, suddenly there is such a thing, even though there is at this juncture only really one place in the UK where you are likely to see it – *Top of the Pops*. Nevertheless, in the spring of 1975, Stig Anderson has asked a twenty-nine-year-old Swedish television comedy director called Lasse Hallström – who will later direct award-winning movies including *My Life as a Dog*, *The Cider House Rules*, *Chocolat* and *The Shipping News* – to make four short film clips to send to TV stations for promotional purposes. And over two days, at a cost of merely £5,500, Hallström has shot clips for 'SOS' and three other tracks from the *ABBA* album, including 'Mamma Mia'.

Those films pretty much establish what we might now think of as the standard ABBA video palate: the use of an outdoor location, nominally requiring coats; the deployment of close-ups of the band as couples, one in profile, the other face-on, with the focus shifting between them; a preference for anyone who is not singing to be giving a look of sympathetic concern to the person who is; a sense, running rather contrary to the general ABBA way, of un-dressiness, and an overall vibe which is relaxed and personal, rather than starry and showy.

In the clip for 'SOS', we come back repeatedly to Agnetha, who is shot in close-up, in sunny daylight and ruffled by a mild breeze, and who gazes straight into the camera with pained eyes. In between, there are fancy mirrored images and the band's faces get passed through some unflatteringly gloopy hall-of-mirrors effects and whisked around like washing on a spin-cycle. But always we return to that simple, tight shot of Agnetha, carrying the burden of the song, and the overall effect is direct, honest, unmediated.

It's only really in the chorus, when the camera shoots the band steadily from above for a couple of bars, that you fully appreciate that Benny is in a red velvet jacket with puffed sleeves and leopard-print lapels; that Agnetha seems to be in some sort of Bavarian dirndl; that Frida is in a faux ocelot evening coat and white loon pants; and that Björn has got off lightly for once and been allowed to wear a grey bomber jacket with some jeans.

Or perhaps he arrived late and didn't have time to change.

Still, I'm not sure that many of us were fully aware of it at the time, but Hallström had just more or less single-handedly invented the pop video. That autumn, the band Queen would release 'Bohemian Rhapsody' and would commission Bruce Gowers to make a promo clip for it, for £3,500, of which, Gowers once claimed, just £465 was his fee. The resulting work, which took only three hours to film, featured various shots of the band's strikingly up-lit faces spun though various kaleido-scopic lens attachments. It received its premiere on *Top of the Pops* that November, and I can still recall whichever disc jockey was presenting the show that week (Dave Lee Travis maybe?), shaking his head afterwards in gurgling amazement and saying, 'Try making *that* at home on your Super 8 camera.'

And, of course, now you look at it and think, 'Give me 20 quid and an iPhone and I'll have something back to you by 5.00 p.m.' But back then . . . well, we had never seen the like and a watching nation's mind was well and truly blown.

Except that we *had* seen the like – back in the summer. That was 'SOS' pushing those promotional boundaries before it was 'Bohemian Rhapsody'. That was ABBA before it was Queen. That was ABBA becoming ABBA.

12

Devon-sent

And here are ABBA in August on BBC1's brand-new Saturday-night variety show, *Seaside Special*, a travelling variety show filmed in a big top belonging to Gerry Cottle's circus and pitched this week in a field in Devon. And light entertainment in the notorious TV dead-zone of summer surely doesn't get any better than this: a show which has dancers in branded *Seaside Special* t-shirts and (at least going by its title sequence) its *own helicopter*, and which offers a prospect so deliriously exciting that we hear the audience clapping along to its theme tune (written and sung by Mike Batt of Womble fame!) even before we see the audience themselves or know that there *is* an audience.

And here are ABBA, inside a hotly lit tent in Torbay, introduced by a perma-grinning Tony Blackburn and welcomed onstage between a set of impressions by Janet Brown and a number from Lulu, and shortly after the New Edition dance troupe in those aforementioned t-shirts has flung itself around to a medley of three songs including The Goodies' 'Funky Gibbon'.

Here they are on a set with a fairground backdrop and velvet-curtained entrances, the hokum, old-timey nature of which chimes just about as dissonantly as it possibly could with

Agnetha and Frida in their knee-length white boots and their white, belted, radically slit, underwear-revealing mini-dresses with : . . what's this? . . . are those? . . . yes, they are! . . . their white, belted, radically slit, underwear-revealing mini-dresses with *drawings of cats on*. Frida's cat is yellow, Agnetha's cat is blue. The dresses come, like much of ABBA's stage wardrobe, from the clearly febrile imagination of the Stockholm design team of Lars Wigenius and Owe Sandstrom, and the cats (I can tell you, courtesy of *ABBA: The Official Photo Book*) are based on drawings of the latter's pet cat, Kissen.

ABBA are travelling these days with two versions of this outfit, including a more demure, floor-length cat-dress for conservative television stations (in Germany, for instance) where cats are fine but a pre-watershed display of thigh and/or underwear is not looked for. But here on racy, pacy *Seaside Special* – which has its own helicopter, remember – the thighs and the underwear get clearance for family viewing, so the cat mini-dresses are *on*.

And here are Frida and Agnetha together in the chorus of the song, producing co-ordinated 180-degree turns from right to left and back, at which point we can observe that, as well as cats, the dresses have their names writ large in a flowing grey script across their backs. Which is handy for anyone still struggling to separate them by more respectful means than 'the blonde one' and 'the other one', as many British people in 1975 seem to be.

Handy further hint: Frida tends to dance with the song's rhythm; Agnetha tends to move with its melody. Something to keep in mind, maybe, for those tricky occasions when they don't actually have their names written on their clothing.

And here's Björn strolling about in the limited hope of some camera-time in a white silk suit with a matching silk scarf around his neck, and also an electric guitar. And here's Benny, seated at a small electric keyboard in some kind of white ferry captain's outfit, smiling out into the audience as much as into the camera, when it bothers to stop by, and seeming to enjoy himself – at least at the appropriate moments in the song, viz the chorus and its coda. For those achingly mournful verses, the camera mimics the Hallström video, closing in on Agnetha's face and staying there for the duration, filling the screen and bringing a sad, lovelorn and lip-glossed Agnetha into the UK's sitting rooms in greater and less ignorable detail than at any point thus far.

Thanks in part to these unstinting promotional efforts in primetime, 'SOS' will land ABBA in the UK's Top 10 for the first time since 'Waterloo' a year earlier, and set the band so firmly on track that their next seventeen singles will go the same way.

But that's all up ahead. On this particular Saturday, even before Tony Blackburn closes out the show with his own perfectly miss-able rendition of 'Tie A Yellow Ribbon (Round the Old Oak Tree)', I've heard and seen enough. I'm thirteen and it's time to take my relationship with ABBA onto the next level. Forget buying the single. This time I'm going all-in.

I'm going for the album.

13

Tape dispenser

It's easy to lose sight of this in the age of streaming and easy
internet access to music, but buying a whole album by an artist
in 1975 required you to dig deep − into your wallet, clearly,
albums being an eye-watering £2.99 at the time, but also into
yourself. It required pocket money, yes, and possibly a supple-
mentary income stream from (in my case) a Sunday paper
round. But it also took character and fibre.

After all, you were about to make one of the biggest purchases
of your life to this point − one which would, no question at
all, radically restrict your short-to-medium term spending power
in the sweet shop at the top of Church Lane on the way home
from school. And yet the thing you were about to blow that
money on was, quite likely, almost wholly a mystery object as
far as you were concerned.

For what did I know of ABBA's 1975 *ABBA* album before
I bought it? I knew 'SOS', of course. But beyond that? Only
the song 'I Do, I Do, I Do, I Do, I Do', which had come out
as a single earlier in the year and which a review in *Melody
Maker* had claimed was 'so bad it hurts'. And though I wouldn't
have gone that far myself, I didn't exactly love it either. Those

bleary saxophones, that slightly seasick rise and fall in the melody, that gentle, suspiciously parent-friendly, sway-along feel . . . Whatever those things were, they weren't really what I was looking for at this time.

Nor many other British people, it seemed. 'I Do, I Do, I Do, I Do, I Do' mildly grazed the UK Top 40 in the spring of 1975, reaching number thirty-eight before (like everything else ABBA had released in the UK since 'Waterloo') it drifted away into obscurity again – for now, at least. There was nothing in that song to dissuade anyone, really, from the theory that ABBA had shown the best of themselves in Brighton a year ago and that we could all now safely move on.

So that means that the *ABBA* album contained one song I knew I adored, one song I knew I was largely indifferent to, and nine songs I knew nothing about at all. The question, then, was whether those unknown songs would cleave more closely to the 'SOS' model of ABBA, or to the 'I Do, Do, I Do, I Do, I Do' model. And my hunch – based on absolutely nothing, really, apart from sheer hope – was the former. And I was prepared to back that hunch. And with my own money.

I bought *ABBA* in the summer of 1975, upstairs in Harper's Music – not on vinyl, but rather on what we lumberingly referred to as 'pre-recorded cassette', or, to use the industry's jazzy coinage for this format, 'musicassette', though I don't think that was a word that ever passed my lips, or the lips of anybody I knew.

Now, it barely needs saying that, by comparison with vinyl records, pre-recorded cassettes were very much the inferior format. Next to the generous facilities provided by 12-inch albums, with their big, square sleeves and gatefolds and inner sleeves and inserts and even entire *posters* to browse, a pre-recorded cassette was a niggardly and inscrutable scrap of plastic. Furthermore, cassettes didn't sound as good as vinyl records, the music on them seemingly having been compressed to death in the process of squeezing it onto the tape, shearing off the high end and the low end to leave only an unexciting, foggy stream of the resonances in the middle. Only eight-track cartridges were less romantic and more absurd as a music format than pre-recorded cassettes, but eight-track cartridges at least implied to the world with some certainty that you owned a car (the only place in which people played them). Your cassette wouldn't even do that for you. Indeed, it would do nothing for your reputation whatsoever. Entirely without dignity or stature, it might as well have come free in a box of cereal.

So how had I become a consumer of this patently inadequate product? A simple shortage of hardware, I'm afraid. I had entered a period of my life when I had no functioning record player, the latest in the small series of family cast-offs which had sustained me since about 1970 in that respect having recently packed up. True, my older brothers had working record players, in their own bedrooms. But negotiating access to those was a task for which I had historically lacked the necessary diplomatic skills – and would continue to lack them, I realised, short of a decade of experience with the police in high-pressure hostage situations. Those doors were closed to me.

Of course, I could have played records on my parents' stereo in the sitting room. But obviously that would have raised scheduling issues in relation to other people's television-watching. It would also have been discouragingly public – and this was perhaps the most important factor of all. Increasingly in this period, my feeling was that music was something I had to listen to in my bedroom, on my own. Pop music, although clearly at heart a communal art form, designed to bring people together, also seemed, in my case, to release a more contemplative side – my inner monk, if you will. It was apparently something I needed to be alone with.

What I did have, since a couple of Christmases before, was a Philips cassette recorder, which had been a faithful accomplice so far in all manner of acts of musical piracy, enabling me to tape music off the radio and occasionally off the television, even though a low buzz of electro-static made anything recorded that way virtually unlistenable. The obvious solution to the present hardware crisis was to press that machine into further service – indeed, to legitimise it by now using it for the private consumption of legally acquired, industry-endorsed tape products.

So home I went with the cassette version of *ABBA*, the sleeve in its paltry plastic case taking the form of a glorified postage stamp with that image of the band luxuriating in the back of the posh car. Bringing this together with my copy of the 'SOS' sheet music, I now owned not one but two utterly inadequate reproductions of the sleeve of *ABBA* – and was still none the wiser about its tart, nose-thumbing implications. (I don't think I thought too hard about the implications of the album's title, either, although it was obviously intended to mark some sort of reset: forget what went before under the name of ABBA – *this* is ABBA.)

I housed this tape with a handful of others in a snap-together plastic box, the size of a briefcase, with a sepia-tinted lid, which when closed made it look as if the cassettes inside were wearing shades. Cool! Meanwhile thirty specially moulded dividers, in two rows of fifteen, allowed me the comfort of knowing that my collection, even if it ever swelled that far, would continue to be held in perfect rank, and the literally handy handle on the leading edge ensured that I would never be without the music that I loved, in any setting, near or distant.

Not that I can remember taking my tapes anywhere. It wasn't really something you did, as a pre-recorded tape owner. Blank cassettes, of course, were different. Blank tapes were a sharer's medium. But not pre-recorded ones. Vinyl collectors enjoyed a busy and convivial social life, with their padded-plastic, handle-topped singles and albums boxes permanently ready to move brightly from house to house in accordance with a packed diary of music-related engagements. Pre-recorded cassette owners stayed at home, feeling slightly foolish about themselves. And quite right.

Anyway, up in my bedroom I scanned *ABBA*'s tracklisting, as displayed in vanishingly small print in the weird wraparound rear-window thing that the backs of cassettes went in for. And on this list, I was both surprised and pleased to see that ABBA were experimenting on this album with the musical part-work. The last track on side one was something called 'Bang-A-Boomerang Part I', and the first track on side two was 'Bang-A-Boomerang Part II'.

Highly encouraging, I felt. Strange title, of course. But two parts? It suggested mature, progressive ambitions and a definite move away from those perceived Eurovision 'roots'. My hunch about this album was already looking good.

Indeed, maybe these tracks would be something akin to 'Une Nuit a Paris', the three-part mini-operetta with which, just that spring, 10cc had opened their *The Original Soundtrack* album, and which, after relentless exposure to it over a two-month period, I could reproduce by heart – all eight minutes and forty seconds of it.

So I stuck the *ABBA* cassette in the machine and pressed play.

The album's first track was a song called 'Mamma Mia', which seemed to have something about it. Then there were two other tracks which were less immediate, but which I thought could possibly be 'growers', which was the technical term at the time for songs that you came to like through sheer exposure and force of will and because you had spent so much of your money on them.

'SOS' was next – brilliant, obviously; good to have it – and then another song, 'Man in the Middle', which was like an extremely watery version of Stevie Wonder's unmatchable 'Superstition' from 1972, and which had a vocal by Björn.

Hmm . . .

(In the winter of 2023, when the International ABBA Fan Club conducted a poll of its members to establish their Top 100 ABBA Songs, 'Man in the Middle' would be one of the thirteen ABBA numbers that didn't make it into the 100. We'll return to that poll later.)

And then 'Bang-A-Boomerang Part I' duly began and I readied myself to hear ABBA in their new, experimental phase.

The song started conventionally enough – bright, poppy, no radical departures in terms of mood, rhythm or instrumentation. However, when it reached the start of its second verse, I was slightly surprised to hear it fade out. A few seconds passed while the tape finished spooling in silence and then the machine clicked off.

Odd.

I pressed eject and turned the cassette over. There was another period of silence and then the song from side one – but now officially 'Bang-A-Boomerang Part II' – *faded back in*. A little under two minutes later, with no change of musical feel or shift into another gear, it finished.

Not a bold new direction for the band, then; a piece of gobsmacking meanness by Epic Records. Had I had a vinyl version of the album to hand, I would have discovered that it simply sticks all three minutes and five seconds of 'Bang-A-Boomerang' at the end of side one, and fires up side two with 'I Do, I Do, I Do, I Do, I Do'.

The problem with doing that on a cassette tape version was that it would have made the sides of unequal length. You would have ended up with about three minutes of blank tape on side two. And tape is money, of course. Better, from Epic Records' point of view, to snip 'Bang-A-Boomerang' in half, bring the two sides more or less in line with one another, length-wise, and cut their losses.

Unbelievable. Returning to the other pre-recorded cassettes in my collection, I mused dryly on the formal warning in tiny print on the sleeve of my cassette version of Paul McCartney & Wings' *Band on the Run*: 'To make a convenient break in the programme, the recorded sides may be of unequal length. Please spool to end of tape before playing other side.'

Or, as my copy of 10cc's *The Original Soundtrack* courteously informed me – both in tiny writing on the insert and, thoughtfully, in even tinier writing on the cassette itself – 'There will be an extended run-off at the end of Side 2.'

That was how you did it, surely. That was customer care. And respect for art. Not to mention respect for my pocket money.

According to the Discogs website, there have been 251 versions of the *ABBA* album in various formats down the years, on different labels, all around the world, and many cassette versions, including a German one, a Greek one and a Spanish one. And only the UK cassette version drives a bulldozer through the middle of one of the tracks in order to save money.

But what could I do? I just had to suck it up. I had one of the world's only self-fading ABBA albums. And I guess there were critics of the band at that time – working for *Melody Maker*, for instance – who would have gladly paid extra for that. Also . . . well, at least 'Bang-A-Boomerang' was the track that this indignity had been inflicted upon, rather than 'SOS' or 'Mamma Mia', which would, in my thirteen-year-old opinion, have been a disaster.

I mean, no disrespect to 'Bang-A-Boomerang', nor to any of the fans who voted it all the way to number sixty-six in that International Fan Club Top 100 ABBA songs poll. And one certainly doesn't wish to be harshly critical of what is, relatively speaking, an item of juvenilia in the ABBA catalogue. But if you felt you had to snap any of the songs on 'ABBA' in half, this would probably be the one to choose. How to put this? The chorus of 'Bang-A-Boomerang' rhymes 'dumby-dum-dum' with 'hummy-hum-hum'. As I listened to that chorus go round for the first time, I felt slightly queasy, very glad to be alone at that point, and inclined to withdraw still further into myself. So much for my hunch. I was a Eurovision-adopting ABBA fan who was determined to hold his head up and back the band moving forward. But . . . *dumby-dum-dum*? And *hummy-hum-hum*? Hello? Fully four years earlier, Middle of the Road's utterly pervasive 'Chirpy Chirpy Cheep Cheep' had proved too saccharine for even my nine-year-old teeth, and this seemed to be in gratingly adjacent territory, lyrics-wise. What was this? Some kind of skipping rhyme? What was I meant to do with a skipping rhyme – especially one that clicked off in the middle?

And what could it possibly mean, anyway, to bang a boomerang? True, Marc Bolan of T. Rex had sung about banging a gong in 'Get It On', a single with a hallowed place in my collection since 1971. But, as so often in Bolan's work, by sheer force of concentration and with an exorbitant amount of pouting and a splash of glitter paint, he seemed to be able to turn what was patently nonsense into something that sounded sultry – vaguely dangerous even. Here, the blended voices of Agnetha and Frida were cheerfully aloft, proudly waving these words like a flag from the top of the song.

And frankly the verses weren't much better. A mere moment's thought seemed to have brought together 'warm and tender', 'return to sender' and 'please surrender' to form what I think even my thirteen-year-old self would have recognised as a notably content-light stanza.

And, of course, the song was catchy. It was an ABBA tune, after all. Even at this early stage, it was apparent that, whatever else they were, ABBA were specialists in catchiness – the question only ever being how much you, the listener, wanted to catch what they were spreading. So 'Bang-A-Boomerang' – both parts of it – was without question a tune you could hummy-hum-hum. And all credit to the band for that because such things aren't easy to come up with. They are, in fact, vanishingly difficult to conjure. But, at the same time . . . well, would it be all right with everyone if we *didn't* use the term 'hummy-hum-hum'?

All in all, there was lot for me to digest here – and a lot that I didn't know at the time. If 'Bang-A-Boomerang' had the title, the melodic feel and the commitment to booming verbal inanity of a potential Eurovision Song Contest entry, that's because it *was* one. Björn and Benny had originally written the song for a duo called Svenne & Lotta to sing at the 1975 Melodifestivalen, the Swedish Eurovision heats. Who knew? Not me. But however keen they might have been at this point, a year after 'Waterloo', to distance the ABBA project from its connection with Eurovision, Björn and Benny obviously weren't averse to keeping in touch with the contest as songwriters.

Svenne Hedlund, incidentally, was one of Benny's bandmates in his '60s group The Hep Stars, while Lotta was a former member of an American R&B vocal group called The Sherrys, who also sang for a while with The Hep Stars. She and Svenne were married. On the happy couple, Björn and Benny now bestowed 'Bang-A-Boomerang', with their very best wishes. Although it was equally, in Svenne & Lotta's version, a tune you could hummy-hum-hum, the Swedish jurors largely preferred not to. The song finished third. Björn and Benny then took it back for the *ABBA* album.

It's probably a good job I *didn't* know all this at the time, in fact, because I would have felt pretty let down. Wasn't the plan – both for ABBA and those of us who felt drawn to them – to get shot of this unhelpful 'Eurovision act' tag? Didn't we have an agreement here? Weren't we moving on together?

My friend Nick from over the road was also a pre-recorded cassette person; it was one of the things we shared, along with an interest in booting a ball up and down a garden and playing Subbuteo on the carpet until our knees bled. But while I was listening to *ABBA* by ABBA, Nick was listening to Cockney Rebel's *The Psychomodo*, a rare blend of glam rock with psychedelic weirdness and the album which had 'Mr Soft' on it, with Steve Harley's off-kilter, balloon-vowelled vocals. It also had 'recorded sides . . . of unequal length', so that it actually played all of its advertised music without fading any of it out in the middle.

It was by far the cooler item to own, there could be no denying. Did that matter? It seemed to. Quite a lot. There were moments when the *ABBA* album appeared to me to be almost overwhelmingly great, but unquestionably there were also moments where it went 'dumby-dum-dum', and clearly other music was available – Cockney Rebel's *The Psychomodo*, for example – which did not do this.

Of course, with hindsight, Steve Harley's vowels were *so* balloon-like that he might as well have been singing 'dumby-dum-dum' himself a lot of the time for all the sense it made. But it was different somehow.

And he certainly wasn't singing 'hummy-hum-hum'.

A long and vexing period of self-examination followed. People, no question, would judge you on these things. And how did I, at thirteen, wish to be judged?

It does me no credit, but I reacted to the pressure. I hid who I was.

I mean, I carried on playing it, obviously. I had too much invested, both spiritually and financially, to do anything else. Plus, I really did want to hear 'SOS' – and a lot. And that 'Mamma Mia' song, too.

But reader, I placed my copy of *ABBA* by ABBA in my deluxe sepia-tinted cassette carry-case spine downwards so that it presented as a blank strip of anonymous grey plastic to the casual observer and no one would know it was there.

14

Though I try

In due course, 'SOS' would famously earn praise from Pete Townshend of The Who, whose public support the band had never formerly been able to rely on but which would presumably have pleased them when they eventually received it. That praise was generous but also typical of the way that endorsements for ABBA tended to operate at the point it was delivered – which is to say 1982, just as ABBA were tailing away as an operational concern.

Townshend recalled to *Rolling Stone* magazine catching 'SOS' for the first time on US radio and eventually realising that the song he was listening to was by ABBA.

'But it was too late,' Townshend said, 'because I was already transported by it.'

Too late! In other words, had Townshend only known beforehand that the song he was hearing was by ABBA, he might have been able to take some kind of evasive action, heading the problem off at the pass somehow and sparing himself the embarrassment of his transportation. There should have been a label or an alarm or something. If only trigger warnings had been around in 1982.

Credit, of course, to Townshend for his commitment, albeit some seven years after the song came out. But such were the razor wires that appreciation for ABBA had to wriggle under in those times. The music of ABBA was not something that self-respecting rock musicians openly talked about listening to without offering some mitigating circumstances.

Accordingly, it wasn't until 2012 that Glen Matlock, the guitarist with the Sex Pistols, fully and openly acknowledged the part played by 'SOS' in the genesis of the Pistols' three-minute punk calling card, 'Pretty Vacant'.

This was in the spring of 1976. Matlock had the idea in his head to write a song that would cut right to the nub and make a band-defining musical statement – perhaps even a culture-defining statement at that pivotal point in musical history. He had the concept for it, which was inspired by a song Richard Hell had written and performed with the American new wave band Television – a song called '(I Belong to the) Blank Generation', the title of which Matlock had seen reproduced on a flyer and which chimed loudly with him and his sense of the general mood among his peers. He also had a title, which had come to him during a Sex Pistols soundcheck at the Nashville Rooms in London when he looked across at his bandmate Johnny Rotten, bathed at that moment in a green light, and found himself thinking he looked 'pretty awful'. And that reflection had combined in his mind with the thoughts he was having about the general vacancy of things to produce the phrase 'pretty vacant'.

But he was still missing one thing.

'What I needed,' Matlock wrote, 'was one particular musical idea which would echo the lyrical idea.'

And that musical idea apparently dropped into his lap a little later, courtesy of the work of Björn Ulvaeus and Benny Andersson, in a bar called Moonies on Charing Cross Road.

'I was there one lunchtime, drinking my way through that week's dole money,' Matlock wrote in his autobiography, 'when ABBA's "SOS" came on the jukebox. I heard the riff on it, one simple repeated octave pattern. All I did was take that pattern and alter it slightly – putting in the fifth, to be technical. *Got it*, I thought. *What could be simpler? I'm the Marcel Duchamp of the fretboard, creating my ready-mades.*'

It's a thrilling thought, not least for those of us who were still furtively nursing our copies of the *ABBA* album while these storm clouds were brewing – that ABBA, in whose music there was felt to be not one iota of raw rebellion, found their way into the imagination of a Sex Pistol and gave the punk generation a riff it could unite around. For those of us who loved Benny, Björn, Agnetha and Frida but struggled to let that love be known in an age when our peers were sticking their hair up with egg whites and patching their jeans with stolen pub beer towels, vindication could hardly be sweeter.

Got to be honest here, though; I've struggled to hear it. And that's despite the very best efforts of the BBC's 2013 documentary, *The Joy of ABBA*, which patiently set the allegedly relevant passages of the two songs alongside each other and ran backwards and forwards between them a couple of times to demonstrate the link.

Here was the bottom of Benny's descending piano intro and the ensuing spangly guitar figure; and here was Matlock's distorted riff. And then back to Benny; and then the Matlock again. Get it? The effect, to my ears, was uncanny. On first hearing, the two pieces were nothing like each other: no audible relation whatsoever that I could make out.

Yet, incredibly, on second hearing . . . well, they were even *less* like each other. Plus, the bit of 'SOS' the producers used in that sequence wasn't a 'simple repeated octave pattern' anyway.

Wrong bit, then? Maybe. But if so, what was the right bit? Given that what we were dealing with here was without question the most improbable example of ABBA's reach and influence beyond their own musical sphere, it seemed important to understand it properly. But, in the light of Matlock's revelation, I kept listening back to 'SOS''s major decorative features and getting nowhere.

Indeed, at one point I began to wonder whether the ABBA song on the jukebox in Moonies that fateful day when the Pistols' guitarist was visited by the spirit of Marcel Duchamp wasn't 'SOS' at all, but was actually 'Mamma Mia'. True, the tick-tock marimba part at the top of that song isn't a 'simple repeated octave pattern' either. Yet something about the way it insistently pogoes along could plausibly have inspired Matlock's three-note twang, couldn't it? At a stretch? If you were in a bar in Charing Cross Road and a couple of drinks in?

For that matter, isn't there a guitar accompaniment beneath the second verse of 'Fernando' that travels across an octave and which could have lent itself, in another life and another mood, to a song about feeling blank about things? And 'Fernando' would have been freshly released and jukebox-ready in 1976 when Matlock was walking into Moonies and going up to the bar.

In fact, when you started thinking into it, virtually any ABBA track in the catalogue up to that point could reasonably have furnished a punk guitarist with the rudimentary material for an era-defining anthem, as long as they had drunk enough.

Eventually, though, I think I found the bit of 'SOS' that Matlock must have meant. Unhelpfully, it's not one of the song's major hooks – neither the opening piano figure over the pulsed bass note, nor the guitar spangle. It's in the power-chord coda to the chorus, that third phase in the composition that we talked about earlier – the passage (at 1.03, in the first instance) where the bass synth and guitar vamp together on two deep notes, low to high, after each of the two lines about trying to go on. That, at least, is a 'repeated octave pattern' to which, on a good day and if they had a mind to, a guitarist could add a fifth and end up with the culture-altering intro to 'Pretty Vacant'.

Let's not get hung up on these finer details, though. We have ventured into a realm of fiercely protected legends and myths here, and sometimes you have to set cold analysis (or your own exhausted ears) aside and simply take people at their word. The larger point is that the ABBA of 1975 would eventually find themselves in some way present inside the genetic make-up of perhaps the greatest opening guitar riff and general call-to-arms of the punk rock revolution. Eventually, this would be talked about and generally, if not accurately, understood.

And that's enough. Indeed, it's more than enough. If I'd known this at the time, I wouldn't have furtively turned my cassette of the *ABBA* album around. I'd have safety-pinned it proudly to my forehead.

15

Skin in the game

Early in the autumn of 1975, a journalist from the West German magazine *Bravo* finds the members of ABBA at the headquarters of their operation in the diplomatic area of Stockholm, where there are soldiers on the street, albeit protecting the Chinese embassy next door rather than the plush new centre of Stig Anderson's Swedish music empire.

ABBA are around a table in the conference room with Anderson discussing promotional strategy and their next steps. Things seem to be coming together in all sorts of ways. The four have recently moved from the modest terraced townhouses they owned in the suburb of Vallentuna to less modest – but by no means grand – places. Frida and Benny have taken an apartment in central Stockholm, high in a building in Old Town with views over the harbour. Agnetha and Björn, with their two-year-old daughter, have moved into a detached villa in Lidingo, an affluent island suburb east of the city which is perhaps the closest thing Stockholm has to a Beverly Hills.

'At our home,' Agnetha tells *Bravo*, 'things don't look as organised as at Anni-Frid's place. Toys and clothes are lying around on the floor, but I gladly accept that . . .'

They have come through an underwhelming tour of West Germany, Switzerland and Austria in the autumn of 1974. Not one of the dates sold out and at the Stadhalle in Vienna, they attracted just 1,200 people to a venue seating 5,600. 'There weren't any real storms of excitement,' claimed an Austrian reviewer that night. And this despite a show bold enough to incorporate machine-blown soap bubbles. (The reviewer was even more gently damning about the Swedish/Polish support act, Beatmakers: 'quite nice in the background'.)

In the deathly words of one German writer on another night, '[the audience] sat there and hardly moved'. Still, another German reporter found at least one positive to emphasise: 'ABBA showed so much skin. More than any group before. The most courageous were Björn and Anni-Frid. Björn wore a skin-tight glittering suit in a Mick Jagger style. Anni-Frid appeared in a short bolero and a mini-skirt slashed eighteen times.'

In Nuremberg, Frida would find herself commended for knowing 'how to showcase a sexy navel'. However, a reviewer in Bremen conceded to some confusion that 'it is difficult to tell . . . whether whistles at such a concert express enthusiasm or displeasure'. 'Their songs disappear like the snow,' said a reporter in Innsbruck. And so did the entire show in Zürich and the one in Düsseldorf, due to slack ticket uptake.

But things have picked up in 1975 with a Scandinavian tour, commencing in Oslo in January, where, incidentally, a journalist called Mats Ollsson from the Norwegian paper *Expressen* has become the first writer (not counting the more obscurely allusive Clive James in the *Observer*) to go into print on the subject of Agnetha's bum, noting that in her 'enormously tight, white overalls', she would now be in a position to give Suzi Quatro a run for her money 'for the title of the most handsome backside in pop'. Here's a talking point which will continue to generate copy for almost the entirety of ABBA's career.

They have spent the summer on a fourteen-date tour of the Swedish folkparks, appearing before sell-out outdoor audiences of 3,000–4,000 and causing gridlock in Stockholm on the evening of their show in the Gröna Lund theme park, for which, perhaps unwisely, 19,200 tickets were put on sale at the door.

And they have found room for a brief holiday. Agnetha and Björn take Linda to Crete, Frida and Benny head for Los Angeles.

And now they sit and discuss the promotion of 'SOS', the song that seems to be unsticking the jam and moving things forward for them. 'We have received four offers for US television shows that we could do at the end of November,' Stig Anderson tells them.

Television knocks touring out of the park in terms of reach, time and cost. It's hard to fathom nowadays, when touring is the prime and sometimes only earnings mechanism for most major bands, but ABBA's tour of Germany, Switzerland and Austria at the end of 1974 operated at a loss, and that summer tour of the Swedish folkparks, with far lower overheads, made only a negligible profit, leaving (according to Carl Magnus Palm in *Bright Lights, Dark Shadows*) £27,500 to be split four ways.

Television, on the other hand, allows you to fly in, reach millions of Americans with one mimed performance and be back home with your two-year-old daughter very soon afterwards. So, in November 1975, ABBA perform 'SOS' in the US on a new weekly late-night comedy show, just five weeks old, called *Saturday Night*, which will eventually be known better as *Saturday Night Live*. They go on directly after the monologue by the show's host, Robert Klein.

I found some photographs online of ABBA on the set of *Saturday Night* and was surprised to see them casually dressed – jumpers, slacks, t-shirts, jeans. A different approach for the US, clearly.

But then I realised the photos were taken at rehearsal. Come performance time, Agnetha has donned cascading white bell-bottoms and a bright green mini-cape trimmed with ostrich feathers; Frida is in an ivory mini-skirt and matching knee-length boots. Benny is in an oddly luminescent jacket, which it's tempting to describe as animal-print, though I would struggle to put my finger on which animal, exactly; and Björn is once again a touchingly silky symphony in bridal white. All these outfits seem to have been pulled directly from the wardrobe for the band's tour at the beginning of the year.

The set is intended to look like the ballroom on the *Titanic*. ABBA then come back at the end of the show and perform 'Waterloo', while water comes gushing through the portholes and the ship 'sinks'. The implication seems to be that ABBA are the band that plays on regardless after the iceberg has been struck – which you could read a number of ways.

Still, great exposure, no question. And exposure is what it's all about at this stage. Exposure, exposure, exposure. This may sit more comfortably with some of the members of the band than with others.

Frida, who is interested in psychology, tells the German interviewer from *Bravo* that 'it's revealing in which position one sleeps. I always sleep on my back, completely stretched out. This means that I'm not afraid of the world and I feel secure. Agnetha, on the other hand, sleeps on her belly, snuggled into her pillow. [This means] she is in need of affection and needs a lot of love and always wants to be protected.'

16

Living forever

SPOILER ALERT. *Please skip this next chapter if a) you have yet to attend the ABBA Voyage show, b) you have plans to do so, and c) you don't want some blabbermouth telling you beforehand how it ends.*

When the Voyage show comes to a close on that opening night, the four members of ABBA come out onto the stage and take a bow. Naturally, it's a big moment. The whole show, in a way, has been about causing time to dissolve, and now time dissolves again, those projections of the band's younger selves melting into the darkness and giving way to the band as they now are, with getting on for forty-five additional years on the clock. They stand humbly to one side of the stage and the hall rises to greet them in a gale of acclaim because . . . well, thank you for the music, obviously.

And, also, congratulations on this show, of course, which has indeed been 'a little strange', as predicted, and yet which has also been a musical blast, and quite the most startlingly beautiful thing to look at, and most definitely like nothing which any of us has ever seen, and which has somehow – surely its most noteworthy and unlikely achievement – managed to conjure warm emotional engagement out of, literally, thin air.

But also, how often are you going to get the chance to express your gratitude to ABBA for having been ABBA, in the presence of actual ABBA? At current rates, the next in-public total band re-assembly isn't due for another decade, minimum. You have to seize these moments.

So, naturally, we stand and applaud with our hands high, and there's an awful lot of love in the room and it's a highly emotional moment. And as the four of them wave, embrace each other, wave some more and then turn and walk off in the direction they came from, I'm not ashamed to say that I'm teary.

And then the members of ABBA come out. The real ones this time. Because the first ones, we now realise, were just the conclusion of the show – its final magnificent, digital and motion-captured illusion.

And of course, now I think about it, when the four of them took that first bow, they were wearing different clothes from the ones they had been wearing at the start of the evening when I stood ten feet away from them: the silk Fendi, the flowing coat of many colours, the tight dark suit . . .

This should have been a clue, I suppose, but it wasn't. And such is the completeness of the illusion that ABBA Voyage creates and the extent to which you enter the world the show builds that, by the end, you genuinely don't know what is and isn't real, even when it's been standing right in front of you.

Friends that I talk to about it in the coming days will ask me how convincing the ABBA-tars were. And the only thing I'll be able to tell them, really, is that in a room which I knew to contain ABBA, I still mistook the ABBA on the screen for ABBA.

It's the same for lots of people, it seems. Over the next few days, I will see a few excited tweets from concert-goers at the ABBA Arena: 'I'm at the Voyage show and ABBA just walked on!'

And, of course, they didn't. Not that night.

Except in as much as they did. That night, and every night the show plays.

It's quite the revival, all in all. An article on the Bloomberg website put it well. ABBA, it pointed out, were 'early to music videos', as we saw, and also 'early to jukebox musicals', as we'll see in the next chapter. But now, in the shape of an unprecedented concert experience, which they could walk away from and simply leave running, they appeared to be on the verge of surpassing both those pioneering achievements and pulling off the greatest trick of all: being 'early to the art of living forever'.

17

The customer journey

In late April 2023, I head to the Novello Theatre in London to see *Mamma Mia!* the musical. Given that the show is in its 24th year in the city, I could be accused of being a little late to this party. I could even be accused of bringing along with me almost a quarter of a century of reluctance to expose myself to this special evening's phenomenally popular and long-lasting twist on the ABBA back catalogue. And those accusations would be fair.

But any attempt to understand ABBA's continuing hold on the ears of the world must clearly reckon at some point with this behemoth of the musical theatre, despite the fact that it's not about ABBA, and they don't appear in it in any form, live, fictional or virtual. So I have shopped online for a cheap ticket ('Slightly restricted view due to safety rail'), and I've opened my mind as wide as I can and here I am. I'm going in.

Crossing Waterloo Bridge in the warm evening sunlight, I am experiencing, I confess, a certain amount of trepidation at the possibility of seeing some very good pop songs badly mangled by trained actors. But I'm experiencing much more trepidation about what I might be about to walk into from a personal safety point of view. For, as unlikely as it may seem, in the spring of 2023, it has been kicking off like never before in the stalls and the circles of musical theatreland. Indeed, there's probably never been a more dangerous time to go to a musical than this.

Quite recently the police have been called to break up a fight during a performance in Edinburgh of *Jersey Boys*, the musical about the formation of the vocal group The Four Seasons. This came hot on the heels of at least two reported incidents of unruly singalongs at a production of *Tina*, the Tina Turner musical, in Birmingham, with performances being forced to stop and at least one show abandoned.

And then, just a couple of weeks ago, at the Palace Theatre in Manchester, two squad cars and a police Transit van were needed to assist in the eviction of members of the audience for *The Bodyguard*, the musical adapted from the movie of that name and featuring the songs of Whitney Houston. The performance had already been paused once, during the first act, when, according to the *Manchester Evening News*, it was necessary to remove 'a handful of people who would not refrain from singing'. It was stopped again near the end when some audience members made a determined attempt to out-sing the lead, Melody Thornton, a former member of the Pussycat Dolls. The curtain came down and, amid scenes of widespread disgruntlement, the show was called off with ten minutes remaining.

'We wanted to carry on,' a member of the cast told Sky News, 'but it had become a major incident.'

'Cannot believe what I've just witnessed at palace theatre,' posted a patron on Twitter. 'A mini riot after the show was stopped because audience members were trying to sing over the cast. Police riot vans have been called in. Chaos.'

Inevitably, people in the news media have been trying to work out why this kind of thing is happening and what it means. Some seem to be seeing it as yet further concrete evidence of general social decline in a bitterly divided and increasingly angry nation, and one more sign that Britain is well on its way to hell in a handcart. But, to be honest, these seem to be the people who say that about most things, whether it's NHS waiting lists or the disappearance of the green ones from boxes of Quality Street.

Other voices, perhaps more persuasively, are giving weight to the idea that people forgot how to behave during the isolation forced on them by the pandemic of 2020 and are perhaps still releasing pent-up energy from two lockdowns and adjusting to restored freedoms. So far as I can see, there's no consensus on whether this trend will shortly self-correct or whether it's a longer and deeper tendency that will at some point need political intervention.

Meanwhile, people in musical theatre have been mustering their own responses to this new and utterly unlooked-for climate for their work. Just recently we have seen the announcement of *Ain't Too Proud*, a musical based on the career of the great Motown act The Temptations, the producer of which has given a newspaper interview in which he thanked his lucky stars that The Temptations' major hits are much harder to sing along to in an all-out, several-vodkas-in, drown-out-the-performers kind of way than, say, Tina's 'Simply the Best'.

Nevertheless, the producer also spoke about the importance, even for this Temptations show, of 'getting the messaging right' and ensuring that 'people don't think they're coming to a hen do'. Elsewhere, a spokesperson for the Ambassador Theatre

Group, the UK's largest theatre operator, assured the *Guardian* that they were now 'taking a multidisciplinary approach to tackling challenging audience behaviour, covering all points of the customer journey, including how we market shows'.

And so here I am, on my own customer journey, heading for *Mamma Mia!* in the West End on a Friday night. *Mamma Mia!*, I should add, sits just an angrily tossed gin and tonic from the theatres staging *Tina: The Musical* and *The Lion King*, in a zone on the edge of Covent Garden that could plausibly be regarded as the very ground-zero for challenging audience behaviour, 2023-style, albeit with the five-star Waldorf Hotel offering a bit of a buffer in between.

This is where we seem to be, though, and no doubt, as they always say about football hooliganism, it's just the actions of a tiny minority spoiling it for the rest of us. Nevertheless, as I broodingly reflect, walking to a musical has never had more in common with making your way down the Seven Sisters Road to see Tottenham play Chelsea, and now comes with recognisably similar levels of worry that, if you're not careful or you simply get unlucky, you might find yourself caught up in something quite nasty.

To steady my nerves, I try to concentrate on the slogan that arrived with the email containing my *Mamma Mia!* ticket: 'You already know you're gonna love it,' it said, which should be reassuring, I suppose. The truth is, though, I don't know that I'm gonna love it. I'm not sure whether I'm even gonna *like* it, actually. The music of ABBA, but not performed by ABBA, and in an entirely non-ABBA-related context? That's by no means a slam-dunk for me, whatever the promoters seem to be inferring from my purchase of a ticket.

So I refocus on another line of encouragement from the accompanying literature: 'By the end of the show, all the ABBA songs will be stuck in your head.'

Well, OK. But that, too, when you think about it, is one of those promises which could also be interpreted as a threat. *All* the ABBA songs? All stuck in my head at *once*?

Anyway, I've reached the theatre now, where all seems, as yet, perfectly calm, with people mingling peacefully enough on the street and in the foyer, and with a generally benign pre-match atmosphere in the air. I begin the long climb, via multiple staircases, to my cut-price seat, pausing only to observe that the merchandise stall on the first landing is offering, among its various branded key fobs, mugs and t-shirts, a souvenir *Mamma Mia!* beach ball, which seems to me to be inviting trouble at this particular moment in British history, but let's hope they know what they're doing.

My seat is at the very end of the front row in the Novello Theatre's steeply-raked uppermost circle, and is an austere and strangely papal affair with a high, red back. From its vantage point, the stage is definitely in front of me, but, far more significantly, below me. My position also affords, as advertised, an unrivalled view of the balcony's safety rail, but I don't mind because that rail is plausibly the only thing standing between me, a momentary nod-off in the second act and an ugly death on top of the show's conductor.

I settle in with my programme and, as nonchalantly as possible, cast a wary eye over my fellow attendees. Next to me is a young Italian couple with their small daughter, who is perched on a chunky booster cushion. They don't *look* like trouble, but these days how can you tell? Generally speaking, the portion of the audience that I'm in a position to observe covers a broad range of ages, with people in their forties and fifties perhaps edging it as the dominant age-group, and with women perhaps edging it over men. There are even some adherents to the ancient belief that a night at the theatre is something to dress up for – people in jackets from the brighter end of the spectrum and open-necked white shirts; some floral dresses and heels – and there is a strong smell of cheerfully colliding perfumes and aftershaves.

The ushers vacate the room, the doors softly close and a recorded voice says, in an avuncular tone: 'You may be tempted to sing along with the songs, but please leave that to the cast.' There is no outright threat of ejection nor any mention of the possibility of riot vans, but we can consider ourselves warned. And with that, the lights go down and the band strikes up.

18

Opening-night ovations

'I thought ABBA was dead,' Björn Ulvaeus once told an interviewer. 'Maybe not into oblivion, but forgotten, like so many groups of that era. ABBA was frowned upon so much in the '80s that it was almost uncomfortable.'

He was speaking about the time when the producer Judy Craymer began trying to persuade him that it would be a good idea to make a musical of some kind out of ABBA songs. Craymer had got to know Björn and Benny when she was an assistant to Tim Rice, the lyricist who worked on the 1986 musical *Chess*. So these conversations started in the late 1980s – the absolute ABBA dead zone, the period in which, as far as Björn could see, what lay ahead for his technically defunct band was a series of waning half-lives as the stuff of 'gold' radio programming and tongue-in-cheek disco compilations. Craymer's first approach raised the possibility of some sort of television special, but that came to nothing. She went back to them with a musical theatre suggestion in 1992.

Not making Craymer's task of persuasion any easier was the fact that ABBA's songs had already been turned into a musical entertainment once, and few had really noticed. Christmas 1982 had seen the broadcast of a French/Belgian television co-production called *Abbacadabra*, a children's show put together by, among others, the French lyricist Alain Boublil, who had just written *Les Misérables*. Boublil was known to ABBA because he had provided the lyrics for the French-language version of 'Waterloo', and Björn and Benny granted him permission to take twelve of their songs and add entirely new, French words to them in order to create a tale in which a book of fairy tales drops off a school shelf and its characters spill out and come to life.

The result was ... well, quite strange, even by the reliably psychedelic standards of children's television. The Belgian punk artist Plastic Bertrand, whose boldly monotonous 'Ça Plane Pour Moi' made him a creature of some fascination in the UK in 1977, played Pinocchio. That meant he got to sing the adapted version of 'Money, Money, Money' – 'Mon Nez, Mon Nez, Mon Nez' ('My Nose, My Nose, My Nose'). Do you see what they did there? 'Dancing Queen', meanwhile, became a song called 'Carabosse Super Show', Carabosse being the wicked fairy of the *Sleeping Beauty* story. And on the subject of *Sleeping Beauty*, Frida herself was persuaded to take that role and to join the French singer Daniel Balavoine on the remodelled version of the song 'Arrival', which now had the title 'Belle'.

Their duet was released as a single and reached number fifteen in the French chart, but otherwise the show seemed to leave few traces. Still, the producer Cameron Mackintosh saw enough in all this to organise an English-language version of *Abbacadabra* in London a year later, in 1983.

Ah, 1983: as the honey-toned disc jockey Simon Bates immortally put it one morning, during an edition of 'The

Golden Hour', his 'guess when?' slot on Radio 1: 'It was the year we lost Sir Ralph Richardson – and gained *this* from Kajagoogoo.'

Well, swings and roundabouts, clearly – and it's an ill wind that blows nobody any good, though whether the loss of one of English acting's greatest talents was straightforwardly balanced by that Leighton Buzzard band's gift to the nation of the single 'Too Shy' may ultimately be down to historic forces greater than 'The Golden Hour' to decide. What 1983 certainly was, however, was the year we lost ABBA, or at least the year they went into what would turn into an almost four-decade hibernation, leaving the stage to the likes of Kajagoogoo and other synth-driven, twentysomething newcomers who suddenly made ABBA look a little tired in the hairstyle department and distinctly short of mohair jumpers. Whoever imagined that ABBA could be out-fought at the level of hair, make-up and wardrobe? And yet this was pop music, and with grim inevitability, that day had come.

Abbacadabra opened at the Lyric Theatre in the run-up to Christmas with a starry cast that included Elaine Page, Phil Daniels and Sylvester McCoy, who would shortly become the seventh Dr Who. The venerable songwriter Don Black and Mike Batt of The Wombles (who, I must admit, is making more guest appearances in this book than I had envisaged) provided rejigged lyrics. With a nose pun out of reach, Pinocchio's 'Money, Money, Money' became 'Battle of the Brooms'. Other alterations were less radical, yet somehow all the more curious for being so: 'Thank You for the Music' became 'Thank You for the Magic', while 'My Love, My Life' from the *Arrival* album – surely the greatest ballad in the ABBA catalogue and a hot contender for the best vocal performance by Agnetha on record – became 'Like An Image Passing By', a title directly lifted from the original song's chorus.

The French version's 'Belle', meanwhile, turned into a number called 'Time', and although Frida did not reprise her Snow White role in the stage show, she recorded the song, this time with the Scottish singer BA Robertson, whom UK record buyers may recall as the creator of the manically jumpy 1979 single 'Bang Bang' and its 1980 follow-up 'Kool in the Kaftan'. 'Belle' failed to break into the Top 40, despite Frida and BA doing their level best to hawk it on *The Russell Harty Show*. The stage show completed its limited run in January 1984 and did not transfer. Beyond a couple of barking-looking Dutch and Portuguese television adaptations in 1985, *Abbacadabra* pretty much vanished – almost, you might say, as if someone had waved a wand.

Still, it had potentially provided a useful service by posing the question: what happens if you take ABBA's songs and replace all the lyrics, making them about something else altogether, and give them to other singers? And the answer seemed to be: you end up with something nobody much cares for (including, apparently, Björn and Benny. It seems that neither of them ever saw the London stage production of *Abbacadabra*).

None of this would have made any easier Judy Craymer's task of persuading the members of ABBA that a new stage exploitation of their songs was the way forward. But, of course, there were already plenty of other reasons out there to be wary of such a project. *Mamma Mia!* would one day be widely credited with turbo-charging the restoration of ABBA that had got underway in the early '90s. But at the point of the show's

conception, the odds on it running the band and their reputation at speed up a siding and parking them there must have
surely looked good, to say the least.

The key question, obviously, was what form should an ABBA
musical take, assuming there should be an ABBA musical?
Should it recount the story of ABBA, with the band as characters? That was clearly working for *Buddy: The Buddy Holly
Story*, which had its first London performance in 1989 and ran
for twelve years, overlapping with *Mamma Mia!*. (Incidentally,
West End audiences clearly weren't above outbreaks of lairy
behaviour even in those days. Shortly after *Buddy* opened,
structural engineers had to be summoned to the Victoria Palace
Theatre to assess the soundness of the circle because people
were bouncing on it every night.)

But the members of ABBA shut down the biographical
route immediately. They had no desire to see themselves
portrayed on stage – and no conviction, perhaps, that their
story even amounted to the kind of material from which
musical theatre could comfortably be made. Perhaps they were
familiar with George Harrison's reaction to Willy Russell's
musical about The Beatles, *John, Paul, George, Ringo . . . &
Bert*, which opened in Liverpool in 1974 and then moved to
London, where it was successful enough to run for a year.
Harrison, who attended the premiere with his business associate Derek Taylor, lasted until the interval and then told
Taylor, 'We have to leave now or I'm gonna jump on that
stage and throttle those people.'

Harrison later described the show as 'awful stuff, all these
idiots acting out people' and said it was 'so inaccurate it was
nauseating'. In protest, he withdrew his permission for the use

of his song 'Here Comes the Sun', which had to be hurriedly replaced with Lennon & McCartney's 'Good Day Sunshine'.

No thumbs-up from George, then. Then again, John Lennon allegedly walked out of the movie of Rodgers and Hammerstein's *South Pacific* starring Mitzi Gaynor, and (according to Paul McCartney in his book, *The Lyrics*) thought there was only one musical really worth bothering with – *West Side Story*. So clearly The Beatles were a tough crowd for musicals. Potentially even a disruptive one.

Anyway, the ABBA story was off the table. Nobody in the band had any appetite for it. However, Björn and Benny conveyed to Craymer that, if a wholly separate story could be devised through which the songs could be successfully threaded, then perhaps they would be prepared to get involved.

But, by the way, unlike with *Abbacadabra*, the lyrics were to be left untouched. The songs were not to be bent to fit the musical; the musical was to be constructed to fit the songs.

In certain ball sports, this would have been called 'a hospital pass'. Indeed, it's hard not to think that those terms were as close as Björn and Benny could possibly have come to not granting Craymer permission to use their music while still granting her permission.

After all, if the ABBA story was off the table, what story *could* you tell with these disparate songs that you weren't allowed to alter, and how much would you have to contort yourself and your audience in order to tell it? Obviously Craymer would have felt encouraged that the songs themselves were cherished and, this being, by now, the mid-'90s, and with the *ABBA Gold* compilation available and selling well, increasing numbers of people seemed willing to admit it. But when is the strength and popularity of the song catalogue alone any kind of guarantee in the world of the jukebox musical? *Good Vibrations*, with a story built around a road trip across the United States to California, and featuring no fewer than thirty-two Beach Boys songs, opened on Broadway in February 2005 and faded away in a welter of indifference after fewer than three months.

And then there was the following year's *The Times They Are a-Changin'*, which had access to the not notably underappreciated song catalogue of Bob Dylan. The piece was intended to tell 'the timeless story of two generations at odds' in the form of 'a fable that exists in a dreamscape populated by the members of a struggling circus'. Personally speaking, I spot about seventeen red flags in the second of those sentences alone, but no matter. The musical was free to help itself to Dylan's songbook: 'Mr Tambourine Man', 'Like a Rolling Stone', 'Blowin' in the Wind', 'Lay Lady Lay', 'Knockin' on Heaven's Door', 'Forever Young' . . . so what could possibly go wrong?

Well . . . let's just say clips are available on YouTube for anybody with some spare time and a strong enough stomach. 'Like a Rolling Stone' is sung out to the audience by the show's lead, Michael Arden, who touts an enormous and unabashedly fake wooden guitar for the purpose. Behind him, dancers dressed as circus performers somersault and stretch. As we reach the chorus and the first appearance of the simile which is the song's title, grey workout balls roll across the stage – those all-important rolling stones which the song is talking about – and the dancers pick them up and variously swing them around, squat on them, etc.

Reviews ranged from 'utterly wrongheaded' to 'a stoned nightmare'. Ben Brantley in the *New York Times* said it gave Dylan's songs 'a systematic steamrollering'. Rob Sheffield's review for *Rolling Stone* begins: 'How awful is *The Times They Are A-Changin'* . . . ? What if I told you that 'Don't Think Twice, It's Alright' gets sung to a dog? And what if I told you that the dog is played by a mime wearing floppy puppy ears?'

The show lasted less than a month and departed with the verdict of the *Wall Street Journal* ringing in its ears: 'so bad it makes you forget how good the songs are'.

From this side of the mountain of *Mamma Mia!*'s success, it's easy to underestimate just how easy it would have been for an ABBA musical to make us forget how good the songs are. Just one part for a floppy-eared dog . . . But, of course, that's not what happened. Craymer brought in the award-winning play-wright Catherine Johnson, who had already written a piece, staged at Bristol Old Vic, about the music of her youth, *Too Much Too Young*, which showed she could blend existing songs and new stories. And Craymer appointed the director Phyllida Lloyd, who made time for this project between productions at the Royal Opera House. And the three of them fashioned the now-familiar, women-forward story about the single mother, the daughter who reads that mother's diary, the three men of whom one must be that daughter's father and whom she secretly invites to her wedding in order to find out, and the mother's former singing-group pals who are also on the guest list. All of this going down over two hours and thirty-five minutes, including a fifteen-minute interval, in the broadly relatable and suitably audience-warming location of a small Greek island.

That location, incidentally, put a line through the musical's working title – *Summer Night City* – but didn't, apparently, preclude the use of *Mamma Mia!* as a substitute. A Greek island, an Italian title . . . some musical-makers might have baulked at the slight muddle of that, but now, of course, it seems thunderously pedantic even to notice it, let alone mention it.

When it was clear the show might work, Björn, in a tiny backtrack – and presumably feeling he'd held out long enough – made some small adjustments to the original lyrics.

Benny, for his part, seems to have been sceptical all the way through the project, right until it opened. He read the first draft of Johnson's book and announced that he couldn't tell whether it was good or bad. After the material was given its first workshop, he said he felt the same way: was this thing going to knock 'em dead? Or was it going to die on its backside? And how would you even know until it happened? At that moment, he had the right to pull the plug. But his lack of a strong feeling in either direction kept both options open. Craymer and Benny agreed that, on opening night, one of them would be able to tell the other, 'I told you so.' They would just have to wait to find out which one of them it would be.

Mamma Mia! opened at the Prince Edward Theatre in London on 6 April 1999, twenty-five years to the day since ABBA sang 'Waterloo' in Brighton. Björn and Benny were in attendance. The show was up against *Miss Saigon*, *Les Misérables* and a new musical in town, *The Lion King*. But it was pretty clear from the instant ovations it received that it was going to be able to hold its own. During the curtain call, Björn, Benny, Craymer, Johnson and Lloyd went out on stage to take a bow, and as the acclaim rained down on them from an audience on its feet, Benny turned to Craymer and said, 'OK, you can say it.'

She leaned into his ear and, through the noise, said, 'I told you so.'

And after *Mamma Mia!*, the deluge: its success opened the sluices for an unprecedented gush of jukebox musicals in various forms in the first years of the new century: the Queen musical *We Will Rock You*; *Movin' Out*, based on the songs of Billy Joel; *Our House*, the Madness musical; *The Cher Show*; *MJ the Musical*, built from the music of Michael Jackson; the story of Gloria and Emilio Estefan in *On Your Feet* . . .

But nothing in this line has come anywhere near it. Twenty-five years after that opening night, *Mamma Mia!* is the sixth-longest-running show in the history of London's West End and the ninth-longest-running show in the history of Broadway, has been seen by more than 65 million people and has generated more than $4 billion in revenues.

You would call it a spin-off, except that spin-offs don't commonly get to spin quite so fast nor grow quite so huge.

19

Marimbas in, cymbals out

Before it grew an exclamation mark and became a record-breaking stage musical, two massively grossing films featuring Meryl Streep and a pair of soundtrack albums, 'Mamma Mia' was, of course, just a three-and-a-half-minute pop song.

Moreover, it was a three-and-a-half-minute pop song which, when the band listened back to it, seemed to be lacking something.

This was in March 1975 at Metronome Recording Studio in central Stockholm where ABBA were trying to finish what would be the last track in the sessions for the *ABBA* album. They sat in the control room and listened to a rough mix that Michael B. Tretow, the sound engineer, had prepared for them.

'Well, that's OK,' Benny later remembered thinking, 'but it's not really a record, is it?'

It was still short of a vital ingredient, something special to set it alight.

It would have been shortly after this that Benny, casting around the studio for inspiration, noticed among the instruments piled out of the way against one of the walls: a marimba.

How many artists in 1975 would have examined the pop

record they were making and diagnosed a marimba-shaped hole? Not many, surely. The freestanding, lower-voiced wooden sister of the xylophone was not in high demand as an instrument for chart-friendly pop in the mid-'70s. OK, so Benny would almost certainly have been aware that Brian Jones had played one very prominently on the introduction to The Rolling Stones' 'Under My Thumb'. But that was nine years earlier, in 1966, and it had hardly started a worldwide run on marimbas. What Benny couldn't have known was that, even as he was reaching for the mallets in Stockholm, an American band called Starbuck (no relation to the coffee chain) were preparing to release a single entitled 'Moonlight Feels Right', which features an almost comically prodigious marimba solo. But that was in the US, and Europe only caught up with that song much later, if at all. It was also, perhaps not coincidentally, Starbuck's only hit.

The fact is, when a marimba appeared on ABBA's 'Mamma Mia', it was the first time many of us who were in our early teens had really heard one outside of Tom & Jerry cartoons, where it would normally be soundtracking some terrible accident for Tom the cat involving a staircase and/or the loss of teeth. As far as we were concerned, it was a joke instrument.

Still, clearly none of these considerations fazed Benny, and none of them would have fazed Michael B. Tretow, either. Tretow was only a year older than the oldest members of ABBA: he was thirty at this point, to Björn and Frida's twenty-nine (Benny was twenty-eight and Agnetha was just short of her twenty-fifth birthday). But in the pop recording context, it's frequently the destiny of sound engineers to appear older and wiser than their years – to seem like the adult in the room. And photographs would suggest that this was true of Tretow in relation to ABBA.

Bearded and studious-looking, and with a carefully parted mop of hair, he wore thick-framed rectangular spectacles and was frequently in shirts with the cuffs not rolled but carefully folded back from his wrists. In several images, he is to be found expressionlessly surveying the mixing desk's disarmingly vast array of buttons and sliders while smoking a pipe.

For a further sense of the dynamic between Tretow and ABBA, it might be helpful to know that Benny and Björn used to take great pleasure in hiding Tretow's clogs on top of one of the studio's tall speaker stacks. It also seems that they enjoyed booby-trapping his matchbox, re-inserting its tray upside down, so that the next time he opened it to refire his pipe, its contents showered onto the floor. What larks, never gets old, etc. But then ostensibly mature and focused studio staff patiently tolerating the japes of slightly bored musicians is essentially the story of rock 'n' roll on record since George Martin first knotted his tie and set off to work with The Beatles, and doubtless since before that too.

However, as with Martin, the notion that Tretow was there to fill the essential lab-coated straight-man role in the ABBA operation won't quite cover it. Consider the album Tretow released under his own name in 1976, entitled *Let's Boogie*. Easily located online, this maverick collection, recorded with some help from ABBA members, includes a painfully growly Dr John-style New Orleans jazz spoof called 'That's the Way the Cookie Crumbles', an aggrieved complaint about country singers who get away with talking through their songs ('He Can't Sing') and a track called 'Robot Man', in which Creedence Clearwater Revival appear to have gatecrashed the theme from *The Benny Hill Show*. It represents, shall we say, an unusual and actually quite challenging listen, even before you reach track twelve, a honky-tonk western skit entitled 'Don McGurgle's Babylonian Lizard Tooth Oil'. But it's beautifully recorded, of course. And it's not the work of a straight-man.

Rather it feels like the work of someone who was both a purist and an eccentric, which is perhaps the ideal combination for a sound engineer. It meant Tretow knew extremely well how things ought to be done, and had the higher degrees of patience required to do them that way, while equally knowing that it was a good idea to do things differently whenever you could. He had engineered Björn and Benny's 1970 album, *Lycka*, and, before that, some tracks with Björn's early band, the Hootenanny Singers. His time with ABBA commenced when tape editing was done by hand with a razor blade and sticky tape. But he then carried the band forward through a decade of hectic advance for audio recording, all the way through to the automated mixing desk and the digital hard-drive recorder which were used to realise *The Visitors* before its release as a compact disc. The basic and irreducible truth about ABBA – that at no point in the band's career after 1975 do their records sound like anybody else's – must be significantly ascribed to the presence in the studio of Tretow.

Consider his practically allergic aversion to that staple excitement-generating ingredient for pop music, the cymbal crash. ABBA tracks, despite being uncommonly busy with dynamic transitions, shifts from dark to light and soft to loud, are unusually cymbal-lite zones. Hi-hats are low in the mix, if they are audible at all, crashes barely ever occur and the tinging propulsion of a ride cymbal, beloved of jazz players and rock drummers in sensitive moods, is heard, to the best of my knowledge, not once in the entire ABBA catalogue. And all of this would appear to be down to Tretow.

'I do not regard the cymbal as a musical instrument,' he told *International Sound* magazine in 1980. 'I regard it as a tool with which the drummer can ruin a good drum sound. It's about time somebody put a stop to them. Put a tax on cymbals.'

In the same interview, Tretow expounded at length on his preferred methods for recording a piano, going into great detail as he described his equipment choices, his preferred microphone positions, etc. 'And that,' he concluded resoundingly, 'is what makes it possible for the engineer to turn a $20,000 grand piano into a $100 honky-tonk upright. Amazing how you can make technology work for you.'

Historically, sound engineers in the world of pop have not always got full credit for their input. But just as some singers (Frank Sinatra would be the emblem here) were always humbly careful to mention the writers of the songs they performed, so Benny and Björn have been diligent about mentioning Michael B. Tretow when they talk about their records. They might have messed about with his clogs and his matches, but they also knew how central he was to the whole operation – the 'fifth ABBA member', to borrow a phrase.

It was Tretow who had been reading the British writer Richard Williams's 1972 biography of Phil Spector, *Out of His Head*, and it was Tretow who had lapped up the descriptions of Spector's enthusiastic multi-tracking of instruments – multiple drum kits! An entire section of electric guitars! – before trying something very similar on the earliest ABBA records: tentatively on 'People Need Love', more confidently on 'Ring Ring', and with panache on 'Waterloo'.

And now it would be Tretow who carefully mic'd up Metronome Studio's underexercised marimba to find out if it would bring anything to the mix.

'Mamma Mia', we can now observe, is the sound of ABBA finding themselves as recording artists. No more throwing great handfuls of sound at the tape machine and seeing what stuck. This is the track on which ABBA start to become something more singular and deft, and set the pattern for their future. As Benny later put it, '1975 was when we learned what to do. "Mamma Mia" was the first song we arranged tightly. Almost all the songs after that had the same type of arrangement. All the instruments contribute something that deviates from the melody line. Listen to the marimbas, listen to the guitars. They're playing their own defined lines. We worked and worked on that.'

On 'Mamma Mia', everything seems to count; everything brings something to the party. Nobody is just in the background, strumming along and filling time and space. Every component, you can tell, has had at some point to justify its existence and everything is there by design and for a reason. OK, so Björn and Benny's 'oo-ee-oo-ee' backing vocals (in the chorus repeats from 2.29) could possibly be hard to rationalise on the basis of *absolute* necessity. But even they add another texture and (that crucial ABBA ingredient) late-in-the-song variation.

And in parallel with that new approach, this is the track on which ABBA firmly up their game as arrangers. 'SOS' had pulled the classic schlager move of a bare verse releasing into a full chorus. 'Mamma Mia' went the other way, the full verse dropping right back to a bare chorus – no drums, just the voices over the chattering piano and that marimba – at least for its first half before everything comes back in and the song accelerates away again.

Reverse schlager! Benny has never seemed particularly interested in talking up his own work, but even he had to admit that this had been a killer move. When he speaks about that chorus in an interview around the launch of the *Voyage* album in 2021, he smiles and his voice drops about two octaves. 'It was *so* clever,' he says.

And so also, of course, was that last-minute burst of marimba. Crucial, in fact. Applied to the introduction, it adds a coat of scratchproof gloss to the piano underneath it and instantly becomes the song's calling card, leaping out of high-end stereos and tinny radio speakers alike, tapping on your ears for your attention. Ostensibly, it's the simplest device – an upwards tock-tick movement between the root of the chord and the fifth, which then modulates to a flattened sixth while the root note remains where it is. There's a major key version of the same trick in 'Waterloo', under the first line of the verse (0.10), where elements of the chord rise a tone but the bass stays right where it is, so you get this sense of the song straining against its anchor.

But in 'Mamma Mia', the additional gift in that tock-tick motif is that it doesn't sit squarely in the bar, which might have been the natural thing to do if you had wanted to give the intro a regular bounce. Instead, the lift comes early in the bar, on the fourth off-beat, so that the motion reverses in relation to the beat, appearing to go from upward to downward, from tock-tick to tick-tock, before switching back again in the same way. It's not a huge thing, and it may even have been arrived at instinctively rather than consciously, but it does slightly mess with your expectations and put a tremble in the ground under your feet. And it means the marimba seems to be leaning forward into the rhythm as if determined to gallop ahead of the song, giving the whole thing an extra flick of urgency.

The lyrics were by Stig Anderson who, just as he had for 'Hasta Manana', reached for a conveniently barrier-busting foreign-language catchphrase and took it from there. But the music was, as ever, Björn's and Benny's, composed in the library, apparently, of Benny and Agnetha's house in Lidingo. It was written on guitar and piano, although, as Benny later pointed out, this was one of the ABBA compositions that didn't really lend itself to a simple rendition on those instruments, being a piece that only really came alive when layered-up in the studio, and with added marimba.

It's understood to be one of the great truths of music that any pop song worth its salt will continue to sound good when played on just a piano. And, of course, it's one of those great truths which is, in fact, absolute nonsense, as anyone who has tried to play Prince's 'Sign o' the Times' that way will eagerly attest. See also Snoop Dogg and Whiz Khalifa's 'Young Wild and Free', The Prodigy's 'Firestarter' and ABBA's 'Mamma Mia'.

But, busk-able or otherwise, the song reflects, as so frequently, Benny's and Björn's roots in catchy '60s pop as much as it does their love and feel for anything more contemporary. Indeed, at the risk of putting an unwanted idea in your head, I hear a debt in 'Mamma Mia' to David Bowie's early, Anthony Newley-style novelty song 'The Laughing Gnome' from 1967 – both in that tock-tick rhythm and also in the very '60s-period oboe figure which chats back at the melody between the lines of the verse (0.18–0.22 in the first instance, 0.25–0.29 in the second). Play them back to back if you don't believe me. Or just quietly move on, if you'd prefer, and forget I ever mentioned it.

There's also perhaps a more respectable, or certainly cooler, lift from the calliope circus riff from Smokey Robinson & The Miracles' 'The Tears of a Clown', which Robinson wrote in 1967 with Hank Cosby and a seventeen-year-old Stevie Wonder. And, like 'Mamma Mia', 'The Tears of a Clown' makes the counter-intuitive move of stripping the drums out for the chorus and bringing back the instrumentation from the introduction to carry the song at that point, so maybe the seeds of that idea were quietly sown there.

By contrast, the guitar leads on 'Mamma Mia', by Björn and Janne Schaffer, one of the small band of regular ABBA contributors, are pure '70s in flavour. One day, historians will be able to explain in full the mid-'70s appetite for twin-guitars playing lines in harmony, and link it to something in the economy, maybe, or peoples' diets, or the after-effects of an under-reported natural disaster somewhere, or whatever. In the meantime, Queen's Brian May has a fair amount to answer for, clearly, along with Thin Lizzy from 'Whiskey in the Jar' onwards – although The Beatles had been there well before either of them in 1966's 'And Your Bird Can Sing', and so, on numerous occasions, had The Yardbirds, whose twin-guitarists happened to be Jimmy Page and Jeff Beck, neither of whom were slouches.

But 'Mamma Mia' bristles with electric guitars generally, not least in the bridge (0.42–0.50), with its chuntering power chords and the classic guitar-hero swipe up the fretboard with which it gives way to the chorus. As with the post-chorus passage of 'SOS' that seems to have enthralled Glen Matlock of the Sex Pistols, it's easy to overlook just how thick and heavy the underpinnings of these seemingly frothy pieces of pop actually are.

As for Agnetha and Frida, they deliver an entirely dual lead vocal, sung in tight unison, as on 'Waterloo', 'Ring Ring' and 'Honey, Honey' before it, which suits the poppy lightness of the melody and also lessens the burden of the lyric to an extent. After all, in the twin-vocalist format, no tale of woe about being helplessly attracted to someone who is a cheater is going to feel directly confessional from the listener's point of view. On the contrary, it's going to sound like a problem already shared.

The other thing you notice is how the women's paired voices grow ever more confidently steely over the course of these four singles. Indeed, the soft, ingratiating warmth of the 'Honey, Honey' vocal, from just eighteen months earlier, is practically the sound of another vocal group altogether at this juncture. We have yet to hear Agnetha's soprano and Frida's mezzo-soprano combine to rip through the air to devastating effect as they will on later recordings, but there's a strong suggestion in 'Mamma Mia' of that force beginning to gather itself, both in the snappy, determined delivery of that bridge at 0.42 and in the boldly linear backing vocals, mixed loud for the chorus (0.50–1.03).

All this is in the context of what is, relatively speaking, an untaxing ABBA song to sing. As Christopher Patrick points out in his excellent analytical book *ABBA: Let the Music Speak*, there is no melody more economical in the ABBA catalogue. The simple two-note modulation used at the top of the chorus – the basic chirpy birdsong of 'Ma-ma Mi-a' – happens thirty-four times at various points throughout the melody in these three and a half minutes. Yet because those repetitions are spread across a constantly shifting arrangement, in which the chorus alone works its way through three separately developed phases on the way to its ultimate resolution (the drum-less section at 0.50–1.04, the drum-driven extension at 1.04–1.15, and the concluding combination of those two at 1.15–1.22), the melody never feels static nor in any way limited. (Top karaoke tip: select 'Mamma Mia' and impress your friends with the ease and accuracy of your delivery.)

Michael B. Tretow nominated 'Mamma Mia' as his favourite ABBA recording. 'It's the whole idea of ABBA put together in one track,' he said. The reviewer for *Rolling Stone* seemed to be making a similar point when he weighed up all those hooks, all those links, all those decorative details, and described 'Mamma Mia' as 'a greatest hits album in three and a half minutes'. Some sense of the attention-grabbing power of what they had created here at least prevailed in the band's decision to make it the album's opening track. Yet by the time the song was completed, 'So Long', 'I Do, I Do, I Do, I Do, I Do' and 'SOS' were ahead of it in the queue to be released as singles off the *ABBA* album, and 'Mamma Mia' might not have been sent out into the world as a single at all if it hadn't been for the pestering of RCA Records in Australia. Executives there had noticed strong reactions to the song when the album arrived, and begged the ABBA office in Stockholm to be allowed to release it as a follow-up to 'I Do, I Do, I Do, I Do, I Do'. Stig Anderson resisted for a while, fearing that carving another song off the album would risk bleeding it dry. But RCA were insistent and eventually he relented. 'Mamma Mia' went to number one in Australia and stayed there for ten weeks.

Meanwhile, back in my bedroom in Essex, I watched with quiet satisfaction as the single barged its way up the UK charts in the first weeks of 1976; watched it take down the last, sadly lingering decorations from the Christmas just passed (Greg Lake's rather awesome 'I Believe in Father Christmas'; Mike Oldfield's piece of antic carolling, 'In Dulce Jubilo'); watched it ease aside the pleasingly eccentric but quickly irritating Sailor, who had for some time been urging us to get together with them over 'a glass of champay-un'; watched it see off a late but doomed challenge from 10cc's 'Art for Art's Sake'; and then, as January ended, for its last glorious trick, watched it topple Queen's 'Bohemian Rhapsody' from the number one slot, in which it seemed to have been cemented for as long as most of us could remember.

That ABBA cassette of mine was a cheap and embarrassing plastic box, clearly, but who could dispute that it contained jewels?

By the age of seventeen, Agnetha Åse Fältskog had been performing in bands for four years and had written and recorded her first Swedish number one single.

Anni-Frid Synni Lyngstad had her first gig as a singer at thirteen, diverted to jazz combos at eighteen, and was the winner of a national talent contest in 1967 at twenty-one.

Björn Kristian Ulvaeus spent the '60s listening to The Beatles but also acquiring a degree in business and law and doing military service.

Göran Bror Benny Andersson from central Stockholm, self-taught pianist, former building-site worker, accordion player and aspiring rock star.

Björn looking clean-cut and cheerful
in his appallingly named but highly popular
'60s outfit the Hootenanny Singers.

Benny on keyboards with Swedish chart act
The Hep Stars. Lots of hair, but clean hair.

Agnetha and Björn's wedding in July 1971 was a big celebrity story for the Swedish papers.

ABBA looking unusually mean and moody soon after realising that two couples could make a pop group.

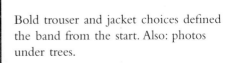

Bold trouser and jacket choices defined the band from the start. Also: photos under trees.

A pre-Eurovision cross-promotional opportunity in 1974 with labelmate Uncle Bulgaria of the Wombles.

Agnetha's spangled Eurovision outfit with Womble and Stan Laurel allegiances made clear.

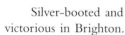

Silver-booted and victorious in Brighton.

The winners of the 1974 Eurovision Song Contest at one of the other Waterloos.

The vast human drama of the *Greatest Hits* 'kissing/ not kissing' cover shot. Ownership of that album was practically enforceable by law in the UK in 1976.

The scene in 2023, poignantly captured on the author's iPhone.

Stig Anderson, ABBA's boldly mustachioed manager, holding some most likely deeply disappointing sheet music.

The sound engineer Michael B. Tretow has a strong claim to be regarded as 'the fifth ABBA'.

Cat dresses – demure version. And Björn drawing a typically short straw in tight yet bell-bottomed white dungarees.

Cat dresses – risqué version – modelled by an alarming ABBA doll set displayed at the Waterloo battle site's ABBA Expo, 2023–24.

Pink, navel-revealing peek-a-boo onesie, reptilian-patterned stack-heel boots, exotically shaped guitar . . . ABBA in the mid-'70s never failed to spoil us.

Going for a slightly cooler all-black satin look as the '70s fade.

Evening wear a-go-go at the photoshoot for the *Super Trouper* album sleeve, 1980.

Eighties hair and brave faces as the end looms. ABBA in 1982.

The perfect comeback: ABBA regroup for the opening night
of ABBA Voyage, London, May 2022.

20

Always with the music

And here are ABBA in early 1976 on the pop show *Der Musikladen* (The Music Shop). Here they are, miming on West Germany's equivalent of *Top of the Pops* with its superbly well-named presenter, Manfred Sexauer. (Every man in a bomber jacket presenting a mid-'70s pop show seems to wish he was called Manfred Sexauer, and very many look into the camera as though they are.)

Here are ABBA promoting 'Mamma Mia' in four matching blue satin suits and bow ties, looking like the hired entertainment at a wedding. Here's Benny at the piano, of course, off to one side but rocking his shoulders compliantly from a seated position and smiling, and here's Björn beside him with an unplugged electric guitar around his neck, pretending to be comprehensively absorbed in the act of delivering music from its unamplified strings.

And here, centre stage, are Agnetha and Frida holding slim silver microphones with wires that go nowhere and rotating their hips and snapping their fingers. Occasionally, as the song transitions, they turn and lean back-to-back and then spin to face each other up close, at which point, just as on the Eurovision stage, smiles threaten flickeringly to disrupt the straightness of their expressions, suggesting that they need no reminding of the sheer daftness of all this.

Frida in particular seems to need no reminding. Eventually we get to the traditionally awkward moment in any mimed television performance where the song fades (there being no received way in which to mime a fade, except, perhaps, by walking off into the sunset, which isn't always practical). And while everyone waits for the camera to complete its obliging pull-out to the distance, Agnetha continues to sway slightly absently, but Frida takes the chance to waddle satirically in a large circle around the stage, taking tiny, stiff-legged steps with her feet together and her arms straight down beside her like a wind-up toy.

All this will be shown in a regular episode of *Der Musikladen* and then form part of a bigger ABBA special for West German television, *Musikladen Extra: The Best of ABBA*, with other hit singles, and other outfits, including some plum-coloured velvet onesies, and some interview segments, including this one:

INTERVIEWER: What does it start with? With the words or the music?

BENNY: With the music. Always with the music.

INTERVIEWER: With the music. And who writes the music?

FRIDA: Björn and Benny writes the music.

INTERVIEWER: And who writes the words?

FRIDA: It's our manager called Stikkan Anderson.

INTERVIEWER: And what do the girls do in this whole thing?

AGNETHA: Nothing.

MY MY!

At which there is a burst of laughter from the rest of band while the interviewer laughs too, and does his best to work out whether he's in on the joke or the butt of it.

21

'We're not splitting the atom'

Inevitably, I spend quite a lot of my Friday-night performance of *Mamma Mia!* monitoring the audience around me for signs of insurrection and wondering which number might prove to be the flashpoint that ultimately upgrades this peaceable evening at the theatre to 'major incident' status.

There is some scattered singing along to 'Mamma Mia' on its appearance (after brief glimpses of 'Lay All Your Love On Me', 'Money, Money, Money' and 'SOS' among others) in the instrumental overture pumped out by the orchestra under the floorboards. But the house-lights aren't even fully down at that point, and the cast nowhere near the stage, so it can hardly count as crowd trouble.

The opening of 'Chiquitita' brings out my Italian neighbour, who sings along for a line or two. But he does so as if he simply can't help it, rather than in the manner of someone determined to halt the show. Moreover, he stops singing seemingly as soon as he remembers where he is, and shows no sign of losing control of himself again, so it's hard to feel he's a major threat to the smooth running of the evening or in need of careful stewarding.

Elsewhere, to the best of my knowledge, nobody anywhere in the theatre at any point during the main action is anti-socially on their feet. The last chorus of 'Thank You for the Music' inspires a robust clap-along – but only from one member of the audience who possibly feels a little foolish afterwards, or perhaps just let down by the rest of us who didn't get in behind her/him. It's the chorus of 'Take a Chance on Me' that really gets people clapping in time, or thereabouts, but even at this point, with widespread tumult threatening, everyone respectfully backs off again for the verses.

As for the vocal accompaniment that rises softly from the stalls during 'I Have a Dream' . . . well, it's certainly nothing to call the police over. In fact, from where I'm sitting, up near the lights, it's rather moving – a gentle communal moment there in the theatre's perfumed warmth, rather than an out-and-out heist.

The show ends with the principal cast members in '70s satin and the rest of the company on the stage with them, belting out reprises of the title song and 'Dancing Queen' and, finally, 'Waterloo', which could not be fastened into the storyline, but without which, somehow, the evening's secondary purpose as a celebration of ABBA and ABBA-ness in general would not be complete. And now, finally, the audience is completely free to leave its seats and occupy the aisles and sing its hearts out without risk of ejection, which it duly does. And if you're not stirred from your own seat at this point – even your seat with a restricted view on a precarious ledge, several miles up – and at least bopping self-consciously at the knees, then it may be that there is something blocked inside you which it is beyond the power of pop music alone to reach.

Phyllida Lloyd, the director, has spoken of 'a *Mamma Mia!* factor' and has said she thought it was 'a certain lack of coolness or pretension that makes the show so special'. She also said, 'We're hoping to create pure pleasure. We're not splitting the atom.' And there's no question about it: absolutely no atoms get split in the performance of *Mamma Mia!*. There's also no question that a huge amount of pleasure gets created by the show in a way that is neither cool nor pretentious. So, mission accomplished, no?

And yes, it seems the sound of overdriven electric guitar emanating from an orchestra pit in a West End theatre will always yield a certain amount of cringe from me, akin to the feeling I get when manifestly posh politicians develop glottal stops and start dropping their t's. But that's almost certainly inverted snobbery on my part.

And yes, too, there's no denying that the songs are hammered into the show with an almost gleeful absence of subtlety – but who would try and deny this anyway? Critics of *Mamma Mia!* tend to produce this supposedly undermining observation with a drum-roll, as if it's something the show hasn't noticed about itself – something the show doesn't actually play with and *embrace*, even. The brazenly opportunistic lead-ins to the big numbers will chime readily enough with those of us who automatically think, recite, or possibly even, in the right circumstances, sing the first line of 'Fernando' at the mere mention of anyone called Fernando, or called anything that sounds even remotely like Fernando. Are we not constantly shoe-horning pop songs into our lives at moments which they sort of but don't quite fit? Isn't this how pop songs visit us all the time? Given the puzzle that *Mamma Mia!* has set itself (or, rather, been set by the iron-clad stipulations of Björn and Benny), this solution seems pragmatic – and possibly even more than that: pioneering. Confronted with the age-old problem for musicals of managing the transition between speech and song, *Mamma Mia!* actually finds a method which you might even go so far as to say feels natural, if naturalism is what you're looking for from your musical theatre.

In fact, almost any way you want to come at *Mamma Mia!*, it's kind of ready for you. You want to accuse the show of pushing our buttons by deploying a set of established musical triggers rather than diligently earning our emotional response with something fresh? But this is a show whose very motto, tagline and all-purpose *cri de coeur* is: here I go again. It's *about* your helpless assent. It's already seen you coming from that direction and headed off your objection.

And do you want to hold it against *Mamma Mia!* that it's not Sondheim? Well, OK, but it would be a strange waste of energy, surely, and akin to holding it against Björn Ulvaeus that he's not Oscar Hammerstein and then, in turn, holding it against Oscar Hammerstein that he's not Shakespeare. And once you're in that particular critical death-spiral, what are you ever going to relax enough to enjoy?

Still, as I gather my things, head up the aisle for the Novello Theatre's exit and begin the long descent to street level, there are aspects of *Mamma Mia!*'s loudly ringing domination of the modern conversation around ABBA which I can't deny that I feel a touch uneasy about – and which perhaps anyone who feels historically invested in ABBA will automatically be at least mildly unsettled by.

Because, in the words of *Vogue* magazine in 2023, the combination of the musical and the movie have turned *Mamma Mia!*

into 'a shorthand for "campy feelgood escapism"'. And it's hard to argue with the plain truth of that, not least when you are leaving a theatre surrounded by people who have just watched *Mamma Mia!* and are manifestly feeling good, campy and escaped.

But, by extension, is that now what ABBA themselves are a shorthand for? For campy, feelgood escapism? And *only* that?

On the way to ABBA Voyage not long ago (my third trip, her first), my daughter said she really hoped that the show would include 'Slipping Through My Fingers'. I broke it to her as gently as I could. But at the same time, I permitted myself a small moment of pride that I had played a part in rearing the kind of person who would travel to an ABBA show in the hope of hearing not just one of the obvious ones from *ABBA Gold*, but a deep cut from the band's conflicted late period. Lord knows, I cannot by any means claim to have got everything right as a parent. But I'll take that.

Then I realised that, of course, my daughter knows 'Slipping Through My Fingers', not through diligent exploration in her own time of the darker corners of the ABBA catalogue, but because of the number's prominence in the *Mamma Mia!* movie, where it gets sung by Meryl Streep and someone even more significant: Amanda Seyfried from *Mean Girls*. Bear in mind that the DVD of that film, which came out in 2008, was estimated at one time to be owned by one in four British households, and its soundtrack has been percolating with an endless succession of gurgles into the culture ever since. Consequently, it goes without saying that there is a whole portion of the *Mamma Mia!* demographic who, like my teenage daughter, are pretty much word-perfect on ABBA's greatest hits, but who came to this music through the film and, what's more than that, in some cases were under the impression (and may remain under it) that this music was written *for* the film.

In other words, whisper it, but there's a generation out there who didn't realise these songs even *had* a life before Pierce Brosnan sang them. This would place them in stark contrast to older people like me who worried that the songs might have no life after he did so.

Contemplating this development and all the sobering things that it implies – about the world, about the position of ABBA in that world, about how goddamn old I seem so suddenly to have become – it's hard for someone in my position not to feel a burst of self-redeeming worldliness coming on and to spot a 'teachable moment' in which yet further redemption may lie.

For what, pray, do these children know of ABBA who only Pierce Brosnan know? Set down your phones and earbuds, my innocent ones, and heed, I bid you, the truths contained in this vinyl copy of *The Visitors* . . .

Here's the thing, though: at the time of writing, the Streep/Seyfried version of 'Slipping Through My Fingers' has been sought out on Spotify on nearly 25 million more occasions than the original ABBA version. It's Streep/Seyfried 146 million and counting, Agnetha/Frida 122 million. And what's the greying ABBA veteran going to do, confronted with a stat like that? Just suck it up, I guess. I mean, it's hardly my business to tell these kids they're looking down the wrong end of the telescope, much though I'm itching to do so. On the contrary: I'm a sixty-one-year-old whose children are now way past the age of majority, and dignity alone insists that it's my business at this stage to concede that whatever control I ever had over the telescope and which way round anyone ought to be holding it is gone for good.

However, let me at least work through some (I think) more than merely elderly discomfort at this idea that ABBA in 2024 – the ABBA I know and revere – have become, in the minds of many, including those who will be in charge of everything in the imminent future, a one-stop party kit, a hen-do's satin sash. Again, obviously I understand that I would have less of a problem with this if I were someone who was likely to be organising a hen-do any time soon. Yet I wonder how *Vogue*'s indisputably accurate 'campy feelgood escapism' label sits with something Benny Andersson once said about ABBA, about how 'even our happiest songs are melancholy at their core'.

Now, the presence of melancholy by no means precludes camp, clearly; it may even be one of camp's prime ingredients. (Indeed, is there camp *without* melancholy? I would say not, but it's an argument for another day.) And melancholy certainly doesn't rule out escapism.

But 'feelgood'? Isn't 'feelgood' by definition on a mission to trample melancholy underfoot, possibly in a big galumphing pair of retro stacks worn as fancy dress? When the feelgood balloon goes up in the sitting room, doesn't melancholy, along with everything else, get squeezed out into the kitchen and told to stay there eating peanuts until it's stopped feeling quite so melancholic?

Or, to put it another way: what happens to that delicious but delicate chill in the ABBA air when the songs are getting heated up and served with a sprig of tinsel and a shot of vodka for quick-release fun?

And where does this leave those of us who were there for

this stuff the first time around – we old musicassette soldiers who now see the layers of kitsch and slatherings of cheese, against which we so selflessly armed ourselves, eagerly stripped from the ABBA story and held aloft like plundered treasure? Held aloft, indeed, as though they were *the whole point.*

Was it for this that we fought in the ABBA wars of 1975? So that our children could have cheese? Cheese and vodka shots?

And what happens to 'the whole idea of ABBA put together in one track', as Michael B. Tretow expressed it, if 'Mamma Mia' now means not something mysterious and faintly cold emanating from the north in three and a half densely packed minutes of pop perfection, but endless and riotous good times amid the scent of thyme and the snap of bikini bottoms on ouzo-blurred holidays in the Greek sunshine? What's the whole idea of ABBA *then?*

Emerging from the theatre with these various discomforting thoughts rolling around in my head (along with, yes, exactly as promised by the producers, bits of 'Waterloo', scraps of 'Dancing Queen' and, especially strongly, the drum-free part of the chorus of 'Mamma Mia'), I step gingerly through a cordon of fairy-lit bicycle rickshaws waiting for post-theatre custom and head for the tube. There will be a time to think about these things, but right now I'm in London in the spring of 2023 and I've got to get safely home through the West End's teeming lawlessness.

I walk quickly, of course, with my eyes lowered, but the streets seem calm enough. I notice, glancing quickly back, that there are no riot police in attendance at *Tina: The Musical,* and no squad cars on the pavement outside *The Lion King,* either. Only more rickshaws, in fact.

My shoulders go down a little. This particular Friday night

on the mean streets of London's musical theatreland appears to be passing off peacefully.

So, whatever *Mamma Mia!* portends for ABBA and the listeners of tomorrow, this, at least, is something to feel unequivocally positive about. Order seems to have returned to the stalls and circles in general, and maybe all that ill-temper and anti-social weirdness was, as some people said, just a moment, a post-lockdown thing, an uncomfortable phase over which we've all agreed to draw a veil.

Or maybe not . . .

BBC News website 26 November 2023
Police are investigating a fight which broke out between theatregoers at a performance of the hit musical *Hamilton*.

A man and a woman in the audience were thought to have been involved in the fight at Palace Theatre, Manchester, on Friday.

A Greater Manchester Police (GMP) spokesman said officers were called following a 'report of an assault'.

He added: 'An investigation is ongoing at this time with no arrests made.

'Thankfully, injuries sustained are not believed to be life-threatening.'

22

A walk in the park

Elizabeth, who will be our guide, is waiting for us at the cemetery gate. We are a group of thirty, all carefully wrapped against Stockholm's surprisingly cold May air. One of us is wearing an ABBA Voyage bomber jacket and there is a smattering of ABBA caps and hats in various styles. We are here on this bright Friday morning in 2023 to do the ABBA Walking Tour, organised by the nearby ABBA Museum, where we have picked up our tickets and been issued with our joining instructions.

Elizabeth gets us all to say where we're from. We are substantially from Germany and Holland, with a fair showing from the UK, and representatives also for Finland and Switzerland – a decent spread, then, although Elizabeth reports that she recently had someone along from the Philippines, letting that hang in the air for a moment before adding, 'Wow'. None of us in the party, I would hazard, will be seeing forty again, and at least a couple of us will not be seeing sixty again. But nearly all of us, I feel somehow certain, will be seeing ABBA Voyage again.

Elizabeth adjusts her headset microphone and cranks the volume on the small speaker that's belted to her waist. She says that, before she starts, she wants to apologise, but she's going to be keeping her phone switched on during our walk. She is expecting a parcel at her apartment and will need to buzz the delivery person through the door. She hopes none of us mind. We all give her our enthusiastically nodded blessing. And with that, our ABBA Walking Tour begins.

'We are gathered here because of four people,' says Elizabeth.

She withdraws from her canvas tote bag some laminated 10 x 8 headshots of the members of ABBA – 'the ABBAs', as Elizabeth refers to them. The shots are from 1976, when ABBA are in their pomp, and Elizabeth shows them to us one at a time, holding each one above her head and turning it slowly through 120 degrees while she sketches the backgrounds of the individual ABBAs for us.

So here is Agnetha Fältskog from Jöngköping, a small lakeside city in southern Sweden; Agnetha, the middle-class daughter of a department store manager, with her ten years of piano lessons and her place in the church choir and her ambitions to become a psychiatrist, before the music intervenes and takes over.

And here is Björn Ulvaeus, born in Gothenburg to a Swedish naval officer and a nurse, and raised in Vastervik, a coastal town 180 miles from Stockholm; clean-cut, readily smiling Björn, with a degree in business and law from Lund University and a year of military service behind him; Björn, 'the mother-in-law's dream' as Elizabeth describes him.

And here is Anni-Frid Lyngstad, whose life story would continue to read like a novel even if you removed the chapters in which she joins ABBA and becomes one of the world's biggest pop stars; Frida from Ballangen in Norway, who is the offspring of an affair in the dying days of the Second World War between a nineteen-year-old Norwegian girl and a sergeant from the occupying German Wehrmacht; Frida who, in a post-war national mood which does not look kindly on 'collaborators', is for her own safety swept off to Sweden at the age of two with her grandmother; Frida, whose mother eventually joins them there, only to fall ill and die at twenty-one; Frida, who grows up in the tiny steeltown of Torshälla, believing both her parents are dead, only for an article about ABBA in *Bravo* magazine in 1977 to be seen by the German half-brother she didn't know she had, beginning a chain of enquiries which leads to Frida meeting her father for the first time at thirty-two.

'Wow,' says Elizabeth.

(And we haven't even got to the bit in 1992 where she marries a prince.)

And here is Benny Andersson, the engineer's son from Vasastan in central Stockholm; Benny, who teaches himself the piano, grows his hair, takes up smoking, does pick-up jobs on building sites by day and fancies his chances as a rock star by night; Benny, who has (though Elizabeth doesn't get into this in detail) two children by the age of eighteen, both with his girlfriend, Christina Grönvall; a son, Peter, born in 1963, when Benny was sixteen, and a daughter, Helene, born in 1965.

'Not a mother-in-law's dream,' says Elizabeth.

'Or not for her daughter, anyway . . .' she adds.

Elizabeth slowly lowers the picture of Benny.

'That these four people met each other, found friendship, love, changed the world . . .' she says. 'Wow.'

Elizabeth tucks the pictures back in her bag and leads us through the gate and into the cemetery. A beautifully tree-filled plot in the shadow of the large and ornately domed Nordic Museum, this memorial garden holds mostly navy-related graves, some of which date back to 1750. However, our destination is a more recent tombstone over towards the chapel.

We leave the path and cross the grass, treading as respectfully as we can, and assemble around a modest rough-hewn stone with a treble clef carved into it and marking the final resting place of Stig Anderson, 25 January 1931–12 September 1997. That's Stig, raised by his mother in a cottage in conditions of near-poverty in a small Swedish town called Hova; Stig, who was in a teenage rock group called Stig Anderson & His Mashed Creampuffs; Stig, the sleeves of whose solo records in the '50s find him with an acoustic guitar, a moustache, a smile and a bold combover; Stig, the workaholic whose daughter Marie once joked that she first met her father when she was seven. Stig, the writer of some 2,000 songs in Swedish and English, and the manager of ABBA.

He founded the Sweden Music publishing company in 1960 and Polar Music two years later, whose annual revenues would so famously, at the company's peak, come second only to Volvo's in Sweden. And so broadly did he bestride the Swedish record industry that he was known simply as 'The Business'. When he died from a heart attack at sixty-six, his funeral, at St Jakob's Church in Stockholm, was broadcast live on Swedish television.

By which time, of course, the story had taken a turn for the entirely typical, with the relationship between the manager and his globally successful pop group eventually souring through the 1980s into arguments and lawsuits. Stig's complex mesh of imaginative off-set investments and international payment-in-kind deals had attracted the interest of the Swedish tax authorities and the furious ABBA members sued him for mishandling their affairs. The case was settled out of court.

Nevertheless, the cameras tracked the arrival at the funeral, through back-pedalling news crews, of Björn and Benny, mournful in dark suits, with their second wives, Lena and Mona. Frida also attended. Agnetha was unwell but sent flowers. During the church service, a vocal group sang one of Stig's songs, 'Vackra sagor är sä korta' – 'The beautiful stories are always too short'.

Elizabeth has photographs for us here, too. One is of the impressive detached house in Stockholm that Stig's unstinting labours bought him. The other is a portrait of Stig in 1981 at his 50th birthday party, in a mostly unbuttoned white shirt, with a garland of flowers around his neck and seated on a gold throne.

That seems to have been quite the birthday, all in all. At 7.00 a.m., Anderson was awoken by the arrival in his bedroom of a women's choir in fishnets, including Agnetha, Frida, Björn's second wife Lena, and Görel Hanser, the vice president of Polar Music. Björn and Benny, the latter carrying an accordion, then used the balcony to climb through the window and serenade Anderson some more.

At the party, the band would present him with the record they had made in his honour, featuring a song called 'Hova's Vittne' – 'Hova's Witness'. The song paints a broad picture of Stig's character, alluding to his virtually professional interest in sausage consumption, his persistent belief (not particularly shared by ABBA) in the value of lifting a song's key near the end for an extra burst of energy ('Hova's Vittne' itself, naturally, lifts a key at this point), and – the best detail of all, I think – his apparent habit of getting out the vacuum cleaner to signal to guests at his house that it was time for them to leave.

Two hundred copies of this masterpiece were pressed on red vinyl for the guests at the party, and good luck acquiring one of those now. Along with 'Säng Till Görel' ('Song for Görel' – a one-sided, blue-coloured 12-inch that ABBA and Anderson pressed in honour of Görel Hanser on the occasion of her 30th birthday in 1979), it's the most sought-after item in the ABBA catalogue. At the time of writing, I can see one copy of 'Hovas Vittne' for sale on the Discogs website. Its Swedish seller is asking £3,250 for it.

By the grave, we soberly muse a while on Stig and mortality and (perhaps) the importance of marking your birthdays with parties while you can. And then we move on.

As we leave the cemetery, I get alongside Elizabeth and talk to her a little. She is a qualified Stockholm tour guide, who designs and leads walks around the city's historic buildings, and who was approached to see if she had any interest in developing an ABBA walk. This was during the lockdown, when the ABBA Museum had to close but when outdoor gatherings were allowed. Elizabeth says she gave it 'at least twelve seconds' before saying yes.

I ask her if she has ever met any of the ABBAs and she says she has not, nor set eyes on any of them in the flesh. I sense from the slightly wary look in her eye when she tells me this that she's wondering if there is any side to this question of mine, but there really isn't. I'm just curious, and also, clearly, labouring under the naïve impression that if you live in Stockholm, you must be bumping into members of ABBA all the time. Anyway, Elizabeth's authority on the subject of ABBA and her city is manifest, and the guide on the Dr Johnson walk I once went on in London hadn't met Dr Johnson, either. I don't recall any of us feeling the walk suffered for it.

Not having left Stockholm since the pandemic, Elizabeth has not yet seen the Voyage show, but she says she is desperate to do so and seems keen to hear what I thought of it. She quotes reviews she has read, including one in which the critic felt cheated because ABBA weren't actually there. We agree this was ridiculous.

At that point, Elizabeth stops to draw everyone's attention to the back of the Nordic Museum, currently on our right. There's no ABBA connection here, unless you count the fact that the museum, a quarter of a century ago, hosted an ABBA exhibition – cat dresses, platform boots, Benny's eye-wateringly expensive Yamaha GX1 synthesiser, etc. – which planted seeds for the idea of the permanent ABBA Museum up the road. But Elizabeth thinks the building is worth a look anyway, and she's right.

We now cross the road and the tramlines and enter the Djurgarden – the vast, green royal game park, where the medieval Swedish kings once did their elk- and reindeer-hunting. It switched to more general recreational use in the eighteenth century, before reaching what many would perhaps regard as the crowning moment in its history when it showed up briefly in the sun-dappled dream sequence in *ABBA: The Movie*, the part-documentary, part-comedy film the band made in 1977. ('Have you seen it?' Elizabeth asks. 'Just a few times,' comes the dry reply from a Dutch woman in silver trousers.) So, once we've passed through the ornate blue gate with its hunting emblems, which Elizabeth also bids us observe, we pause on the path and absorb our proximity to the stretch of water down which ABBA and the journalist so thwartedly pursuing them for an interview (played by Robert Hughes – the actor, not the art critic) floated at that point in the film, some forty-six years ago.

It's as we're continuing along the park's path and absorbing the distant view of the television tower and the National Maritime Building, both scenes of prominent ABBA photo-shoots (Elizabeth again produces from her bag the illustrative evidence), that Elizabeth's phone goes. 'Ring ring,' the woman in the silver trousers says brightly. Elizabeth then enters into a brief conversation before hanging up. 'I heard him open the door,' she confirms, and we all cheer the safe arrival of Elizabeth's parcel.

We loop back on ourselves through the park for a while and then Elizabeth brings us to a halt by a park bench under a tree whose trunk has a distinct lean to the right. It's clear that we have reached the walk's big moment – its major reveal. The Djurgarden is not short of benches and trees but these, Elizabeth assures us, have been forensically checked against the pictorial evidence, and there's no question about it, they're definitely the ones: we're standing at the scene of the photograph of ABBA that is wrapped around the 1976 *Greatest Hits* album, the image known in ABBA lore as the 'kissing/not kissing' photo.

Elizabeth doesn't need to ask us if we know where we've seen this tree and this bench before. It would be like that moment in *Wayne's World 2* when Wayne's girlfriend Cassandra finds a copy of Peter Frampton's *Frampton Comes Alive!* album from 1976 in a garage sale, and makes the mistake of asking Wayne if he knows it.

MY MY!

WAYNE: Exsqueeze me? Have I seen this one before? *Frampton Comes Alive!?* Everyone in the world has *Frampton Comes Alive!*. If you lived in the suburbs, you were issued it. It came in the mail with samples of Tide.

And, of course, that *Frampton Comes Alive!* album was all over Britain in 1976, too. It was the album on which Frampton pioneered the Talk Box, a foot-pedal with a long plastic tube emerging from it which he could clamp between his teeth and thereby magically blend the sound of his voice with the notes coming from the strings of his electric guitar. And OK, when you listen to it now, after half a century of rapacious advances in the electronic generation of sound, the resulting noise sounds pretty unimpressive – a bit like someone twanging an elastic band while trapped in a drainpipe. Plus, the tube always made Frampton appear to be gasping into a life-support machine, which wasn't, in retrospect, a particularly great look. Yet we didn't feel that then. Indeed, the sound of Frampton burping at length into this game-changing addition to the guitarist's armoury was for many of us a feature of the '70s soundscape to rank with the tinny crackle of astronauts calling in from Apollo space capsules and Muttley's snigger in the *Wacky Races* cartoon.

So, yes, there were plenty of copies of *Frampton Comes Alive!* around at that point in the UK, too, and, like Wayne, we also bowed before its altar. But if you lived in Britain in 1976 – and certainly in suburban Essex – it was, surely, ABBA's *Greatest Hits* that appeared to have been delivered door-to-door to every household, like the telephone directory; ABBA's *Greatest Hits* that appeared to have been issued to at least one member of

173

every family at birth. And worthy of reflection though the sleeve of *Frampton Comes Alive!* was (portrait format for the image across the gatefold, rather than landscape? Interesting . . .), it was the picture on the front of the ABBA album that properly commanded our attention.

There was just so much to take in, not least from a fashion point of view. The generous quantities of Lois denim; Björn's airy flares and the body-straddling lapels on his denim jacket; the chunky four-inch heel on his and Benny's matching black boots; Agnetha's rolled-up jeans and her turned-in feet in her knee-length brown suede boots; that green cap she's wearing at an angle; Frida's white crocheted shawl, which is exactly the kind of garment my mother, moving on from quilting, had taken to producing with Stakhanovite determination, at all hours of the day and night, for herself and for anyone else who would wear one.

Beyond the clothes, though, what was actually happening in this image? And what was it trying to tell us? It seemed important to know. At one end of this park bench, Frida and Benny are literally wrapped up in each other, not just kissing, *snogging*, Frida's face almost entirely invisible, pressed into Benny's beard. At the other end, while Björn placidly reads some kind of paper and gives every indication of being several hundred miles away (and perhaps in need of the biggest elbow-in-the-ribs ever delivered), Agnetha sits alertly, staring straight out at us with an expression of . . . well, what exactly? Disapproval? Longing? Mournfulness? A dawning sense that she's . . . *with the wrong person?*

So much to interpret, so many interpretations . . . The fallen leaves in Agnetha's lap and, comically, on top of her cap . . .

Are they intended to signal that she's been sitting like this for some time? That she's gathering dust/leaves? Nobody else is at all leafy, and especially not Benny and Frida . . . What is the significance of Björn's oh-so-absorbing reading matter, which seems, if you look closely, to be a Swedish medical paper on the use of antibiotics? Allegedly this document was simply lying on the bench when they came to take the photo. (And so was Agnetha's green cap, apparently.) But even so . . . That didn't make those items any less open to interpretation, nor any less likely to lead us to some central truths, surely, about the chemistry of this band made from two couples, an arrangement which was, for us onlookers, somehow entirely mundane and weirdly exotic at the same time.

Passion blowing hot, passion blowing cold; connection, disconnection; velvet and corduroy or double denim . . . you could be many hours decoding the messages here and yet somehow nowhere near exhausting the intrigue. I had friends at this time (and some brothers, definitely) who had grown deeply enthralled by the prism image on the sleeve of Pink Floyd's epic prog rock album *The Dark Side of the Moon* and who seemed to think that, if you stared for long enough at that talismanic artwork, it would unlock many, if not all, of life's most profound mysteries. And that image still enjoys enormous kudos today, being typically the first port of call in almost any consideration of 'the art of the record sleeve'.

But here's my contention (and I would have made it then as I'm making it now): that prism picture was just an old sweet wrapper pulled from the bottom of a coat pocket by comparison with the broiling human drama contained in the 'kissing/not kissing' shot on the front of ABBA's *Greatest Hits*.

Anyway, thanks to Elizabeth's guidance, here we all are, some forty-seven years later, by that very bench, from where I can report that there's now a car park behind the tree, slightly spoiling the background. And whereas the bench on the album appears recently to have had a fresh coat of green paint, here only the metal arms are green and the seat is back to the bare wood. But that's time for you, I guess.

And what else are you going to do when you suddenly find yourself on location with your past like this? How else are you meant to solidify your utterly nonsensical but definitely tangible feelings at such a juncture?

Along with everyone in the group, I hold up my phone and take a picture of the empty park bench and its accompanying tree.

23

Compulsory purchase order

By the time ABBA's *Greatest Hits* came out, I was back on the vinyl. My eighteen-month phase as a user of pre-recorded cassettes was over, that wholly regrettable interregnum having been brought to an end by the arrival of fresh hardware – a departing brother's cast-offs.

There are definitely things I can't recommend about being the much younger sibling in a family and watching your three older brothers clear off – all three of them, within weeks of each other – accelerating away into adulthood and leaving you behind at home to twiddle your thumbs for another *five years*. It changes things. You'll notice, for instance, how deathly quiet the house has become, how much less frequently the phone rings or the doorbell goes, and how, suddenly, very little seems to be happening altogether, on account of the fact that all the people who came free with your brothers – their friends, their girlfriends – have automatically relocated, too. You'll notice how much you're looking out the window for the arrival of those brothers' cars on the Sundays when they can be persuaded to tip up for lunch. You'll notice that your parents have gone a bit quiet, too, like the house, and you'll wonder whether they're suffering from some form of empty-nest syndrome, even though that would be a bit previous of them, given that the nest isn't empty yet. But you'll absolutely get it, because, yes, the nest isn't empty, but it *is* unquestionably more roomy, containing gaps, indeed, which cannot be filled.

Swings and roundabouts, though. There was absolutely no other way at this stage of my life that I was going to come by a perfectly serviceable Garrard turntable, an Amstrad amplifier with a missing treble-control knob (but you could still twist the protruding silver metal bit that remained) and a pair of mysteriously unbranded, possibly even home-made, speakers. So that was definitely a plus, and I could genuinely wish my eldest brother every happiness for the future in his newly wedded life with the vicar's daughter, as brazenly treacherous as that whole development definitely was.

The fact that I was back to vinyl had massive repercussions for my personal standing among my peers, of course, and for my state of mind generally. And it very specifically assisted my meditations around the cover image on ABBA's *Greatest Hits*. Naturally, it meant I had unlimited access to the full-sized cardboard item without which, we know, meditation on album cover images is a loser's game.

But, importantly in the context, it also gave me access to the picture inside the gatefold. That internal image showed the band broadly smiling under a sharply backlit chestnut tree – actually laughing, in the case of Benny and Frida – and could have been designed to settle a few nerves. Have no fear, it seemed to be saying: all is well with these people. That business on the front, where half of them seem to be in crisis while the other half probably need to get a room? They're just larking about! Look – here they are, laughing! They're fine!

No such reassurance would have been available to me had I been still been in my pre-recorded cassette period, because that second image doesn't appear there. In fact, everything would have been really confusing because, in another act of quite breathtaking shoddiness on the part of Epic Records – fit to rival their self-fading *ABBA* album of the previous year – the cover used for the cassette box shows, like the front of the vinyl, the end of the bench with Agnetha and Björn on it. But flip it over and . . . well, nothing. Benny and Frida, with their lips locked? Absolutely nowhere to be found on the paperwork with this item.

So, as far as the poor cassette user is concerned, then, that's half of the band snipped off and removed from consideration. These days we have social media to ensure that we go about most of the time in a cloud of misinformation and enervating half-truths. Back then, we had pre-recorded cassettes and I refer the jury to my earlier allegation that the format was a stain on society, and rest my case.

Still, it could have been worse: we could have had the Swedish version of the *Greatest Hits* album. There the park bench shot merely forms the image for the inside of the gatefold. On the cover, meanwhile, is a gothic cartoon, rendered in comic-strip blues and blacks, known to ABBA cognoscenti as the 'glam monsters' image, and which must be about the most bizarre visual rendering of the band ever to see daylight.

On one side, Benny, depicted in a psychedelic leopard-skin suit that gives way for no explained reason to a pair of three-clawed feet, pumps away smilingly at a piano while a drawing of Frida, next to him in black, reptile-scaled stockings and suspenders, and a substantially diaphanous bat costume featuring the pelts of a number of black kittens, bawls into a bulging fish-headed microphone. Meanwhile Stig Anderson, dressed as Napoleon, grins from under the piano lid. (Something to reflect on here: it's true that Anderson made indispensable lyrical contributions to the songs on this album, but has any other band's manager been positioned on the cover of their client's greatest hits record? In cartoon form and dressed as Napoleon, or otherwise? Perhaps some measure of the man there.)

On the rear, where this gruesome panorama continues, Björn, largely topless, happily strums what seems to be at least a seven-string guitar whose body appears to have been fashioned from some kind of extinct reptile, while Agnetha sings alongside him in a vaguely owl-shaped leotard with goggling eyes for breasts, and in a pair of knee-length boots that have each spawned a nest of other knee-length boots in a kind of stack-heeled hydra effect.

Also in attendance are various flying creatures, a pair of legs which seem to be functioning as a music stand, and a grinning feline with piano keys for teeth, and the whole thing seems to be poised at some uneasy point where the Marvelverse meets *Top Cat*. This is ABBA as you have never seen them before – and perhaps as you never wish to see them again, albeit that the ABBA Museum once had the image done as a giant board through which visitors could poke their heads for photo purposes, and a lot of people seemed to enjoy doing so.

Anyway, Sweden's unusually illustrated fourteen-track hits collection had emerged in November 1975, too early to include the single 'Fernando' which ABBA had only just finished recording at that point. But the UK version, despite coming later, almost missed that song, too. The intention was to copy the tracklisting on the Swedish release, but when 'Fernando' came out in March 1976, became a UK number one and sold a million copies, it suddenly seemed a bit remiss to be releasing an ABBA's *Greatest Hits* album in April that didn't include it.

So 'Fernando' was quickly bashed onto the end of side two. Unfortunately, the sleeves had already been printed for the first batch of pressings. Consequently, neither the inside nor the outside of the finished record cover said anything about 'Fernando'. Instead, my copy bears silver stickers, on the front and on the rear, stating, in three desperately clashing fonts: 'EXTRA TRACK – THE HIT SINGLE – FERNANDO'.

Cassettes that faded in and out; LPs whose sleeves couldn't tell you what was actually on the record . . . You could be forgiven for thinking that ABBA releases in the UK were a bit of a mess.

Even with 'Fernando' on board, though, and added to 'Waterloo', 'SOS' and 'Mamma Mia', it was possible from a UK perspective to wonder what ABBA were doing, laying claim to the 'greatest hits' treatment at this early point in their career. Sure, the band were three albums old by now, but not really to audiences in Britain, where the first two of those albums had gone practically unnoticed. So what went by the name of 'greatest hits' here was that quartet of bona fide smashes, padded out with a mixed bunch of international releases which UK record buyers had either chosen to ignore or not even been given the chance to: 'Honey, Honey', 'Ring Ring', 'Another Town, Another Train', 'Dance (While the Music Still Goes On)', 'Nina Pretty Ballerina' . . .

Nobody seemed to mind, though. On the contrary, we couldn't get enough of it. ABBA's *Greatest Hits* was the biggest-selling album in the UK in 1976, outperforming Rod Stewart's *A Night on the Town*, David Bowie's *Station to Station*, the Beach Boys' *20 Golden Greats* and, yes, *Frampton Comes Alive!*. In a year when ABBA also had three number one singles, *Greatest Hits* was number one on the album chart for eleven weeks, and the era of ABBA saturation was well and truly underway.

For me, as an owner of the *ABBA* album already, and the possessor of the 'Waterloo' single, there was quite a lot of overlap there which could plausibly have stayed my hand by the counter at Harper's Music. Six of the fifteen tracks, in fact. Yet it didn't, and consequently I now owned a version of 'Bang-A-Boomerang' without a mid-point fade. For what it was worth.

And anyway, the matter was completely out of my hands. In 1976, in suburban Essex, you had to own ABBA's *Greatest Hits*. It was the law.

24

Character error

The essential premise of *The Martian*, the 2015 Ridley Scott movie starring Matt Damon, is: what if a NASA astronaut were to find themselves stranded on Mars with little hope of rescue and only a bunch of '70s pop songs for company?

Damon plays Mark Watney, a NASA botanist who is left behind when the rest of his crew flee a ruinous Martian storm. Utterly isolated and months from home, Watney does at least have access to the downloaded music library abandoned by Commander Lewis, played by Jessica Chastain. Unfortunately for Watney, Lewis is a disco-loving ABBA fan with a framed sleeve of the *Arrival* album on her wall at home, and Watney likes neither disco nor ABBA.

'Jesus, Commander Lewis,' we hear him say to himself at one point. 'You couldn't have packed anything from *this* century? I'm gonna die up here if I have to listen to any more goddamn disco music.'

Incidentally, finding the actorly truth in this moment may not have been a stretch for Damon. Promoting the movie, he told an interviewer from the Canadian magazine *Macleans* that he comes down 'even more firmly on not liking disco than

Mark Watney does'. 'Damon's a Stones guy,' the piece explains. 'A Springsteen guy. A U2 and Pearl Jam guy.'

The Martian, then, offers a celebration of ABBA ('Waterloo' plays at length in one sequence) which, at the same time, openly acknowledges that some people are driven completely nuts by them. ABBA positivity, where we come across it in the culture, very often seems to have this kind of double-edged nature. We see a very similar kind of balancing act going on in *The Adventures of Priscilla, Queen of the Desert*. Released in 1994, Stephan Elliott's drag queens' road-trip movie is frequently grouped together with the film *Muriel's Wedding*, from the same year, and Erasure's EP of ABBA cover versions from 1992, *ABBA-esque*, as the key agents in the initial stirring of the ABBA revival. And no doubt that's accurate. The film's climax is a warmly affirmative song-and-dance routine set to 'Mamma Mia', matching the equally affirmative and uplifting 'Waterloo' karaoke sequence in *Muriel's Wedding*. And this was at a time when the reviewer of *Priscilla* in the *Washington Post* had to remind his readers, in brackets, whom he meant by ABBA: '(as in, the kitschy pop group)'.

However, Guy Pearce's Adam (stage name, Felicia Jollygoodfellow) is an ABBA fan to a degree that makes *The Martian*'s Commander Lewis look positively hesitant. A framed *Arrival* sleeve? Kid's stuff. Adam can claim to have made a 'pilgrimage' backstage at an ABBA show, seeking an audience with 'Her Royal Highness Agnetha'. Although he was frustrated in that ambition, he did manage to enter the loo that the singer had just vacated and claim what has become his 'most treasured possession in the whole wide world', and which he now carries with him everywhere in a glass sample jar.

So, that's all a little . . . troubling? It's certainly something to bear in mind when people are crediting *Priscilla* with instigating a late-twentieth-century burst of unalloyed ABBA rapture.

And let's not forget the scene – a comic highlight of the movie for many – where Adam fills an idle moment by putting on a tape of 'Fernando' and reaching for his acoustic guitar. He barely gets to the end of the first line before Terence Stamp's Bernadette snaps off the machine.

'I've said it before and I'll say it again: no more *fucking ABBA*.'

Again, as endorsements go . . .

Still, for all the scepticism floating round up there, at least the script for *The Martian* allows Commander Lewis to have the unqualified support, in her ABBA fandom, of her doting partner. In a video call between Earth and Lewis's spacecraft, her husband sends news that he has a present waiting for her when she gets back: a vinyl copy of ABBA's *Greatest Hits*.

We see him hold the 'kissing/not kissing' gatefold open for her approval.

'I found it at the flea market,' he says. 'Original pressing.'

Lewis cries out with delight and claps.

Hate to disappoint her, though . . .

The Internet Movie Database hosts 'Goofs' pages for movies, where eagle-eyed and/or pedantic viewers can log plot holes, continuity errors, factual slip-ups, anachronisms, and so on. As a work of science fiction, *The Martian*, somehow unsurprisingly, attracts some particularly assiduous correspondents to its Goofs page. So, there you will find disputatious postings about the likely strength of planetary winds ('Due to Mars' low atmospheric pressure, the effective wind pressure in Martian wind storms is much lower than shown in the movie, very unlikely to be sufficient to tip a spacecraft'); about the size of the Sun as seen from Mars ('Mars is 1.52 AU from the Sun, which means the Sun looks about 50 per cent smaller than the scene portrays it'); and about Watney's crucial ability to grow potatoes and feed himself out there ('With rover data, we've learned that Martian surface dirt contains roughly 0.5% calcium perchlorate. Before Mr Watney could grow his potatoes, he would have needed to extract those salts'). There are many, many observations such as this.

And there's also this one, posted under the category of 'Character Error':

On a video call when Commander Lewis' husband shows her the ABBA album he bought in a market, he states it is a first pressing. The cover shows 'Fernando' at the top of the tracklist, but the first pressing only had 'Fernando' as a bonus track and it wasn't listed on the cover. What he is showing is the second pressing.

Completely right, of course: no silver stickers.

At the time of writing, 100 readers have tagged this comment as 'helpful'.

25

Island life

In April 1976, shortly after my fourteenth birthday, I watched ABBA perform 'Fernando' on *Top of the Pops*. The women were in floaty, embroidered, white folk dresses and bare feet, the men were sitting on stools in white blouses with what appeared to be handkerchiefs around their necks. Benny was playing guitar. None of this made much sense – not even when fed through one of *TOTP*'s 'fisheye' lenses, a relatively recent innovation which, no matter the time of year, made the bands in the studio appear to be reflected in a bauble off a Christmas tree.

Then again, on the same show, Pan's People danced to the Carpenters' 'There's a Kind of Hush (All Over the World)' by twirling around under a giant globe in Snow White dresses, which didn't make much sense either, and Paul Nicholas, in a bowler hat and a stripy double-breasted jacket and with his blond ringlets swinging, bounced around and sang 'Reggae Like It Used to Be', which *really* didn't make sense, for all kinds of reasons. So maybe it was just the times and the fact that, in those days, if you wanted to be baffling on *Top of the Pops*, you had to join the queue.

Nevertheless, what was this ABBA song, with its fade-in, its martial fife and drum, its slightly stilted lyric? And why were these two young women singing about being old, grey, battle-worn Mexican revolutionaries? The song seemed to have no root in the moment and no connection with anything else around it, least of all Paul Nicholas doing a reggae number while dressed like a Droog from *A Clockwork Orange*.

What was it *like*?

And, of course, it was like nothing, really – except, somehow, ABBA. Listening to it now, you can hear this in the way the melody of the verse is so deftly built out of three ascending climbs (0.26–0.36, 0.37–0.46, 0.47–0.54), each reaching a little higher before dropping all the way back down again; and in the way that, in the middle one of those climbs, Frida's voice suddenly opens up and blows hot (0.40–0.41); and in the way the repeat of the intro is neatly folded under the final notes of the first chorus (2.03); and in the arranging ingenuity that says, 'Why don't we make the bass guitar the lead part in the accompaniment for the verses?'; and in a certain tautness in the harmonies and a certain silvery ring in the open acoustic guitar chords; and in the way this song has a tune so strong and so capable of planting itself in people's minds that it will echo on for fifty years and beyond.

'Fernando' wasn't originally meant to be an ABBA song. Given the working title 'Tango', it was written by Benny and Björn for Frida's 1975 solo album *Frida Ensam* ('Frida Alone'), which Benny produced, and its original lyric was in Swedish, provided by Stig Anderson. No distant drums or sounds of bugle calls coming from afar in that first version, and certainly no crossing of the Rio Grande on any kind of frightful night. Fernando seems to have been the name of a barman in Stockholm that Stig knew, and at this point the song was a fairly straightforward commiseration regarding love lost. Indeed, my trusty online Swedish-to-English translation engine translates the first verse as follows:

Why are you mourning, Fernando?
Why does your guitar sound in a minor key, what's going on?
Is it love, Fernando?
Has she left you, your great, great love, is that so?
Anyone who has loved and lost knows that such things can
    still happen from time to time.

Even allowing for what gets lost in translation engines, this doesn't look like a lyric that's exactly going the extra mile in terms of invention. Yet *Frida Ensam* sold well in Sweden – 130,000 copies – in no small measure because of that opening track, which received a lot of radio play even though it wasn't released as a single. It was clear that, whatever it had to say about losing your great, great love and such things that can still happen from time to time, 'Fernando' had a chorus whose welcoming cadences and strongly signalled resolutions loaned themselves magnetically to singing along. So maybe they should re-record it with an English lyric and see what happened then.

Björn apparently struggled with this project for some time. And then one night, allegedly as he lay on a jetty and looked up at the sky while the tune cycled in his head, the idea came to him of a pair of elderly Mexican soldiers reminiscing about their fight for freedom in the early years of the twentieth century and concluding that, if they had to do it all again, they would, my friend, Fernando.

This would have been on Viggsö, a tiny island an hour out of Stockholm if you had access to a motorboat, and more than twice that if you were using the public ferry, which was forbiddingly infrequent. Stig Anderson had bought a summer house on Viggsö at some point in the '60s; the two ABBA couples followed suit at the beginning of the '70s, before they were the two ABBA couples. There were probably only about thirty properties on the island at the time, no real roads, certainly no shops. It was the private space where they holidayed – boating, fishing, generally grabbing the light and the warmth while it was there in the traditional Swedish manner. (It's a cliché, but the cold, dark winters cause the summer to be embraced with heightened commitment in Sweden. A misunderstanding of this cultural phenomenon – wilful or otherwise – seems from time to time to have led British people to form an image of Swedish people as somehow uncommonly desperate to get their clothes off. Perhaps they are, but not necessarily like that.)

Björn and Agnetha's property included, up a slope above the house, a small outhouse. Made of corrugated metal and painted pale yellow, the hut had windows all along its front, creating what was almost a conservatory, entered from one side. Björn and Benny hauled a small blonde-wood upright piano into it (Sid Bernstein, the legendary American concert promoter who booked The Beatles for their US appearances, happened to be staying with Stig that weekend and found himself requisitioned as a piano shifter) and it became a music workshop. In the morning, Björn, in his kitchen, would hear the sound of piano from the top of the garden and know that Benny had arrived. Then he would take a pot of coffee up there and, looking out across treetops past a shining white flagpole to the water beyond, the two of them would sit and jam and compose some of our lifetime's most enduring pop songs.

Before long, when ABBA's fame had escalated, Viggsö would find itself casually referred to as 'ABBA Island' and getting circled by boatloads of fans craning for a glimpse, at which point its days as an idyllic escape offering guaranteed seclusion were, for the band at least, and also presumably for some of the other residents, over. Still, the hut had done some stout service by then. 'Dancing Queen', 'Fernando' and 'Knowing Me, Knowing You' got their start on Viggsö, as did others. The positioning in the ABBA Museum of a full-size replica of the writing room and its panoramic sunny view is there to meet our natural fascination for this germinal location – smash-hit songwriting as a garden-shed holiday hobby! – but also, one feels, tacitly to discourage further unwanted tourism. In 2019, Malcolm Jack, with the permission of the current owners, visited the hut and wrote about it for *The Big Issue*: 'I played "Dancing Queen" on my phone – cheesy but necessary – and my wife danced with our son in his sling.' But the hut was pink, the flagpole was rusting, the treeline had getting on for half a century of growth on it, and the view of the water was gone.

In a Swedish television documentary made in 1976, entitled *ABBA-Dabba-Doo*, Benny and Björn sit in the Viggsö hut in t-shirts on a sunny day while a reporter leans in through the open window and asks them questions about how their songs come together. There is a tangibly sceptical edge to these questions – certainly nothing straightforwardly celebratory or deferential in their tone – and you pick up a strong scent of the critical disapproval that ABBA's success has brought them in their homeland. 'The problem with ABBA,' wrote the music scholar Per F. Broman in *The Journal of Music Studies*, '[was] not that they lacked skill or talent, but that they were commercial. Sweden is and was a society with strong egalitarian tendencies in which issues of wealth are particularly problematic.' Accordingly, even a TV special designed to feature lavish uninterrupted performances of several ABBA songs simultaneously arches an eyebrow at them.

Benny gamely rides his interviewer's mild air of incredulity and explains the way the songwriting works. The two of them will start to play together, just rotating a simple chord pattern and seeing where it goes, and then maybe 'we hum, and sing in some weird kind of English, which is a pleasant language. Some kind of Hasse Alfredson version of English'. (Hasse Alfredson: Swedish comic actor, famous for 'wildly comic extemporising'. Nearest equivalent in English: Stanley Unwin, possibly, or maybe Kenneth Williams.)

Björn then adds: 'The music is the main thing, after all. Language is just one of many instruments, in a sense.'

They never wrote the music down, and they never recorded anything prior to going into the studio. This might appear casual, but it was actually the acid test. Musicians – and creative people in general, maybe – frequently live in fear of the great idea that arrives but slides away again before it can be captured, a terror which sends them rushing to the notebook and the tape recorder. This never seems to have been the Andersson/Ulvaeus approach. The way they saw it, you were better off trusting the filter helpfully operated by your memory. The melodies and sequences that they had come up with on Viggsö, or in Björn and Agnetha's library, or wherever it happened to be, had to prove their worth by staying in their heads. That's how you knew they were any good: by the fact they stayed with you without further assistance. And if they wouldn't stick in the heads of their creators, why would they stick in anyone else's?

Frequently, the nonsense lyric would still be in place when the song got to the studio; Björn speaks here, and on numerous other occasions, of needing the mood of the developed track to tell him what the song should be about. Sometimes in the studio, a guide vocal would be put down using the nonsense lyric, a process memorably described by Michael B. Tretow in an interview with *International Sound* magazine: 'Either Björn, Frida or Agnetha will sing a guide track with phoney lyrics like "I love you/Please love me too/Don't be untrue/Say I do/ Cause I lo-o-o-o-ve you so."' Then Björn would keep listening until something better arrived.

That could be a lengthy business, too. Sometimes, whole lyrics would be written and recorded, complete with harmonies, only to be taken off and thrown away because they weren't felt to sit quite right with the track. In the case of the song 'Move On' on 1977's *Abba: The Album*, Tretow reports that three complete sets of lyrics were recorded, fully harmonised and erased before the fourth attempt was agreed to work.

Yet there were those, clearly, who would claim there was something underhand in this industry; that these people couldn't possibly be doing this because they enjoyed it, or because it pleased them; that there had to be an ulterior motive that could not be respected.

'We're always met with distrust,' Benny tells the interviewer in the Swedish documentary. '"Oh, you just throw together a song and reap loads of money . . ."'

In another interview, years later, in 2018, on Australian television, Björn says: 'I almost, you know, get angry when people think there is some kind of cunning behind it – some formula or some skill that made us write them knowing exactly that they would be big hits. That was never the case.'

You can see why this kind of critical post-rationalising must have been infuriating – why it would drive the seemingly even-tempered Björn to be 'almost' angry. And if you wanted to mount a case for the defence, then surely 'Fernando' would be a compelling piece of evidence to produce.

Because what kind of songwriter would sit down and think: 'I know what will sell right here and right now, in the aggressively competitive world of chart pop music in 1976: a song representing a conversation between old, battle-worn Mexican revolutionaries, but in the form of a campfire schlager and sung by two women. I know, I know – you're going to tell me it's a world where dance music is having a moment and people seem to want to hear Tina Charles singing "I Love to Love" and Barry White singing "You See the Trouble with Me" and The Fatback Band doing the "Spanish Hustle" . . . But trust me, this song which fades in on a fife and drum has exactly the required levels of magic to achieve pan-global cut-through.'

'Fernando' was a number one in Austria, Belgium, Ireland, the Netherlands, Portugal, South Africa, Switzerland, West Germany and the UK. It sold ten million copies around the world, one of fewer than forty records in the entire history of the 7-inch single ever to do that. And is it entirely fanciful to think that the creators of that song must have been as surprised about the scale of its success as anyone else?

And, of course, 'Fernando' was number one in Australia, too
– number one, indeed, for fourteen weeks, equalling The Beatles'
'Hey Jude' as the longest-reigning single that country had ever
had, a record which would hold until 2017 when Ed Sheeran
came along with 'The Shape of You'. Australia had latched onto
ABBA faster and firmer than anywhere else, and now it was
ready to come out for the band on a major scale – the full
Beatles-style, greeted-at-the-airport, screamed-at-in-the-streets
fan mania. ABBA had arrived in Sydney at the start of 1976
to film a TV special and put plans in place for a concert tour
later in the year. The trip took on something of the shape of
a state visit: a river cruise, some boomerang throwing, a barbecue
and a visit to Taronga Zoo for the inevitable koala photo-op.
And through it all, the band found themselves having to be
smuggled out of buildings the back way, hustled by minders
through grabbing hands, the whole panoply of pop superstar
experiences which, in the main, the male members of the band
appear to have found at best exhilarating and at worst amusing,
and the female members more alarming.

But then their fame was growing exponentially everywhere
at this stage and taking on all sorts of new and unlooked-for
forms. This was the year that a rumour took hold for a while
that all the members of ABBA, bar Frida, had died in a plane
crash at Templehof Airport in West Berlin. Frida, though spared,
had suffered life-changing injuries. Apparently sparked by a
rogue phone call to a newspaper office, this easily disproved
piece of fiction spread rapidly across West Germany and beyond,
where it had the chance to mingle with another emerging cult
theory: that ABBA were actually a set of unremarkable-looking
studio session musicians, and the four people who were the

group's public face were merely actors. Think Milli Vanilli, '70s-style.

Well, now three of those actors were dead – as long as you overlooked the fact that they weren't dead, and they weren't actors. It's hard to disagree with Carl Magnus Palm, in *Bright Lights, Dark Shadows*, that the Templehof plane crash rumour marked a kind of watershed moment for ABBA, the confirmation of (ironically) their safe arrival in the pop stratosphere, proving 'beyond any shadow of a doubt that they had now achieved true superstar status'. You know you've really made it to the top of the tree when people start saying that you're dead. (See also, Paul McCartney.)

The bizarre flavour of their new position, vis à vis the press and the public, did not, of course, escape the members of the band, who discussed it with the Swedish television programme, *Sveriges Magasin*.

Frida: 'They are trying to make a myth out of us . . . it's incredibly annoying.'

Agnetha: 'The real people disappear and the myth gets across instead.'

26

The sincerest form of flattery

In 1976, the Eurovision Song Contest is won by a four-piece group, featuring two women, one blonde and one brunette, and two men, one with facial hair and one without. They are the UK's Brotherhood of Man, and they floor the juries with a sucker-punch combination of the wince-inducingly jaunty 'Save Your Kisses for Me' and a thumbs-in-belt-loops/cocked-knee dance routine, which will instantly open itself to feverish imitation in the clubs and playgrounds of the land.

On the subject of feverish imitation, though . . . Well, it's clearly a sensitive subject how much ABBA have influenced Brotherhood of Man, who have been working as a band since 1969, and with this particular two-women/two-men line-up since 1973. It should also be noted that 'Save Your Kisses for Me' will outsell 'Waterloo' and remains, in 2024, the biggest-selling Eurovision-winning single of all time. It also manages to hold 'Fernando' off the top of the UK chart for three weeks before it succumbs to the inevitable in the first week of May.

So, credit where it's due. Nevertheless, perhaps the band don't help themselves in this area when they follow ABBA's success with 'Fernando' with a single called 'Angelo' in June 1977, the story of which begins high on a mountain in Mexico.

And they probably don't help themselves again when they follow 'Angelo' with a single called 'Figaro' in January 1978. That's Figaro who played guitar in the disco-bar and is clearly one of those untrustworthy foreign lotharios that the expanding army of British holiday-goers in this period seem either worried about encountering or hoping to encounter.

Fernando, Angelo, Figaro . . . it's getting crowded in here. And we haven't even met Chiquitita yet.

And there's no disguising the contempt that we aficionados of ABBA, with their *proper* Eurovision-winning pop and their *proper* Mexican-flavoured fireside ballads, feel for the Brotherhood of Man and their oddly galling raid on the low-hanging fruit in the ABBA orchard.

I mean, not just trading the name Fernando for the name Angelo like that, but landing the chorus firmly on the title as well . . .

And how dare they go lifting Benny's pounded piano octaves – which will also, incidentally, be big with Steve Nieve from Elvis Costello and the Attractions, who will slap them onto 'Oliver's Army' in 1979, and with Johnnie Fingers from The Boomtown Rats, who will use them to ramp up the drama of 'I Don't Like Mondays' in the same year.

And, sure, Benny himself lifted those octaves from Tchaikovsky. But that's different.

It seems important to make a stand here, is all I'm saying. A stand for quality against the palest of imitations.

Also: who takes a guitar to a disco?

27

Blurred at the edges

After our pilgrimage to the park bench in the Djurgarden, Elizabeth's walk leads us to the chestnut tree under which ABBA gathered for the photo which forms that reassuringly cheerful image on the inside of the *Greatest Hits* album. We also pause to observe a patch of grass near a café on which ABBA once posed. And then we head up the hill to the cream-and-pink, and lavishly glass-fronted Cirkus theatre, where Frida performed in that televised national talent contest in 1967 and became a star. The venue is now owned by Björn, who restored it and used it in 2022 for the first production of his and Benny's Pippi Longstocking musical adaptation, *Pippi at the Circus*.

And if we turn around, we can look over the road at the splashy, riotously coloured entrance to the Tivoli Grona Lund fairground, a gift to the people of Stockholm from Germany in the eighteenth century, of course, but, far more significantly for our purposes, the venue for that outdoor show in 1975 when ABBA gridlocked the city.

And with that, our walk is done. Elizabeth, by way of wrapping up, now produces four more laminated portrait photos, taken in 1981, six years after the ones she showed us at the beginning of our journey. So here, again, are those four ABBA faces, but after six more years of being ABBA; six years of circling the earth in fame's cramped capsule and breathing the thin and artificially supplemented air up there; six years which have yielded success and wealth and recognition at unimaginable and unplanned-for levels, as well as the ultimate destruction of two marriages. Agnetha smiles boldly, perhaps even defiantly. Frida's hair has taken a turn for the '80s – some asymmetrical cutting going on in there, and some purple dye – and the face from 1976 (let alone the person in the bubble perm and the glam-folk blouson from 1974) is another woman here. Björn now wears a beard and his expression seems narrower and harder than it did when we saw him at the cemetery gate. And maybe it's the picture, but Benny is heavier about the face and wearier about the eyes at this end-point on our walk, and altogether a bit blurred at the edges.

And OK, these people are only thirty-four and thirty-five in these pictures, and Agnetha is only thirty-one, so it's not quite like looking at photographs of Barack Obama before and after eight years of the American presidency. Nevertheless, here are four faces wearing manifest traces of a long and intense campaign at pop's frontline – four people in a band who have been repeatedly spun around the world and back, and who have understandably grown tired of some of the aspects of that spinning, including, to various extents, each other.

But they're still intact, still themselves, still moving forward, seems to be Elizabeth's point. And one day, forty years later, when all this stuff is a shared past in a set of lives on which time is running out, they will even find it in themselves to get together for a while and make another record and put together a pioneering virtual live show in which they do and don't feature.

What was Elizabeth's takeaway message here? It wasn't, she said, about the music, really, for which she was thankful, of course, but which hadn't come up in much detail in the previous ninety minutes. It wasn't even really about 'the ABBAs', and the quirk of fate and timing that brought those four people together.

No, what was important, Elizabeth said, was the fact that the ABBAs had brought *us* together – had given *us* a reason to meet. So we could be lastingly grateful to the ABBAs for that.

It was, somehow, a very ABBA message. And with that, we all thanked Elizabeth and went our separate ways.

28

Fields of gold

June 1996. On a warm Sunday evening, 30,000 people are gathered in Finsbury Park in London to witness the return to the stage after twenty years of the Sex Pistols.

'We're fat, forty and back,' John Lydon – the former Johnny Rotten, wearing a check suit and green hair – will shortly declare before the band piles hectically into its opening number, 'Bodies' (*Never Mind the Bollocks, Here's the Sex Pistols*, side two, track three).

Is this comeback wise? The question has been widely debated in the run-up to this moment. Indeed, it's probably no exaggeration to say that this mid-life return to action by the leaders of the punk revolution has been identified as a perhaps unprecedented stress-test for ideas and practices around the emergent phenomenon of the rock reunion tour.

After all, it's been enough to raise eyebrows that The Who – who once so enthusiastically agitated on behalf of the advantages of dying over growing old – are dragging themselves back out on the road again in 1996 in the service of their heritage, and that Ozzy Osbourne of Black Sabbath is embarking this year on the self-explanatory Retirement Sucks Tour.

But the Sex Pistols? The band whose overtly declared motivation was to apply a bare electrical wire to a moribund musical
culture and to frazzle the old, the tired and the established?
Where do the Sex Pistols fit on pop's expanding heritage circuit
and would this project thrive on the mountainous quantity of
irony it automatically generated, or simply collapse under the
weight of it?

Three months earlier, at the 100 Club in Oxford Street,
during a press conference at which journalists were served trays
of cheese rolls and jellied eels by a small team of drag queens,
questions for Lydon and his companions about their proposed
rebirth had ranged from the nakedly sceptical to the even more
nakedly sceptical.

'Do you still hate each other?'

Lydon: 'Yes, with a vengeance, but we share a common cause,
and it's your money.'

'This is sad, isn't it?'

Lydon: 'It's sad that an arsehole like you doesn't appreciate
the effort that we've gone to.'

'You said you hated stadium rock bands, but you are one
now.'

Lydon: 'No we're not. What stadium would that be? You
name the stadium and I'll call you a liar. Finsbury Park is not
a stadium. It is *a field.*'

But here we are in June, and 30,000 people have voluntarily
paid £25 to come and stand in what is definitely not a stadium
but a field and experience the third performance on the Sex
Pistols' Filthy Lucre Tour, which is scheduled to last six months
and girdle the globe. (Why had the tour opened in Finland?
Lydon: 'You've got to rehearse *somewhere.*')

Reports of this occasion in the newspapers will not miss the opportunity to describe it as a convention of retired punk soldiers in relaxed-fit bondage trousers. And it's certainly the case that, amid the fast food and drink outlets that ring this temporary arena, a stall is offering t-shirts emblazoned with the slogan 'Old Punks Never Die – They Just Stand at the Back'. In truth, though, the assembled crowd is a broad mix of ages, including people who were there or thereabouts in 1977, some here with their children, and also people who weren't there but are here now, because . . . well, setting all the ironies aside, a bona fide musical legend is a bona fide musical legend, and if you missed it all the first time, why wouldn't you be curious about catching it when you could?

After a supporting set from Iggy Pop (forty-nine and topless in PVC trousers), a paper curtain spattered with Pistols-related tabloid headlines is put up to conceal the stage while it is readied for the arrival of the main act, and anticipation builds.

It's at this point that the PA begins to send out across the heads of the increasingly expectant and slightly restive audience a series of pop hits from the '70s: 'Shang-a-Lang' by the Bay City Rollers, ABBA's 'Dancing Queen' . . .

Phil Singleton, who was in the crowd that day, wrote about what happened next in a blog for the Sex Pistols site, sex_pistols.net:

Ah, I thought. Brilliant! It's a reminder of how awful the music scene was pre-Pistols. A recreation of the conditions that resulted in the Pistols coming into being. Was I alone in thinking this?

Surely not. The Bay City Rollers? They were exactly the kind of grinning, tartan-wrapped lightweights that first set punk's lip curling, weren't they? And as for ABBA's 'Dancing Queen', well, wasn't dance music a genre of music that punk was especially inclined to spit on? For its ubiquity, as much as anything else. And quite by coincidence, on the day 'Dancing Queen' was released — 16 August 1976 — a band called The Ramones was making its first live appearance, at CBGB in New York, a venue originally designed to host country, bluegrass and blues music (hence CBGB), but which had taken the temperature of the times and decided it might be prudent to start booking some of this new wave of harder-edged rock acts.

Meanwhile, back in the UK, 1976 was the year the following bands formed: The Clash, The Jam, The Cure, The Damned, UK Subs, Generation X and Elvis Costello & the Attractions. Even as 'Dancing Queen' came out, a wind of change was already getting up, designed to blow it, and the people who made it, away.

Certainly, here in Finsbury Park, a reflexive murmur of discontent has run through the audience at the onset of this barrage of flimsy pop. Yet that murmur of discontent has turned quite quickly to communal laughter. And that communal laughter has in turn become . . . well, what *is* this?

Perish the thought, but is this . . . wait . . . are people *joining in*?

'I looked around,' Singleton recalled. 'Punk rockers were singing "Dancing Queen".'

29

Thanks a billion

'Dancing Queen' is by most measurements ABBA's most successful song – successful then and successful now; a 1.56 million-selling single and multinational number one on its release in 1976, and the first ABBA track to reach a billion streams on Spotify, a landmark moment which occurred precisely on 11 July 2023, according to the ABBA International Fan Club magazine, which keeps a close eye on these things. In a way that almost every pop song at some level hopes to do, but very few manage at all, 'Dancing Queen' comfortably straddles time and worlds.

It doesn't hang about, either. A headlong slide down the piano keys and we're in, instantly afloat on a bubbling bass line and an air-filled drum-beat, while guitar and piano in unison chop gently at the rhythm and oar it along. Over the top of all this, a melody is being seductively 'aah'd' to us by a blend of synthesiser and high choral voices – a disembodied, faintly eerie noise, calling to us, perhaps, from a discothèque somewhere in the afterlife.

And then a pair of very much embodied voices cut in with an important announcement, informing us that we can dance and, more than that, we can *jive*.

Which came as news to a few of us who were fourteen at the time this record was released, and in whom an unlooked-for outbreak of weapons-grade self-consciousness would render dancing, and definitely jiving, and sometimes even *walking,* problematic for the foreseeable future. I can only speak for myself here, of course, but ahead of me at the point at which 'Dancing Queen' turned up in my life lay at least two years of jive-stifling cramp during a phase when what went by the name of dancing was chiefly girls and boys hopping about stiffly in gender-themed knots, facing each other. This wasn't really dancing, one subsequently realised: it was circling the wagons.

But then part of 'Dancing Queen's magic lay in evoking, however dimly, the possibility of other, more open engagements, somewhere out there – in causing you to begin to wonder whether, despite all evidence to the contrary and the seemingly insuperable objects in your way, maybe you *could* dance, maybe you *could* jive . . .

What was never in any doubt, though, was this: that those first forty-two seconds of music, before the song eases back and gets on with the business of its first verse, were endowed with a superpower. Deployed in any setting in which communal dancing was being encouraged, the opening bars of 'Dancing Queen' quite clearly had the capacity not just to draw people out onto dancefloors, but actually to suction them there help-lessly from anywhere in the vicinity, in the manner of some kind of mammoth cordless vacuum cleaner.

It would be next to impossible to have attended, for example, a wedding reception during the last forty years – in any kind of venue, high-flown or modest, from lantern-hung, country-garden marquee to strip-lit community hall – and not seen the intro to 'Dancing Queen' go to work on the room like a detergent, strong enough to rid the seated areas of even the most stubborn of aunts. It's why Jarvis Cocker once felt able to declare: 'If you went to a wedding and nobody played "Dancing Queen", you'd probably feel a bit short-changed.' And it's why the music writer Tim Jonze could similarly announce: 'There are only two kinds of wedding discos – ones that open with "Dancing Queen" and terrible ones.' Both of these statements, we can safely assert from this particular vantage point in the twenty-first century, will remain true for as long as there is electricity and for as long as there are wedding receptions.

In the mid-'70s, that floor-filling superpower straight away made this single an indispensable tool for the newly burgeoning breed of 'mobile disco' operators. In a way which made me feel profoundly well connected, my brothers were mates with one of that new breed. By day, he was Malcolm Austin, deputy manager of the local Martin's the newsagent. By night, he was Ozzie, the power behind Ozzie's Disco, bringing your best-loved chart sounds to the rec halls and social centres of north-east Essex for ten quid plus petrol.

Now, a fuller biography of Ozzie from Ozzie's Disco would probably have to acknowledge that he was also a man of legendary gullibility. When, for example, Colchester got its first automated cash machine, my brother Simon took Ozzie there and entirely convinced him that there was a man inside it.

But my sense, looking up, of Ozzie's grandeur was undiminished by any of that, and coloured instead by my knowledge that, at any of his professional engagements, Ozzie would be carrying with him, in one of his formidable artillery of boxes and adapted suitcases, *the entire and up-to-date Top 30*, with that week's new entries freshly added.

Owning every record in the chart? It seemed to me that this man was living the dream. As far as Ozzie was concerned, however, it was just customer care – part of the service. If some saddo ever came to him and said, 'Can you play that new one by Brotherhood of Man?' (to pluck the name at random), he was going to be ready for them.

Still, Ozzie knew the facts as well as anyone: if you weren't packing a copy of 'Dancing Queen' in the van with your decks and your coloured lightbulbs and your slightly inadequate microphone, you weren't going anywhere.

And given that it seemed to remove all personal agency from the business of getting onto the dancefloor, the record could be welcomed as a saviour by those of us on the other side of the disco's trestle table from Ozzie as well. Because when push comes to shove, where is the walk to the dancefloor meant to end and the dancing begin? Peter Kay famously studied the physical comedy of this transition in 2004. It comes perfectly naturally to many people (and those are the ones whose behaviour Kay seems to find funniest), but some of us struggled with these things.

The emergence of your dancing self from your non-dancing self . . . is that intended to happen only after you have occupied your space on the dancefloor, with strict separation between the two? Or is it meant to occur in some more evolving way – in a gradual loosening (or, probably, tightening) of the limbs as you cross the dancefloor's perimeter and head for that space?

Or does it occur even before that, in your very rise from the table? Scientifically precise measures of a person's comfort in their own skin could be taken from their handling of this phase in any dance-based gathering.

Kay chose, as the essential soundtracks for this bottomless human drama, the opening bars of 'Celebration' by Kool & the Gang from 1980 and the fanfare that announces Village People's 1978 hit 'YMCA' – that fanfare being essentially the theme from the US TV show *Dallas*, but wearing a leather posing pouch. And both those passages of music have, without question, been amply proven across the years to have bat-signal proper-ties and a strong role to play in dancefloor crowd control.

But he could equally well have picked the first forty-two seconds of 'Dancing Queen', which beat both those others off the blocks by years, which are equally efficient in those departments, and which, by virtue of being practically irresistible, are an even firmer friend to the self-conscious in a time of grave difficulty.

What accounts for the mysterious magnetism of those opening bars? Is it something ultimately ineffable in that combi-nation of those unearthly, seductive voices and that rhythm? Almost certainly. But maybe there's something straightforwardly structural and witting going on, too. Certainly, one should never underestimate the boldness of this record's decision to dispense with the usual niceties – a verse, at least, maybe even a bridge or linking device of some kind – and instead land you straight in the sweet-spot of the chorus.

The point being that we're not merely at the start of the chorus when 'Dancing Queen' opens, but halfway through that chorus, at the point at which it hits its peak. There's no guided ascent in the company of patient sherpas in 'Dancing Queen', the way there is in most pop songs – you're thrust straight into the dizzyingly thin air at the summit.

It's an extremely unusual move, although it's interesting to note that someone who had already tried it was Willy Nagara, the writer of that Austrian schlager 'Du spielst 'ne tolle Rolle', which, as we saw earlier, seemed to inform the making of Björn and Benny's first hit song, 'Ljuva Sextital'. Nagara, too, kicks off with the second, more intense half of his chorus to ensure that the song instantly grabs you by the shoulder straps on your lederhosen. And 'Ljuva Sextital' did the same thing. So that tactic seems to have been lingering in the pages of Björn and Benny's playbook from the beginning, just waiting for them to pull it out and produce the most surprising and euphoric opening to a pop record since The Beatles abruptly hurled themselves chorus-first into 'She Loves You'.

And somehow (and this really *is* the magical thing), after a billion repeats and counting, it still feels surprising and euphoric forty-eight years later.

30

Bad altitude

And here are ABBA in the autumn of 1976, in a television studio in Warsaw, taking 'Dancing Queen' behind the Iron Curtain to the people of Poland. Here they are, as those opening bars ring out, standing at the top of what is surely the longest staircase built for showbusiness purposes outside the one commissioned by Busby Berkeley for his famous 'Lullaby of Broadway' tap routine. (See the movie *Gold Diggers of 1935*.)

White and shiny, this purpose-built monster drops horribly steeply from just below the ceiling to the studio floor, more than six metres below, and would seem, even for the relatively young and agile artistes that ABBA are at this stage in their career (Agnetha is twenty-six, Benny thirty, Frida and Björn thirty-one), to be crying out for a cable car, or at the very least a handrail. As it is, if this all goes wrong – and the odds must be high – the four of them will have nothing to grab except each other.

What's more, starkly increasing the jeopardy, the staircase has been wrapped in a sheet of glistening white plastic, tucked around each of the steps and falling away over the sheer drop on each side. The idea seems to be to create a kind of icy-mountain effect, dramatically enhanced by blue lighting, but the use of slippery plastic as carpeting for a steep staircase is certainly an odd decision from a health and safety point of view. This is no descent for the faint-hearted. And this is surely no descent for anyone in white judo outfits and stack-heeled footwear, which is what ABBA find themselves wearing as they stand on a platform just under the studio's lighting rig and contemplate the treacherous terrain that lies between themselves and the safety of the ground.

Dancing? Jiving? Not at this height, clearly, and not on this surface. With much surreptitious checking of feet, the four band members start to edge their way gingerly down the stairs – Agnetha and Frida leading the way, Benny and Björn one step behind them, strumming at guitars; Björn on an electric, Benny on an acoustic. There are no acoustic guitars audible on 'Dancing Queen' and even if there were, it's highly unlikely that any of them would have been played by Benny, but no matter – this is television, and television rules apply. Plus, it stands to reason that there was no question of Benny attempting to get a piano down these steps – or not without the risk of evoking Laurel & Hardy rather than Busby Berkeley. And the alternative in which the two men, in their matching white outfits, descend silent and empty-handed behind the women, like chaperones at some kind of overimagined wedding ceremony, is clearly worse. So, for the next three minutes and fifty seconds, 'Dancing Queen' has an acoustic guitar in it.

What with the instruments, the heels and the reckless camber, the band's progress is inevitably slow, each step fraught with potentially career-ending risks. Twice during the first verse, they pause completely for several seconds, perhaps to regain their balance, perhaps to allow their ears to adjust to the changing air pressure, perhaps to ask themselves what the hell they are doing, here in Warsaw, on this death-trap of a set, when they could be at home in Stockholm, using more sensible staircases. But each time, with formidable professionalism, they eventually go again, cautiously covering a few more feet in the direction of sanctuary.

Grin and bear it, seems to be the approach. This slot on *Studio 2* is a rare opportunity, after all. How many Western acts get behind the Iron Curtain to promote a pop record at this point in the Cold War? Before ABBA, communist Poland last saw brief visits from The Animals in 1965 and The Rolling Stones in 1967. So politically paranoid and exotic are these cross-border cultural exchanges that a rumour will in due course take hold that the Polish government has paid for ABBA's appearance in a barter agreement with Sweden which has seen wagon-loads of green peas shipped the other way in exchange.

In fact, no peas at all seem to have changed hands in the making of this television special, though a chartered plane was sent to Stockholm to collect the band and will ensure that they are delivered straight back afterwards, following a press conference and some photo opportunities around Warsaw. (Agnetha, however, has flown in separately from Björn, which she chooses to do whenever possible while on ABBA business, being a) terrified of flying and b) terrified of leaving her child an orphan in the plane crash which her terror of flying causes her to believe to be highly likely.)

Polish ABBA fans, it turns out, are legion following the import into the country of the band's first two albums and a handful of regulated TV clips. But like all Eastern European fans of Western pop at this time, they must grab what they can from a strictly limited flow of information and product, and confusions are apt to arise. Accordingly, this trip to Warsaw is a chance for Björn, in particular, to show Poland who he is. The publication in a Polish newspaper in 1975 of the address of ABBA's Swedish fan club has triggered a deluge of fan letters and drawings. And the organisers of the fan club who opened those letters were surprised to discover that some of that fan art appeared to depict Björn with breasts. 'For some reason,' Carl Magnus Palm writes in *Bright Lights, Dark Shadows*, 'quite a few Poles thought he was a woman.' This illusion, at least, will not survive Björn's extended appearance on *Studio 2*, assuming Björn survives it himself.

The band do some more cautious stepping, the floor now comfortably in sight. Eventually, to the relief, no doubt, of anyone watching from the television company's insurers, they're down, reaching base camp on the studio floor exactly at the point the first verse ends and the chorus kicks in.

Yet even here, their challenge is not over: after a short, relieved run across the surface, they must now take it in turns to use a small box to step up onto a plinth, about two feet high and carved in the shape of the number two – as in *Studio 2* – and then complete the song from up there, while standing in a line along the narrow promontory represented by that digit's lowest limb.

The stairs, the plastic sheeting, the novelty plinth . . . the negotiation of all of this without disaster must surely rank among ABBA's greatest gymnastic achievements.

It's also a chastening reminder of one of the perhaps unanticipated consequences for a pop group of seeking to dominate the international airwaves in the middle of the 1970s: that you will find yourself in a television studio in Warsaw, clambering around on absurd furniture in lightly cinched robes and inappropriate footwear.

31

Cut to the chase

Places where 'Dancing Queen' was number one on its first release include Australia, Canada, Denmark, Mexico, South Africa, Czechoslovakia, West Germany, the UK and Spain – as well as the US, where no other ABBA song topped the chart. In Sweden, it was number one for fourteen weeks. In the UK, it would knock Elton John and Kiki Dee's 'Don't Go Breaking My Heart' off the top of the chart and stay in place for six weeks, seeing off Paul McCartney & Wings' 'Let 'Em In', Rod Stewart's 'The Killing of Georgie (Part I and II)', and the Bee Gees' 'You Should Be Dancing'.

Looking at the calibre of those rivals, it's easy to form the impression that the fight for the number one slot in mid-'70s Britain was a permanently raging battle royal between armour-plated super-contenders, all built for the long term. Talk to Ozzie from Ozzie's Disco about it, though. One quick peep inside the record-spinning king's Top 30 suitcase would have informed you that this apparently golden period for innovative and deftly constructed pop music was also a phase in which The Wurzels could have a huge hit with 'I Am a Cider Drinker'.

It would also show you that 'Dancing Queen' was eventually

replaced at number one in the UK in the second week of October 1976 by Pussycat and 'Mississippi', a concertedly unsurprising, mid-tempo country and western number which arrived from the Netherlands and which I can still recall thinking was the dreariest song I had ever heard. The impatient dismissiveness, there, of a callow fourteen-year-old, of course. But having listened to it again just now out of curiosity . . . well, I had a point.

The thing was, 'Dancing Queen' was carrying so much more in the way of energy. Pussycat had, by their own admission, looked for inspiration to the Bee Gees, specifically to their 1967 folk ballad 'Massachusetts', with which the title 'Mississippi' clearly shares several things, including a syllable-count and a reliable berth in spelling bee challenges.

But the Dutch group had chosen to go in that direction exactly as the Bee Gees themselves were leaving folk-pop in the mud and reinventing themselves as the suppliers of elite-tier disco music, modelled on the sounds that were newly leaking from nightclubs in Miami and New York and Philadelphia. In keeping with this mission, the aforementioned 'You Should Be Dancing' signalled to the world the full emergence of the Barry Gibb falsetto, which he had tried out, in a whispery sort of way, on the band's previous album, but which he now piloted with the breath stripped out of it, producing something loud, clear, and on a hitherto undiscovered wavelength that called alike to dancers in discos and DJs at radio stations (and, yes, almost certainly dogs).

The other breakthrough in the band's vocal department was the development of the extreme unison vibrato with which the group's banked voices, juddering like a braking lorry, practically become another percussion instrument, carving its own path through the songs' rhythms. The following year, 'You Should Be Dancing' would be gathered, with five other Bee Gees songs, into the soundtrack for *Saturday Night Fever*, by which point it would be absolutely raining disco music, the whole world over.

'Dancing Queen' revealed that Benny and Björn had been listening to that American nightclub music, too, or certainly to the earliest forms of it. In particular, they seemed to have latched onto 'Rock Your Baby' by George McCrae, released in 1974, a disco trailblazer along with The Hues Corporation's 'Rock the Boat'. For starters, we could note the way in which, in 'Rock Your Baby', the organ glissandos upwards as the vocals come in and glissandos down again in the transition into the bridge, and suggest that this might have given Benny an idea for the intro to 'Dancing Queen'. But Benny had already opened an ABBA song with a glissando – 'He Is Your Brother' on the *Ring Ring* album, in 1973, where he repeats the trick as a linking device after each chorus. And he would do the same thing near the top of 'Don't Shut Me Down' on the *Voyage* comeback album in 2022, by which time, thanks to 'Dancing Queen,' the white-key glissando could practically be thought of as a signature Andersson device.

What 'Dancing Queen' certainly takes from 'Rock Your Baby' is its tempo. Disco music likes to operate at around 125 beats per minute but, as the song metrics data-crunching site songbpm.com will tell you, 'Rock Your Baby' rolls along at just 104 bpm. What that slower pace creates is some extra space in which to feed in another rhythm that runs against the straight 2/4 disco beat – specifically, in the case of 'Rock Your Baby', a samba rhythm, tapped on a woodblock.

'Dancing Queen' moves even slower than that at 101bpm, which earns it a 'somewhat danceable' score in songbpm.com's ratings system. (For comparison purposes, Earth, Wind & Fire's 'September', at 126bpm, secures a 'very danceable' rating.) This is where we reach the limit of this particular branch of maths, of course, because as we've already established, using the evidence of a zillion wedding receptions, 'Dancing Queen' is not just 'somewhat danceable', nor even 'very danceable', but actually 'extremely danceable' – maybe even 'off-the-charts danceable'.

The point is, though, that its rhythm is languid, and even within the confines of the dancefloor's demands for a reliable beat, contains a sense of drift. It also leaves room for something contrapuntal to take place without things getting messy.

There were probably other sources for this idea, too, apart from the McCrae song. The same approach to rhythm-building can be heard, for instance, on Dr John's 'Iko Iko'. Björn and Benny had possibly been able to resist Rolf Harris's 1965 cover of this New Orleans Mardi Gras standard, and, of course, here in 2024, we have subsequently learned to resist everything Rolf Harris ever did. But we know that ABBA and Michael B. Tretow were fans of Dr John's version of 'Iko Iko' on the 1972 *Gumbo* album, which, again, sets a samba rhythm against a straight beat so that it keeps advancing and retreating on itself – three steps forward, two steps back.

It's there, too, in Aretha Franklin's 'Rock Steady', composed by her and released on the 1971 album *Young, Gifted and Black*, where the busy patter of the Latin percussion is set against the relaxed drum-beat provided by Bernard Purdie, with the result that the track seems to be playing in single- and double-time simultaneously. All of this finds a match in those chopped guitar and piano chords that set the rhythm for 'Dancing Queen' and particularly in the accented sets of those chords that sit in the links between chorus and verse (first one at 0.41–0.42).

Yet how thin and rudimentary the McCrae track, in particular, sounds by contrast with the thickly layered, high-gloss sheen of 'Dancing Queen'. The rhythm track of 'Rock Your Baby' has the tippy-tappy feel of an early-generation home-organ rhythm generator (indeed, the original demo recording used exactly that). The synthesisers on that track also have a proto-typical wispiness to them. During its instrumental middle section, held notes on the keyboard seem to be marking a place where the solo will go later and the section risks losing our interest altogether until McCrae lets out his falsetto cry to save it and bring everything back into focus again.

Contrast, on the ABBA recording, the density of the produc-tion and the constantly renewing details at every turn. The arrangement is soaked through with melodic invention, particularly from the keyboards. The verses wriggle with decor-ations between each of the sung lines: the busy arpeggiated synth figure after the first line (0.46–0.48), the punctuation on the piano after the second line and leading into the third (0.52–0.56), the firm chords that echo the vocal line in the fourth (1.00–1.01), and then, ramping up for the chorus, a flowing upward piano run (1.18–1.20) before the strings take over. Then there are those pounded Tchaikovsky octaves that spring up throughout the track, like a series of revelatory 'ta-da!' moments. Best of all, there's the counter-melody, made from a blend of synth, voice and grand piano, which joins the vocal and then carries on rising beyond it causing the entire chorus to bloom (1.50–1.57).

Even more than 'Mamma Mia', you realise, this track is meticulously constructed, right through to the fade and the violin flourish which appears out of nowhere, as the music dissipates (at 3.38) and is never used again. And then right at the very bottom of the fade, just peeping out before the song entirely disappears, there's that final set of Tchaikovsky octaves, sounding even more emphatic this time (3.46–3.48).

But, listening closely now, it's Agnetha and Frida's shared vocal delivery that leaps out at you. How easy it is to overlook the sheer power those vocals were packing. The chorus itself is a simple four-note phrase for the most part. But from the bottom of the verse to the peak of the chorus, the melody travels a full two-octave span, and it's astonishing just how much force those twinned voices are carrying by the time they complete it. The two full choruses even gain an ecstatic scream after the 'oh yeah', a whole octave above (at 1.45 and 2.58), which sounds a lot like the wailing war cry that Tony Visconti managed to build from Mickey Finn's falsetto voice on those T. Rex singles. The singing on this record is altogether off the leash.

The band began recording the song at the beginning of August 1975, put vocals on it in September, and were still working on it in December, trying to get it to sit right. The working title – 'Boogaloo' – was long gone. ('From the people who brought you 'Waterloo' – here's 'Boogaloo'.' It was always unlikely.) Once again, it was Stig Anderson who had conjured something more serviceable from the available syllables, producing a set of lyrics which Björn then reworked. Revisions seem to have been plentiful. At one stage the song had another verse before the second full chorus, matching the two verses before the first full chorus, but that was snipped out. It's a cut that hurries the track forwards. We've been here before with ABBA: in 'Waterloo', where the descending four-note run which chugs down into the chorus each time takes two bars to elapse the first two times it happens, but is squeezed into one bar ahead of the final chorus; and in 'SOS', where the same thing happens with the introductory piano figure when it's repurposed as an outro. And in each of these cases, the cut ensures that the song continues to surprise you, just when you think you're getting to know its patterns.

Another substantial edit: the one that attached the second half of the chorus to the front of the song. Finally, they were happy with it, and just over a year after they had started work on it, 'Dancing Queen' was ready to be released.

I was fourteen when that happened, sunk in the middle of a baking British summer which had turned the lawn Saharan and caused a water shortage, though it seemed important to enjoy it at the time. After all, with temperatures up around the 35-degree mark, this was the hottest UK summer in 350 years, so what were the odds on you seeing another one of *those* in your lifetime?

Anyway, at fourteen, questions about what new sounds were coming out of the nightclubs of the US were of little concern to me. Indeed, the most important sounds coming out of the US as far as I was concerned were emerging from a new comedy show on ITV called *Happy Days*. Those sounds specifically were 'Woah!' and 'Heeey!' and they were made by the character called Arthur Fonzarelli, whom we were encouraged to know more familiarly as 'The Fonz' or, when you really got to know him, 'Fonzie'. Or, when you *really* got to know him, Henry Winkler.

The Fonz was also responsible for the unimpeachable riposte, 'Sit on it', and the extremely valuable rhetorical question, 'Who's cool?'. Plus, he pioneered an important variant on the 'thumbs aloft' gesture – more 'thumbs akimbo', the hands turned outwards from the thighs, and best executed with slightly dropped shoulders and hips. All of this seemed to merit our attention and practice wherever two or more of us were gathered. (The Fonz's habit of summoning girls to his side with a single click of the fingers hasn't weathered well. But he did at least have charm to go with it – and also, we were assured, a rigorously sound moral sense. So there was that.)

Yet even among those of us who were still at least seven years – half our lives again – from being able to set foot legally in the smouldering atmosphere of Colchester's Andromeda nightclub (twenty-one-and-overs only) and who were spending this period going 'Woah!' and 'Heeey!' all the time, disco music did seem to achieve some cut-through. The Bee Gees were suddenly telling us 'You Should Be Dancing' and it seemed polite to at least consider the suggestion, even though it was so hot. The stuff Barry Gibb mentions in that song about his 'woman' being both 'juicy' and 'trouble', and going right on until dawn and properly getting it to him . . . well, all of this made dancing seem very appealing indeed. Or it would have done, had we had any idea at the time that that was what he was singing. (The full adult candour of the lyrics to 'You Should Be Dancing' was only unfolded to me recently in conversation with a friend who had just watched an episode of *Top of the Pops 2* with the subtitles switched on. 'Did you have the first clue?' he said. I did not. You could have knocked over the pair of us with a rolled-up John Travolta poster. Those new falsetto voices were a smuggling device, clearly.)

And very soon after that, ABBA were telling us that *we* could dance, *we* could jive – and again, it seemed highly unlikely and yet one had to do them the honour of at least contemplating the possibility. The directness of the song's appeal to us, the listeners, in those opening lines, demanded that, at a minimum.

Of course, it was only later that you realised there might be layers to this lyric, beyond the mere exhortation to get out there and dance while the dancing's good; that it was open to interpretation in ways that Barry Gibb's going right on until dawn ultimately was not; that there was a plangency attached to that use of the second person; that you could conclude that it was all about memory, or all about fantasy or delusion, or all about the stories that you tell yourself when you want to feel better about things; that it was a song about losing yourself in a song – in the form, conveniently, of a song in which it was entirely possible to lose yourself.

In other words, this was a piece of music, I now realise, that was storing up its poignancy for later, carrying a melancholy payload that could detonate under you thirty, forty, fifty years later. You couldn't possibly have realised it if you were seventeen or younger at the time, because there was no pop single in 1976 that you would have confidently asserted would still be around in fifty years. Indeed, there were many you felt would be doing well to get through the next fifty minutes. But 'Dancing Queen' had cunningly taken out a lease on the future and had gone ahead to wait for you.

32

The dodgy shaker

'But what about the tambourine?' the sceptics are bound to ask. 'Isn't the tambourine a problem?'

Many people down the years have objected to 'Dancing Queen's invitation to feel the beat of the tambourine. Reactions can range from a ripple of unease to full-blown, honking derision. It will be pointed out that the tambourine is not the greatest of all the instruments whose beat calls a dancer to action on the floor – that it's logically the drums that should be getting a shout-out at this moment in the song. Indeed, there's an argument that the lyric takes a turn for the bathetic when it reaches that line, because essentially the singers are inviting us to feel the beat of the little shaky thing familiar from primary school music lessons and which sits in the instrument food chain one step above the triangle and only two steps above the bottle shaker.

In conclusion, the sceptics will tell you that the tambourine is there for one reason, and for one reason alone: because it rhymes with 'queen'.

Well, OK, but if we're going to be pillorying ABBA for this line, let's at least not slander the tambourine along the way. Listen to 'Reach Out I'll Be There' by The Four Tops, and in particular the instrumental bar that introduces the chorus, and then tell me the tambourine doesn't have a feel-able beat. Or listen to the chorus of Grace Jones's 'Slave to the Rhythm' and tell me that there's no beat in the tambourine that suddenly pops up and skims across the song's chorus like a stone across a pond.

Or, if we're really going to go there, listen, even, to Sting's 'If You Love Somebody (Set Them Free)' and tell me that, despite the bass, the drums, the guitar, the organ and the saxophone which are present in that arrangement, the four shifting patterns played on the tambourine at different points as the song evolves aren't its chief means of propulsion – its key plot device, even.

Altogether, I'm definitely with the superprof music tutorial blog which forcefully argues, in an introduction to the instrument for potential practitioners, that 'the tambourine is not to be underestimated' and further declares, importantly, that the instrument 'is not just something whacked lazily by Liam Gallagher'.

Damn right it isn't. Have you ever tried to play a tambourine? I mean, properly and accurately play one? Anyone who has so much as picked up a tambourine off a table knows that those things have a mind of their own. There is almost no moment in its life when a tambourine doesn't actively want to be jingling. Playing the tambourine well and, equally importantly, stopping the tambourine from playing itself, are delicate skills, fit, surely, to be ranked alongside pottery and cat-herding.

I was once, while working as a journalist, able to sit quite close to Ray Cooper, the venerable rock and pop percussionist, during a recording session. As he busied himself among the various tools of his trade, it occurred to me that the ability to cause a tambourine to make a noise *only when you want it to* didn't merely connote supreme mastery of the instrument but may actually have been some kind of sorcery. I realised that I wasn't just impressed by Ray Cooper, I was slightly afraid of him.

Anyway, art is definitely on ABBA's side here, and maybe even religion. To the best of my knowledge, no major piece of religious iconography from a reputable source depicts an angel behind a drum kit, and certainly not behind a drum machine. But angels feeling the beat of the tambourine? They're all over the walls of history. OK, so angels chiefly loved a harp, but according to vast amounts of surviving imagery, the tambourine was, clearly, for hundreds of years, the angelic host's chosen percussion instrument, and maybe it still is – although people don't paint that kind of thing so often these days so it's harder to tell. Either way, art is stuffed with tambourines, from Fra Angelico's *Angel with Tambourine* (c. 1480) through Carl Rahl's *Autumn* (1845) which hangs in the Vienna Opera House, all the way to *Angel with Tambourine on Branch* (unknown painter on Valentine's card, 1904).

Was there anything ABBA could have done to sidestep this tambourine controversy? I guess 'feel the beat of the drum machine' would have satisfied both rhyme and meter, and also the disco context. No drum machine on 'Dancing Queen', of course – but there's no tambourine, either (unless it's buried so deeply with the snare in the mix that I can't hear it). However, if anything was going to snap you out of the euphoric fugue state in which this song aspires to suspend its listener, a reference to something as blankly technical as a drum machine at that peak point in the melody would definitely have done it. They were better off with the tambourine, surely.

But even the staunchest defender of ABBA would have to surrender eventually and admit that, yes, it's a dodgy line. At the same time, though, if you want a demonstration of how time has abetted ABBA in the conversion of something that was once lame into something transcendent, then this business with the tambourine would surely be it. Or what about the fact that I only now discover that the club where the dancing queen is doing her dancing is actually where they play the right music, and not, as I've been hearing it, a club where you are serenaded 'with a bit of rock music'. I always thought that was a dodgy piece of writing: rock music in a disco? And I was right: it *is* a dodgy piece of writing. But also a non-existent one.

This is the thing, though. With enough repetition, and enough goodwill, we listen the lyrics of the pop songs we love into transparency. And with the most-played and the most familiar songs, it's only with conscious effort that we can bring the lyric back into focus. Can we really listen to the words of, say, The Beatles' 'Yesterday' at this point in time? Can we really hear them or think about them, without some counter-intuitive act of will like the one I'm currently exercising? The words just . . . are. The song just . . . is. After a certain point, the language becomes another instrument in the mix – and sometimes, as we heard Björn imply earlier, it always was.

So, feel the beat of the tambourine? Who nowadays even notices or thinks to raise the hobbled nature of that line? Only someone writing a book about ABBA, or the kind of person who would point out to you that *Mamma Mia!* is an imperfect name for a musical set on a Greek island. You've heard it a billion times and now it just whistles past.

33

The soundtrack of solitude

The first castaway to choose 'Dancing Queen' as one of their eight records for the famous BBC Radio 4 programme *Desert Island Discs* was Britt Ekland, the Swedish model and actress, who, in May 1994, asked Sue Lawley if the record could accompany her into exile, along with Bruce Springsteen's 'The River', Tchaikovsky's 'Swan Lake', Captain Sensible singing 'Happy Talk', some Champagne and a pile of magazines.

Ekland wasn't the first person on the show to request an ABBA song. That was Tony Greig, the England cricket captain, a precociously early ABBA adopter, who selected 'I Do, I Do, I Do, I Do, I Do' in May 1976, only a year after its release and only two years into the band's period of pre-eminence, when so much – and, I don't think it's controversial to say, so much better – still lay ahead of them, including 'Dancing Queen'.

Most castaways like their selections to have sat with them for a while, so all credit to Greig for backing his hunch here. At the same time, though, the Sussex all-rounder also picked Ken Dodd's 'Happiness' and 'Welcome Home' by Peters & Lee, lending credence, some would argue, to the theory that the last person on earth you would put in charge of selecting the music for a long car journey would be a professional sportsman. (Twenty years of social progress later, when the Olympic gold medallist Tessa Sanderson picked Tina Turner's 'The Best', Bryan Adams' 'Everything I Do (I Do it for You)' and Whitney Houston's 'I Will Always Love You', it was possible to feel that the age had arrived when the theory had equal purchase for professional sportswomen, too. And not before time.)

But whatever else he was, Greig was an outlier, and it's 'Dancing Queen' that is overwhelmingly the most popular ABBA song among the show's high-achieving castaways. Not 'Waterloo', the choice to date of only the golfer Colin Montgomerie and the Paralympian Tanni Grey-Thompson. Not 'The Winner Takes It All', the choice of only the England football manager Sir Bobby Robson and the novelist Isabel Allende. Not 'Super Trouper', picked by the chef Anton Mosimann and the historian Martin Gilbert.

And certainly not 'Andante, Andante', the choice in 2023 of Lucinda Russell, the racehorse trainer, the only person to date to select an ABBA deep cut (from the *Super Trouper* album). Moreover, Russell was able to regale listeners with the story of being invited one day to a lunch in Majorca at which *Frida herself* was present; and how, an unspecified number of bottles of rosé later, some singing of ABBA songs took place around a piano including, most memorably, 'Andante, Andante', with Frida allegedly to the fore.

Another first for Russell, then: at the time of writing, nobody else who has picked an ABBA song on *Desert Island Discs* has been able to report singing it with an actual member of ABBA.

Since 2003, though, when the actor Sir Ian McKellen became the first person after Britt to select it, 'Dancing Queen' has been the choice of the death-row lawyer Clive Stafford Smith, the explorer Ann Daniels, the businesswoman Karren Brady, the tennis player Martina Navratilova, the sports commentator Jonathan Agnew, the former US ambassador to the UN Samantha Power, the hairdresser Trevor Sorbie, the novelist Kate Mosse, and Kylie Minogue.

And in 2014, along with the Jersey Boys' version of the Four Seasons' 'Walk Like a Man', two hymns and an audio clip from the sitcom *Yes Minister*, it was the choice of the Home Secretary and future Prime Minister, Theresa May.

'My husband and I are sort of the ABBA generation,' May, then fifty-eight, told Kirsty Young. She had danced to 'Dancing Queen', she recounted, in 'flared trousers and . . . a yellow blouse that had huge voluminous sleeves'. She had possibly done so at the Oxford University Conservative Association disco at which she and her husband, Philip, had met. May graduated in 1977, so this must have been when the record was box-fresh. She mildly suggested that she had chosen the song because, in her island solitude, she was going to need 'something to jump up and down to'.

An aggrieved correspondent for *Vice* magazine piled in. '"Dancing Queen" is not just about jigging [sic] up and down . . . "Dancing Queen" is a song about death. It is one of the most evocative, sensual, delicately poised pieces of music ever constructed and if you can't see that, then frankly I'm not sure you have the nuance of mind to run the country.'

Well, fair enough. 'Dancing Queen' is indeed delicately poised, and it is sort of about death, or certainly about memory and the passage of time and our idea of the seventeen-year-old self that we would have loved to have been but never were, or however you come to interpret it. But that doesn't mean nobody ever jumped up and down to this song. And, in her defence, May didn't say anything about what her state of mind might be while she was jumping up and down on her desert island, and it didn't preclude abject melancholy and a sense of life's once-burgeoning possibilities receding before her, or even, possibly, remorse.

Flash forward to 2018 and the Conservative Party conference in Birmingham. A lectern on an otherwise empty stage awaits the arrival of the party's leader for her keynote speech. ABBA's 'Dancing Queen' plays, and Theresa May – for it is she – arrives, dancing. Well, I say dancing. As she moves across the stage, she slightly drops a shoulder, turns her palms forwards and swings her arms a little, as if shooing a spaniel into the back of a Nissan Qashqai. Once at the lectern, she continues to rock her shoulders and at one point, she seems about to *mime along*, but clearly thinks better of it.

I'm not knocking her for any of this. For some of us, as I've already said, dancing is hard – and I wouldn't know, but dancing at a Conservative Party conference must surely be the hardest dancing of all. May also had a purpose here, which was to meet some recent ridicule head-on and thereby, she hoped, turn it around. Not long before this, during one of those agonising 'meet the people' moments on a diplomatic trip to South Africa, May had found herself stiffly jigging in front of a party of school-children and had been broadly mocked for it. So this dance-on in Birmingham was her attempt to join in with the joke and thereby achieve a kind of redemption-through-news-clip.

Reactions to her performance were divided, as ever, according to politics and people's sense of how their own causes might best be advanced. It was 'classy', according to the future Conservative Home Secretary James Cleverly, and 'totally brill' according to the continuously absurd Conservative MP Michael Fabricant. The *Daily Mail* went so far as to suggest that May had 'danced her way back to authority', which would be a first, surely, for any politician.

But the SNP MP Joanna Cherry accused the stunt of being an 'affront to my favourite song' and Diane Abbott, who was then on the Labour front benches, recommended that 'whoever thought of that idea should be sacked'. (Abbott herself would be sacked by her party in April 2023 for having some far worse ideas.)

Watching all this develop, what was the average ABBA appreciator and respecter of 'Dancing Queen' to do, really, except try, along with everyone else, to resist the overwhelming heaviness of spirit that almost invariably descends when politicians decide to show us their 'lighter side'. Irrespective of political affiliation, there might have been one or two mild worries about the possibility of long-term collateral damage to the song – that those images from Birmingham would be slow to dissolve from the memory, and that the record would be lastingly tainted by association.

But you always knew, really, that the song was stronger than that – far stronger. Totally above the political fray, in fact, which is another reason to love pop music. By 2018, 'Dancing Queen' had already seen off three Conservative prime ministers (and three Labour ones) and was about to see off a whole bunch more.

And you also knew that ABBA had survived far worse than having their music fleetingly piped into the auditorium of a Conservative Party conference, and would survive far worse again.

34

Marked forever

You had to get a logo. All the bands in the '70s were getting logos. Kiss, Wings, Chicago, Thin Lizzy, 10cc . . . Even Relic had a logo.

Relic were the band two of my brothers had formed: Jem on lead guitar, Simon on drums, with Mike 'Spiney Norman' Wright on bass, Ian 'Nuts' Nichols on rhythm guitar, and Michael 'Mike' Blanc on vocals. Mike Blanc was, on reflection, a simply tremendous name for a rock vocalist, particularly a vocalist emerging from the suburbs on the cusp of punk. But alas he couldn't really sing and was very quickly replaced by a bloke called Neil, who sort of could.

Relic's debut gig, supporting Plod at Lexden Church Hall, which I witnessed, opened with a cover version of Black Sabbath's 'Paranoid' so loud and disorganised that it ought really to have cleared the room like a fire alarm, yet somehow didn't. Relic could be said to have lacked many of the things required to propel a band from mere hobby-status to the rock stratosphere; things like their own material, and talent. But they didn't lack a logo. It was designed by Jem, or possibly his girlfriend, or was possibly a collaboration between the two of them, and it featured the name of the band in an extremely florid script with an equally florid underlining. This brave trademark appeared on all official documentation relating to the band, which in this case, as far as I could see, was basically my brother's notebook and various bits of doodled-on paper that lay around the house.

ABBA, too, felt the imperative to get a logo, but they got theirs from a designer, Rune Söderqvist, a former advertising creative who had his own studio in Stockholm and worked extensively on ABBA's album sleeves and stage sets. Söderqvist devised the now familiar ABBA trademark – News Gothic Bold with the first B reversed so that the lettering becomes perfectly symmetrical. That reversal had happened once by accident in a TV studio when four display cards with the band's initials on got muddled. But it looked good and it had symbolic value – two couples, cleaving together, just like in the band – so it stuck. The logo made its first appearance in July 1976, on the sleeve of 'Dancing Queen'.

Most band logos were ornate: Chicago with their free-flowing font which seemed to be borrowing from the Coca-Cola label, Kiss with their jagged lightning strikes, 10cc with their patched balloons (later disappointingly, in my opinion, switched for something less art-school, incorporating a star at the centre of the 0). Such things could not be committed in biro to the front of one's school 'rough' book without some concentration and a steady hand. ABBA's new mark, by contrast, was very clean and very slick, and very easily transferred by amateur hands to books/clothing/skin, if you were of a mind to do so, which I was not, though thousands clearly were. (The 10cc logo, on the other hand . . .)

But the purity of the ABBA logo was also something else for people to hold against them. Here was visible proof that there was something about ABBA that was cold, corporate, *commercial.* That they were *an operation.* When you see that logo now, though, whether on the cover of 'Dancing Queen' in 1976, or on the front of *ABBA Gold* in 1992, or beaming like a beacon from the roof of the ABBA Arena in Stratford in 2024, you wonder whether it was simply, like the best design, timeless, and whether it was telling you that ABBA were, too.

35

Flying cars and focus groups

In June 1992, U2's ZOO TV tour reaches the Globen Arena in Stockholm. U2 are promoting their *Achtung Baby* album with an electronic extravaganza designed to satirise media saturation – fizzing screens around the stage, Trabant motor cars used as lighting rigs, appearances by satellite, Bono adopting various onstage personae, phoning out from the stage for a pizza, etc. – all in a direct break with the band's more earnest-seeming past.

Now, you could argue that, as with the politicians who were mentioned earlier, a heaviness of spirit descends when U2 elect to show us their lighter side. But that's a conversation for another time. Tonight, as every night, there's a portion of the show where the band assemble at the end of a long catwalk, which takes them out into the middle of the arena, and play close together, in an 'unplugged' or busking-style format. They do 'Angel of Harlem', sparking the inevitable singalong, and then begin strumming through a chord sequence and humming a melody that's not one of their own, yet is naggingly familiar . . .

Back down the catwalk at the lip of the stage, the lights go up on two slightly portly, bearded figures with mildly unfashionable haircuts, wearing pastel-coloured, open-necked shirts and jackets and relaxed-fit jeans. A forty-six-year-old Benny Andersson is standing at a small table, prodding at a comically tiny portable keyboard; Björn Ulvaeus, forty-seven, is closely beside him, strumming an acoustic guitar. They seem a little self-conscious as the audience goes nuts and Bono, with his slicked-back hair and black plastic trousers, bounces back down the catwalk to be with them.

Björn will later tell *Time Out* about the moment this invitation arrived. 'I assumed we were being sent up,' he said. And why wouldn't he? It's 1992. The biggest ABBA-related presence in the culture at this point is the Australian tribute act Björn Again, whose members go by the names Agnetha Falsestart, Benny Anderwear, Frida Longstokin and Björn Volvo-us. Just two months after this U2 show, Björn Again will reach a career milestone by appearing in front of more than 50,000 people in daylight and a strong headwind at the traditionally rock-inflected Reading Festival – and at the invitation, allegedly, of Dave Grohl of Nirvana, who are also on the bill and who loves ABBA, or certainly Björn Again. Maybe, as with the *Mamma Mia!* musical, the effect of Björn Again's allegiance will be to lead people out and round and back, eventually, to the music. But from 1992, as a Reading audience grinningly bangs its heads to an inch-perfect rendition of 'Money, Money, Money' played by four Australians in costume, you have to say it looks like a long journey.

Yet here in Stockholm, half of the real ABBA is on stage with U2 and many of us – including Björn, it would appear – are trying to work out how this fits. What's the likely cross-over between U2's natural audience and ABBA's, and who is even really thinking about that at this moment in time?

Well, actually, there are *some* people thinking about it, and that's the people in the London-based marketing department at the Polygram group, who have acquired the ABBA catalogue and are wondering what to do with it. And this is the 1990s, so the first step is obviously to commission some market research. A company in Ruislip has been appointed to find out what the public really feel, here and now, about ABBA.

So focus groups are being organised and people in gatherings of eight or so are being offered a glass of wine and asked if they like ABBA songs and, if so, which ABBA songs, and if they would be interested in buying an album with those songs on, and, if they are, what they would be interested in seeing on the cover of that album and, equally importantly, what, if placed on the cover of that album, might actively dissuade them from buying it.

And reports from these focus groups are going back to George McManus, an executive at Polydor Records who has achieved considerable standing in his corner of the industry by organising, just the previous year, a platinum-selling Neil Sedaka compilation at precisely the moment that Sedaka's popularity with the public seemed to have gone the way of the horse-drawn cart and rickets. Furthermore, McManus has just repeated and possibly even exceeded the trick with a collection of tracks by the Greek keyboardist and composer Vangelis which nobody on earth seemed to be crying out for, not even other Greek keyboardists.

Meanwhile, in Stockholm, entirely unconnected with all that, Björn and Benny are on stage with U2 doing 'Dancing Queen' and it's . . . well, let's say we've heard the song played better. The key has Bono scrambling up and down between octaves to try and find a comfortable slot for his voice, and not even Benny, it seems, can make a toy keyboard with miniature keys sound fluid.

But that's not the point, really. The point is what happens when the song ends.

The film *Wayne's World* is fresh in people's minds and, as the audience claps and roars, Bono stands facing Björn and Benny, raises his arms above his head and bows forward from the hips. 'We are not worthy,' he says.

And because this is U2 and the ZOO TV tour, you feel duty-bound to investigate the moment for layers of irony, or for some kind of multimedia twist still to come. But I've done so, repeatedly, using the clip on YouTube, and, try as I might, I can't see one. In the face of Bono's humble gesture of supplication, my carefully assembled scepticism simply dissolves, and I wonder if the same is true at the time for Björn and Benny, who smile back at him a little sheepishly and appear a bit overwhelmed. The endorsement looks, in as much as anything can during a high-tech rock show in the 16,000-seat Globen Arena, spontaneous, and even . . . moving.

Good grief – I find myself gulping back some tears.

Benny and Björn have made their way offstage, waving as they go, and the show is ready to move on and get back to doing its bonkers U2 stuff; indeed, a Trabant has already descended on wires from the ceiling and started turning above the stage. But the crowd can't let it go. They're still singing the opening melody of 'Dancing Queen', and then they're singing it and clapping along with themselves like it's a football chant, and Bono has little option, really, but to stand there and let them go.

'Where's Frida and Agnetha when you need them?' he eventually says.

To which the answer is: probably at home, in bed. At any rate, they stopped doing this ABBA thing a whole decade ago, long before any major rock god had thought to kneel before them and declare themselves unworthy.

Three months later, the *ABBA Gold* compilation is released in its classy black and gold, graphic-only sleeve – because one thing that came back from the focus groups was that, while people wouldn't mind hearing some of those songs again, at this point in time they found images of the band a bit . . . much. And the first track on *ABBA Gold* is 'Dancing Queen', which it simply has to be, doesn't it? It's also put out as a single again and, sixteen years after its original release, 'Dancing Queen' re-enters the UK chart and ABBA, through no real effort of their own, are on their way back into our lives.

36

An absence of irony

December 1986. Elvis Costello & The Attractions' 'Spinning Songbook' tour reaches the Royal Court Theatre in Liverpool. On stage, the giant wheel that will decide what song the band play next rotates. It has previously stopped at the tab denoting the Elvis Presley favourite 'His Latest Flame', and will, shortly after this, randomly generate a rendition of the Costello favourite 'Every Day I Write the Book'. But, for now, the wheel turns and slows and comes to a halt at ABBA's 'Knowing Me, Knowing You'.

The opening chords ring out and Costello begins.

'No more . . .'

There's a video of this on YouTube. The sound is lousy, but the voice cuts through and the playing is tight and punchy.

'Silence . . .'

This is six whole years before Steve Coogan begins the Radio 4 series *Knowing Me, Knowing You with Alan Partridge* – six years before Norfolk's most notable sports-reporter-turned-chatshow-host sets out on the road to television glory with a bespoke offering of 'classic chat with his guests from the worlds of theatre, politics and emotional tragedy'. It's not a moment at which those notorious 'a-ha's are occupying any real space in the national conversation, jocular or otherwise.

'Walking through . . .'

This is eighteen years before the invention of the iPod, before the internet revolutionises the way we access music, before streaming arrives and makes everything available always. And so this is a time when pop music's momentum still seems linear, where there's nothing so unfashionable as what was recently fashionable, and when the point of the new is to plough the recent past under, to a depth where it's hard to reach without effort.

'This is where . . .'

So this cover version is a work of exhumation, in a way. Yet this isn't panto – not some arch, costumed retread in the manner of the Björn Again tribute act, who are still two years away from forming in any case. The gusto of the performance and Costello's absolute commitment to the tune declare an absence of irony or of any sense that the song is being worn as a badge to denote this particular era's cursed wackiness ('You don't have to be mad to lob an ABBA song into your set, but it helps!'). These musicians, you are obliged to conclude, are playing this song because they remember how great it is and how much they loved it and still love it.

Now flash forward three years to 1989. In my new job as a pop critic for the almost equally new newspaper the *Independent* (advertising pitch: 'It is – are you?'), I slip a pen and a notebook into my pocket and take the Northern Line to Kentish Town in London to see the group Danny Wilson perform at the Town & Country Club (now the O2 Forum).

This really is no chore as far as I'm concerned. To a degree probably only surpassed by Prefab Sprout, Scritti Politti and Aztec Camera, the music of Danny Wilson has been accompanying me through the back end of the '80s, not least the single 'Mary's Prayer' (which has now, at the time of writing, amassed around 40 million streams on Spotify), and their singer and chief songwriter, Gary Clark, has become something of a personal cause.

Indeed, four years after this, as a member of the judging panel for the 1993 Mercury Music Prize, then in its second year, I will agitate openly for the inclusion on the shortlist of Clark's solo album, *Ten Short Songs About Love*, declaring in my impassioned pitch to the table that he is nothing less than 'a British Brian Wilson'. At which the head of the judges will snort and reply, 'A British Mike Love, more like', and the conversation will move on to other acts apparently more deserving.

Tough crowd, the Mercury Music Prize jury.*

Anyway, tonight at a packed and enthused Town & Country, Danny Wilson will be playing 'Mary's Prayer', of course, and also songs from their recently released album *Bebop Moptop*, while I, in accordance with my important professional role at these proceedings, make a few notes in my notebook which, typically of notes made from a standing position in the dark at gigs, will look like the work of someone attempting to transcribe Morse code in their sleep and therefore be entirely useless when I come to look back at them.

---

* Just in case you need clarification here: Mike Love, for reasons including, but not limited to, perceived lack of creativity and overt Republicanism, is the least adored of all the Beach Boys. Oh, and the 1993 Mercury Prize went to *Suede* by Suede.

But the band also play a song that isn't their own and which starts with some faintly familiar ringing chords . . . And the drums pick up the rhythm and Clark leans into the microphone. '*No more . . .*'

'Knowing Me, Knowing You' again – still three years pre-Partridge, still a decade and a half pre-iPod. Another exhumation, then; another act of archaeology, knocking the dust and dirt off this twelve-year-old pop song by possibly the least fashionable band on earth at this point. But, again, it's archaeology performed with vast enthusiasm and immense commitment and in the complete absence of irony, by a band with two drummers and an accordion player (Benny Andersson would approve) who have remembered that they just so clearly *love this song*. Clark's marvellous Scottish voice quavers and cracks at the limits of its range, and the snares slap and crash on the skipped beats in the chorus and the place ignites.

I haven't thought about ABBA very much during the '80s. And, indeed, in common with many people, I've grown used to thinking of ABBA as a no-go area in polite society (and definitely in cool society), to be quietly set apart like something embarrassing we all did the night before and from which we are now all extremely keen to move on and never mention again. But this performance seems to be shaking something loose, somewhere down deep, and now, standing in a London concert venue, I'm remembering a few things, too.

Frida in that fur hood. The snowy parkland. The couples in each other's arms and then separating. Those freeze-frames. Those concerned expressions.

And Agnetha in ghostly vignette form, giving Frida's lines a whispery echo.

'*Baaaad days.*'

What was sublime about ABBA at the time often seemed to be fighting this soft undertow of the ridiculous. But, good grief, when you go back to it like this, and strip all that out, or even just roll with it a little, what was sublime really was *sublime,* wasn't it?

37

Cover versions

Released in February 1977, 'Knowing Me, Knowing You' was the third single from the *Arrival* album and it reached the airwaves at a point when Britain's thirst for ABBA and ABBA-y things seemed to be unquenchable. It was the month when the band made its long-awaited first British live appearances – sold-out shows in Birmingham, Manchester, Glasgow and London, where their two concerts at the Royal Albert Hall (a 6.00 p.m. matinee and a 9.00 p.m. evening performance, seating just over 11,000 people in total) attracted, according to the legend, more than three million ticket applications.

Just as the previous year's *Greatest Hits* seemed to paper the land with the kissing/not kissing shot, so it was hard to move in a public space at that moment in history without bumping into some kind of reproduction of the *Arrival* cover shot: ABBA in matching white jumpsuits sitting in the crowded Perspex cockpit of a Bell helicopter. It was, on its own terms, an intriguing image, even though it featured a surprisingly static use of an aircraft (the Bell's becalmed rotor is barely visible against the blacked-out sky), positioned on the edge of a daringly uninteresting-looking Swedish airfield.

But ABBA's album covers, one was learning, were rarely not pointed or suggestive to some degree about their sense of their own predicament – messages pressed to the window of a kidnapper's car, perhaps – and here for our extended consideration was a depiction of the group literally in a bubble.

Something to think about there.

'Knowing Me, Knowing You' landed in a UK chart which had been going through one of those irritating periods where 'slow ones' seemed to be dominating the higher spots. My fourteen-year-old self automatically resented slow ones – mostly for being slow. In fact, *entirely* for being slow. Yet these phases seemed to come around with the weather – the chart equivalent of a 'wet playtime', you could say – and this time the dominant buzz-killers were David Soul's soupy 'Don't Give Up On Us, Baby', Leo Sayer's tremulous yet turgid 'When I Need You', The Manhattan Transfer's positively yawnsome and (worse than that) *French* 'Chanson D'Amour' ('ra-ta-ta-ta-ta', indeed), and Julie Covington's soporific and, of all things, entirely drum-free 'Don't Cry For Me, Argentina'.

That said, I had a personal investment in the success of the last of those singles. Thrillingly, my sister-in-law had been at teacher training college in Cambridge with Julie Covington, and not only had their paths crossed, but Covington had once *cried on my sister-in-law's bed*. Further details regarding this incident were never imparted to me, and nor did I seek them. That outline was plenty; as far as I was concerned, Covington was practically family, which significantly cheered a few slow weeks on *Top of the Pops* in the early part of 1977.

Anyway, 'Knowing Me, Knowing You' – which was itself no stormer, but at least had a discernible beat – had elbowed aside these sluggish bystanders by the end of March and it stayed at the top of the UK chart for five weeks. It would be ABBA's third best-selling single, after 'Dancing Queen' and 1980's 'Super Trouper', which we'll come to.

As usual, the lyric had bubbled up through batches of preliminary nonsense, the chorus having been 'Ring it in, ring it in' for a while, then 'Number one, number one', which must have sounded like some kind of gloating football chant, until Stig Anderson did his usual syllable-count and volunteered 'Knowing me, knowing you'. What Björn then went away and produced to fit the theme and the mood is arguably the best and most poignant of all the ABBA lyrics. Yes, there were the 'a-ha's that Alan Partridge could be so naffly drawn to and squeeze so much wince-inducing comic mileage from, and which, accordingly, are now likely to raise an unhelpful smile at what is meant to be a peak moment for the song's plangency.

But, on the other hand, there are those touching and metrically assured lines about the freshly deserted rooms with their echoes of children playing and the tears in the narrator's eyes. Or 'tizz in my ice', as the blended voices of Frida and Agnetha render it. Those moments in ABBA songs where the Scandinavian accents peep through can, for non-Scandinavian listeners, carry a heart-melting depth-charge. See also 'Thank you for the moossic' in the song of that title, and 'nothing ess can save me' in 'SOS'. They may actually be more triggering in that regard than Agnetha's perhaps slightly overcalculated whispering directly into our ears in this song, an idea presumably conceived in honour of the 'big boys don't cry' passage in the middle of 10cc's 'I'm Not in Love'.

What jumps out now, though, is just how gorgeous this song is built to sound. There's the glossy shine on the opening chords

(0.00–0.08, a blend of acoustic guitar and synthesiser); there's the star-burst of noise that announces the bridge (0.27–0.30); there's the ringing suspended guitar-and-keyboard figure that comes between the vocal lines in that bridge (0.32–0.36); there's the power amassed in the chorus by the hard-sung vocal harmony, with its softer, folded-in male counterpoint, and (again) the surprisingly hardcore electric guitar that's thrumming beneath it all.

Notice also the McCartney-esque bass line, played by Rutger Gunnarsson, which follows and elaborates on the vocal in the verse and is like no other bass line in ABBA's catalogue. And though the production has features which definitely tie it to its period – the wonderfully drifty vamped chords on a Wurlitzer electric piano that underpin the verses (0.09–0.27 and 1.32–1.50); our old '70s friend, the harmonised electric guitar melody (1.14–1.32 in the first instance) – it slips free of fad and fashion in its choices and, by being so purely its own thing, ends up seeming ageless.

With the passage of time, it's no less remarkable that this aching report from the frontline of marital turmoil was ABBA's follow-up to 'Money, Money, Money', which had just seen the band spend the Christmas of 1976 at war with Johnny Mathis and those drape-wearing '50s throwbacks Showaddywaddy for what newspaper articles were obliged to call 'the coveted festive number one spot'. (Mathis, with the undeniably more season-appropriate 'When a Child Is Born', had won.)

Because what, exactly, is the link between 'Knowing Me, Knowing You' and 'Money, Money, Money'? Beyond the name of the band on the label, what ultimately connects them, and in what universe?

'Money, Money, Money' seemed to be ABBA's take on 'If I Were a Rich Man' from *Fiddler on the Roof* by Sheldon Harnick and Jerry Bock, with a few staccato hints of Lionel Bart's 'You've Got to Pick a Pocket or Two' from *Oliver!*, and over the years it seems to have shelved itself in my memory accordingly as a novelty piece – a jingle to break out whenever a television documentary needs music to accompany images of rich people doing rich people things, or a gimmick to oil a dry business story on one of the magazine shows.

But with *ABBA Gold* spinning on the turntable behind me, I now come to appreciate that the song was, in its own quite mad way, packed with risks – the kind of risks which only ABBA took.

For example, which major pop act approaching the peak of their fame attempts to have a hit with what is essentially a tango? Who was the last major act to shoot for the charts by blending a keenly contemporary overdriven electric guitar with dusty cabaret-club ingredients like tack piano, glockenspiel and timpani?

Also, a single which slows to a halt (0.38–0.48)? Doesn't radio run a mile from that kind of thing? (Even ABBA only risked it once. The second time that the verse gives way to the chorus, the song maintains tempo and marches straight on through.) This, you realise, wasn't a pop song so much as it was a piece of musical theatre as bold as those from which it drew its flavours: a tale told across the footlights amid flourishing gestures by the leading actress (Frida in this case), with knowing interjections from the chorus (Frida and Agnetha together). A tale told quickly, too: the single lasts for just three minutes and six seconds – ABBA's shortest since 'Waterloo'. It gets in, it does its business, it gets out. Key change, timpani roll, curtain.

And oh, yes, that's something else that marks out 'Money, Money, Money': it's the only one of the nineteen tracks on *ABBA Gold* that opts for a key change near the end. ABBA, we saw earlier, mocked Stig Anderson for his belief in that classic, song-saving tactic. Tune beginning to flag? Quick, crank up the chorus a tone! The late key change is song-writing's ER-room defibrillator.

Stand clear!

Ker-chak!

And suddenly everyone's back in the room and singing in F#.

It's a piece of equipment that ABBA rarely break the emergency glass on, though – mostly, I would surmise, because the levels of invention in their melodies and arranging are so sustained that that kind of artificial revival never seems to be called for. Whatever you think about the big ABBA songs, you never get to the end of them and think, 'OK, this is just walking the same idea round the block now. It needs a lift.' They're simply better built than that.

And that's true even of 'I Have a Dream', the most daringly minimal of all the big ABBA hits, which for a lot of the time is essentially going backwards and forwards between two chords and might have been exactly the kind of composition that seemed to be begging for an artificial vitamin injection for the last few laps. OK, so what 'I Have a Dream' *does* do in its closing furlongs is introduce a children's choir, which you could argue was another version of inserting a key change – and one which is, in many respects, twice as sappy and possibly even, in some contexts and if you're not very careful, emetic.

(People in Argentina, Belgium, Canada, the Netherlands and all the other places where this song was a number one may want to pick a fight with me over this, but 'I Have a Dream' is probably my least favourite ABBA hit, the one that even advancing age can't quite bring me round to, even though that rise-and-fall melody on the line about believing in angels has a good old go. Returning to the song now, and after many years of turning a wilfully deaf ear to it, I was interested to discover whether my reaction to the children's choir at the end would have been materially altered for me by the experience of having children of my own. I stood solemnly between my speakers, bowed my head and closed my eyes. I discovered that it hadn't.)

However, a children's choir is *not* a key change, so my stat about 'Money, Money, Money' having the only one on *ABBA Gold* stands, and that's obviously the important thing here.

So, then you have to ask: why is it there? A moment of weakness? It doesn't feel like one to me. The shift comes so soon and so abruptly (at 2.28, when we've only heard the chorus twice and have barely learned it, let alone grown bored with it) that it arrives with a jolt, like a slap across the face, becoming another aspect of the song's highly compressed drama. In their pomp, it seems, Björn and Benny could not only take ownership of the glissando, but even reinvent the key change, or certainly perform some alchemy on its tired old currency.

Still, what about the bristling theatricality of 'Money, Money, Money' could have been felt to foreshadow in any way the glistening and melancholy pop of 'Knowing Me, Knowing You'? Clearly ABBA at this time were operating according to laws of their own, from deep inside their own Bell helicopter bubble.

38

Splinters of ice

'Knowing Me, Knowing You' came out when Björn was approaching his 32nd birthday and when Benny had just had his 30th and it's a grown-up pop song – pop with an adult theme, or you might even say a mid-life theme. That's not to do with it being a break-up song; pop is full of break-up songs. But this is the kind of break-up that seems to involve property, furniture and children, and pop, to this point, definitely had fewer of those. ABBA, of course, would eventually supply us with a small catalogue of them to leaf through: 'The Winner Takes It All', 'One of Us', 'When All Is Said and Done' . . . Indeed, the grown-up break-up could be described as one of ABBA's specialist areas.

But the first of them, and the best of them, was 'Knowing Me, Knowing You'. Hindsight is a powerful thing, obviously, but, written at a time when Agnetha was about to become pregnant with her and Björn's second child and when Benny and Frida were happily co-habiting in a new villa in the swish suburb of Lidingo, the song must be accounted a work of imagination, albeit an eerily premonitory one. Talking to Rick Beato about writing this track, in an interview for his extremely good-value YouTube channel, Björn said: 'I could clearly see a man walking from room to room with boxes all packed up – what was going through his mind at that moment, almost cinematic.'

But whatever its relation to their lives and emotions at the time, the song came as a firm corrective for a prevalent UK view of ABBA as purveyors of tacky bubblegum pop. 'Europop' was the usual term, applied with a geographically broad brush by British critics to things deemed to be vapid, unserious and suffering in general from an advanced absence of Britishness. But not even those whose hearts were most firmly set against ABBA and Europe were calling 'Knowing Me, Knowing You' Europop. There were splinters of ice in this song – and that wasn't just about that snowy video location. It had a chilly depth.

Perhaps this ought not to have surprised any of us. The thing was, ABBA always *were* adults. True, some of the early costuming may have provided another impression. But that was really how they stood before us from the beginning: as two couples. As *parents*, even. Grown-ups in the room.

'Mixed-sex bands are very popular with the easy-listening audience because they are safe,' one critic rather haughtily observed at the time. The contrast was with the solo rebels who had been calling out to us since rock 'n' roll's earliest stirrings: 'from Jerry Lee Lewis to Chuck Berry, Gene Vincent to Johnny Rotten . . . Nothing could be further from that than a band consisting of two apparently happy couples.'

Were they in the wrong business, then? This was an industry in which, incredibly, as late as the 1980s, male stars were being encouraged to remove their wedding rings before television appearances lest they unhelpfully hindered viewers' ability to fantasise about their availability. No point trying that with

ABBA. They were unavailable from the get-go. They were paired up. And it didn't exactly earn them credit.

Actually, it was a disgrace. ABBA, in their woefully un-rock 'n' roll coupledom, were deemed to fly in the face of what a pop group was meant to stand for. In its ideal state, as God had surely intended, a pop group was a unit of outlaws or a shipload of pirates – a bunch of people who had come together in some kind of socially unsanctioned union that the rest of us, in our conformity, chained to our jobs and our partners, could only look on at in awe and longing. It was an idea immortalised in the sequence from the movie *Help!*, where The Beatles walk separately up four paths to four front doors in a typical terrace of British housing . . . except that we then cut inside and the doors all turn out to open into one glorious open-plan living space, a band romper room, no less. It brilliantly and lastingly fed the archetypal fantasy about group life: blokes (mostly), bonded by fun in a world where domesticity has been transcended.

ABBA, as an uber-successful pop group, were to a very large extent living that fantasy – jets, limos, gigs, hotels, fame, all the romper rooms they could wish for – but they were doing it as two couples, which sort of destroyed the point. Things you couldn't get from ABBA included a feeling of barely leashed wildness, a manifest interest in hard-drug use, or any sense that one of them had just driven, or might be about to drive, a car into a swimming pool. Benny, apparently, liked cars, and once, as ABBA's fame flared, bought himself a bright-red Maserati Merak SS Coupe, plumbed with a state-of-the-art Blaupunkt stereo. But he never entirely dunked it in water nor even, to the best of my knowledge, got fined for speeding in it. Agnetha seems merely to have liked horses. And for some people, all of this was an offence against the natural order of things.

'When it comes to celebrity couples,' Andrew O'Hagan once wrote, in a piece for the *New Yorker* considering the relationship of Elizabeth Taylor and Richard Burton but also the relationship of David and Victoria Beckham, 'passion and ambition are typically inseparable'. But with the ABBA couples, it never felt that way, nor was it really possible to feel that they were, in another useful phrase of O'Hagan's, 'commandeered by the soap opera of their own lives'. They were just . . . couples. They were coupled up before they were internationally famous, so when those of us outside Sweden think of them as 'celebrity couples', it's not in the usual meaning of the term – the complex alignment of two mighty and probably doomed planets. They were couples on whom global celebrity had descended. Couples before they were famous, parents before they were famous.

This is perhaps why they weren't perceived to be particularly good pop stars. They were just too mature for the job. George Michael, meditating rather brilliantly on fame in an interview with Michael Parkinson in 1998, said: 'It's the things that are missing that make you a star, not the things that you have.' By this, I take him to mean that the pursuit of fame is frequently driven by holes in a person that need filling. This seems incontrovertible – and, when push came to shove, ABBA just didn't have enough missing.

Or maybe not at first. Of course, those (as the *Guardian* put it) 'two apparently happy couples', exuding all their 'safeness', didn't remain that way. In the autumn of 1978, in the face of an unworkable deterioration in their relationship, Björn and Agnetha made plans to separate. And I can think of no greater demonstration of the uniquely testing circumstances in which those two found themselves at that point than the fact that, in between agreeing to separate and performing the actual separation, they had to fly in to London to film an appearance on *The Mike Yarwood Christmas Show*.

'. . . and this is me,' as Britain's most fabled impressionist always said, looking into the camera with a smile and wink before going into his closing number.

'Yeah, and this isn't us,' as Björn and Agnetha may have been tempted to reply.

Anyway, the family celebrated one last Christmas together and then, according to Carl Magnus Palm, Agnetha and the two children got in her car and drove to a house owned by Polar Music and used by the company as a guest house, a few minutes away. Agnetha lived there for the next ten years.

There were, of course, stakeholders, as we would now refer to them, and all of this had to be carefully news-managed. The couple's separation was formally announced in mid-January of 1979, via an interview in the Polar Music offices with the Swedish newspaper *Expressen*. 'It's important to stress that this is a so-called happy divorce, if such a thing exists,' offered Björn, his own qualifications seeming to suggest that it probably doesn't.

Meanwhile, bang in the middle of all of that, after eight years of living together, Benny and Frida went the other way and finally made their relationship formal. One Friday in early October 1978, even as their bandmates were discussing how best to break news of their separation to their children, the other two slipped off to the church in Lidingö and got married in a ceremony witnessed only by their housekeeper, Bitte. (Thank you, again, to Carl Magnus Palm for this impressive detail.) They had arranged a party at home the following day for twenty-five friends, including

258

Björn and Agnetha, Stig Anderson and Michael B. Tretow, intending to surprise them with their 'just married' news. But the wedding was somehow leaked to the press so everyone turned up already knowing – and carrying hastily bought presents.

Was the wedding an attempt to cement a relationship that was already cracking? Or were there entirely mundane reasons for it? (My wife and I married after eighteen years of living together and when our three children were all old enough to complain about having to join us at the register office. And, as incurable romantics, we tend to offer a one-word explanation for why we did so: tax.) Whatever, by 1980, Benny and Frida had separated and in 1981 they divorced. 'We simply grew out of each other,' Frida would say.

These four people – these two couples – had been launched into the ether and taken their relationships with them, obliging them to live out their marriages in the most unnatural con-ditions. And, finally, it had hollowed them out. Yet they decided to . . . well, to be grown up about it, I guess you would say, and to keep working together. For a while, ABBA were a band comprising a pair of newly-weds and a divorced couple, which was pretty fascinating. Then they were a band comprising two divorced couples, which was even more fascinating, because how the hell was *that* meant to work? As Andrew O'Hagan noted: 'Celebrity marriage is an internal combustion engine and audiences love nothing more than to watch it stall or send the car off a cliff.' So the world tuned in.

Did their marriages have to fall apart before the world could fully and comfortably come on board? Did the perfect surface need to crack before we could fully take ABBA to heart? It certainly seems they had to split up before they got taken seriously.

39

Uncrowded house

'Where is everyone?'

The woman, who has just come through the door with a glass of wine in her hand, stops and stands still with a disappointed look on her face. It's a decent question. Here in Screen 3 of the splendid Chiswick Cinema, with only minutes to go before lights-down on this special Tuesday evening 'Fan Event' screening of *ABBA: The Movie*, the waiting audience is made up exactly as follows: the woman with the wine glass, with her friend just behind her, also holding wine; a man on his own, probably in his sixties, in a cloth cap; me, also in my sixties, not in a cloth cap but holding a cup of coffee and a notebook; and approximately ninety-six sumptuously upholstered and entirely empty cinema seats.

Even when, moments later, our numbers are further swollen by the last-gasp arrival of a middle-aged woman with what is possibly her late-teenage/early-twenties daughter, this does not look like it's going to be the biggest, hum-dinging, wall-shaking party night that the Chiswick Cinema has seen.

The newcomers settle quietly into their seats and a complete silence re-descends on the room, broken only by the hollow pop from somewhere of a spectacles case snapping shut.

So, yes, where is everyone? This is the second of two of these ABBA 'fan' screenings, so maybe everyone went to the first one, a couple of days ago, and had an absolute blitz. Or maybe, here in the autumn of 2023, with the ABBA Voyage show doing big business in east London, special fan showings of ABBA's 1977 'mockumentary' with additional 'exclusive footage' are just not the hot ticket they might once have been.

What I would bet good money on, though, is that I am not the only person in this room slightly worrying about what all this portends for the promised post-movie karaoke singalong.

First, though, there's *ABBA: The Movie* to watch. Confession: this is my first time in front of this pretty monumental item in the ABBA archive. I didn't see it in 1977 when it came out, and, beyond the small batch of clips from the film which tend to crop up in ABBA documentaries and on YouTube – Agnetha and Frida backstage, warming up their extraordinarily powerful voices; fans going nuts for ABBA in the tipping rain in Sydney; the famous bottom-related press conference, which we'll deal with in a moment – I haven't seen it since, either.

In 1977, I guess it caught me at precisely the wrong moment. *ABBA: The Movie* coincided almost exactly with the release of *Saturday Night Fever*, with John Travolta and the music of the Bee Gees, which I *did* go and see, taken along to the Colchester Odeon in Crouch Street by one of my brothers and his girl-friend. *Saturday Night Fever* had an X certificate (strong language, violence, sexual content), which meant it was technically out of bounds for me (fifteen going on sixteen) and anyone else under eighteen. But my brother knew how much I liked those Bee Gees songs, so he said he'd have a go at getting me in.

In the nervous run-up to this act of lawlessness, I reflected hard on the ways I could plausibly contribute to its success by making myself look older. Make-up? Prostheses? Hard to organise. Eventually I hatched a plan. I could stuff some socks inside my shoes.

The effect was transformational: where before I had looked very obviously like a fifteen-year-old who didn't have a ghostly chance of getting admitted to an X-rated movie, I now looked very obviously like a fifteen-year-old who didn't have a ghostly chance of getting admitted to an X-rated movie, but slightly taller.

Somehow it worked, though. My brother did the business at the box office while I lingered anxiously in the distance by the concession counter, and the usher who ripped our tickets at the door to the screen while I stared fixedly at the carpet didn't see anything remiss, so I was in.

ABBA: The Movie was a U, so I could very easily have seen it without stuffing anything whatsoever in my shoes and without the complicity of an older relative. That was exactly the issue, though: the undeniable U-ness of ABBA at this moment in history. Who were the out-and-out ABBA fans in 1978? The Australian vox pops in *ABBA: The Movie* make that very clear: it was predominantly young kids and their parents. And if you had been one of the young kids originally but now had your eyes firmly, if prematurely, set on adulthood, that could put you in a slightly awkward position – still drawn to the music, but not keen to *seem* drawn to the music.

So, just as I hadn't applied for a ticket to the Albert Hall show (one of the few people in Britain who didn't, it now appears), I felt I needed to stand quietly aside from the film, too. Going to see it would have compromised my broader vision of myself at that time – as someone leaving U-certificate things firmly behind him and striding out in his sock-enhanced footwear to discover the X-rated world and everything that it so gloriously offered (strong language, violence, sexual content).

Now, clearly, there were various levels of delusion and basic misunderstanding operating there. But, with hindsight, at the level simply of film criticism, I think it's hard to fault my choice. Having now seen *ABBA: The Movie* – having, indeed, enjoyed an exceptionally clear and uninterrupted view of it – well, how to put this? I think *Saturday Night Fever* was probably the better film.

The original plan was for Lasse Hallström to accompany the band throughout their tour and shoot a straight documentary. But somewhere in the process (quite late, one senses), it was decided it would be more fun to fold a story of some kind into the concert and backstage footage. So a narrative was cooked up in which a radio journalist is under heavy manners from his ratings-desperate producer to secure an exclusive ABBA interview – one that gets right to the heart and soul of the band. Off he sets in their wake as they travel round Australia, only to endure a sequence of slapstick run-ins with the band's Australian 'bodyguard' and find himself thwarted in his mission at every turn.

A pretty thin story, then – quite literally. Apparently, the screenplay for the additional fictional sections was just five pages long.

Still, come for the 'family-friendly comedy', stay for the snappily edited concert material. *ABBA: The Movie* certainly has plenty of that. Shots of bands standing tensely in the wings before shows while the audience impatiently claps and stamps, and then, at the given signal, advancing towards the stage and into the light – I'll never tire of those. And if the band are wearing floor-length silver capes at this point, then I'm even wider awake. (The capes get flung off during the introduction to the opening number, 'Tiger', an awe-inspiring piece of stage-business if you hadn't seen Spinal Tap do it in the meantime.)

ABBA live in 1977 sound pretty darned punchy, too – although, of course, the film's sound is so post-produced that you have no real idea how any of this would have come over in the arenas. Naturally the movie watcher is also spared the unique challenge to eyesight and patience which was the giant outdoor show in the days before the invention of the video screen. Until God made the JumboTron, what was going on onstage was a distant battle in another country, as far as at least two-thirds of the audience were concerned. Nowadays at big gigs, we are essentially sitting down with the band to watch television. People might have something to say about the sterility of that, but at least you can see.

What the film does viscerally convey is the level of hysteria that enveloped ABBA on that Australian trip: the screaming, the rending of clothes, the swarming of streets under hotel windows. Australia, you conclude, fell first, and Australia fell hardest.

And then there's the bottom question. It gets asked by a genuine Australian journalist during a genuine press conference.

'I read somewhere that you are the proud owner of an award which declares you as the lady with the most sexiest bottom in Europe. Is that true?'

Agnetha replies: 'How can I answer to that? I don't know . . . I haven't seen it.' The room erupts with laughter.

This moment seems to have passed into ABBA lore as a classic, snappy Agnetha 'own', but I'm still unsure whether she means, wittily, that she hasn't seen her bum (because it's behind her), or whether she means she hasn't seen the story the journalist is referring to. And, consequently, I remain a bit baffled about who is laughing with, or at, whom in this sequence.

Anyway: SPOILER ALERT. Having exhausted himself trailing the band all over Australia, without getting the exclusive interview with the band that his producer wants from him, our hero the radio journalist (played, as previously mentioned, by Robert Hughes, but not the art critic) – his race run, his interview unsecured, his recording equipment dangling forlornly from his shoulder – is miserably trudging back to his hotel room to pack before getting ready to return home in despair and professional ignominy. Then the lift doors open and who should be inside but . . . the four members of ABBA! The doors close and the reporter is gifted thirty floors of lift-travel in which to secure his scoop.

And in that interview, we see the band open up, one by one, and tell the journalist everything about themselves, their hopes, their dreams, their deepest fears, their true feelings about each other, leading us to understand them personally at a new and deeper level which . . .

OK, no we don't. While that interview is meant to be going on, we watch a montage of cartoon images and listen to the song 'Eagle'. It's a version of one of those seduction scenes where we see the couple talking and laughing and growing inexorably fonder of one another . . . but all set to music, sparing the scriptwriter a lot of hard graft.

And I guess you could argue that, in a light film like *ABBA: The Movie*, this was all rather daringly self-referential – meta, as we would now say. What the film ends up proposing, courtesy of those vox pops, is that ABBA exist most strongly as a bunch of other people's feelings about them, as a collage of opinions, projections, conjectures; that the reality is always out of reach and impossible to convey, and that ABBA, and perhaps all pop groups, are ultimately destined to be, first and foremost, the products of our thwarted curiosity.

Too much? What's definitely true, though, is that even in a movie which is about them and of their own devising, ABBA end up slipping quietly away.

40

The big cheese

The last song you hear in *ABBA: The Movie* is 'Thank You for the Music'. It would have been brand-new to audiences on that 1977 tour, and was only released later, on *ABBA: The Album*. On stage, it formed part of a somewhat bizarre mid-set interlude – a four-song mini-musical, entitled 'The Girl with the Golden Hair', featuring a narrator in Joker-style make-up and portraying the music industry and fame in general as a macabre trap. Whether a fifteen-minute neurotic art-rock freak-out was what the punters had come to an ABBA show for is not clear, but that was what they got, including a performance of the agitated threnody 'I'm a Marionette' with Agnetha and Frida flitting manically around the stage in matching wigs and doll outfits. Most nights, this passage in the show seems to have inspired bewilderment and/or a general drift in the direction of the bar.

'Thank You for the Music', however, was clearly destined for greater things. Only in a handful of countries was the track ever released as a single, and in the UK it only appeared in that format in 1982, as part of the promotion for an ABBA compilation album. Yet its magnitude within the catalogue has expanded to the point where it is now quite widely regarded as ABBA's signature tune and calling card (this while being, I was interested to note, only the 25th-best ABBA song, according to the International ABBA Fan Club's most recent poll of its members).

It's music about music, a song about singing, like The New Seekers' 1971 hit, 'I'd Like to Teach the World to Sing (In Perfect Harmony)', and also like the 1972 Melodifestivalen entry that Björn and Benny wrote for Lena Andersson, which was called 'Sag det med en sang' ('Say It With a Song'). Their interest in music as a subject for music would continue all the way up to 'I Let the Music Speak' on the final ABBA album, *The Visitors*.

In 'Thank You for the Music', however, that interest seems to meet another founding ambition of theirs: the pursuit of a song that everyone can cotton onto, an easy singalong. And I get the nobility of the cause, yet tremble slightly at the prospect of the music that can follow from it. Because when a song wants to open its arms so wide, things can quickly get a little corny – cheesy, even. Indeed, to try to defend 'Thank You for the Music' against the accusation of cheesiness would be like trying to defend cheese against the accusation of cheesiness, and for many years I wouldn't have even bothered trying. If you're in the wrong mood, this song can appear to be encouraging a kind of glazed swaying which something inside me seems reluctant to sign up for. There have certainly been periods in my life (and certainly at sixteen, when the song came out) when I have heard 'Thank You for the Music' get underway and thought . . . well, to quote the song itself, that I could live without it.

Indeed, it strikes me that, here in 2024, 'Thank You for the Music' presents a unique test case for ABBA and embarrassability, here in 2024. Because clearly, in an age when ABBA have ascended to international treasure status, we are mostly past the point where anything like shame needs to attach to an appetite for ABBA songs. We have come through that dark period when the band was a 'guilty pleasure' and have emerged into the light, where we can all stand, gloriously liberated in a new atmosphere of tolerance, and proclaim our ABBA inclinations without too much fear of reprisal.

Indeed, I would suggest that one of the great advances of our time has been the considerable diminishment of the whole idea of 'guilty pleasures' in general. Every weekend, *The Times* newspaper continues to ask people, in a questionnaire on its arts pages, to tell us their 'guilty pleasure' – and practically every time nowadays the respondent will make a little preliminary speech about how the notion doesn't really exist for them anymore, and that they just simply unapologetically like Westlife, or whoever. This is a good thing. We have most of us reached an improved position on the dire waste of energy involved in making people feel bad about what, or who, they love.

And yet, undeniably, there's still 'Thank You for the Music'.

I write quite a lot in cafés and I'm familiar, as I'm sure you will be, with that modern jeopardy wherein someone fails properly to connect their Bluetooth headphones to their device, so that, until they realise, whatever they are trying to listen to is broadcasting at volume to the rest of the room. And during the writing of this book, I have found myself wondering how I, personally, would react if that happened to me at the precise moment that I was investigating 'Thank You for the Music'.

Would I have the calm self-possession to meet the disturbed gaze of people on other tables with a defiant look and a slight tilt upwards of the chin that said, 'Yeah, "Thank You for the Music". Want to make something of it?' and then calmly reconnect my headphones and carry on?

Or would I smash my hand down on the laptop's mute button, pluck the buds from my ears and call out, with a craven smile, 'Sorry, *sorry*! Just . . . researching, obviously . . . writing something . . .'

And it does me little credit to admit it, but, even now, after all we've learned and all we've gained, I believe I would have reacted in the second of those two ways – which would not have been the case with literally any other track on *ABBA Gold*.

And yet, and yet . . . Listening to it now (with headphones carefully connected), I hear how that song shares the sonic shimmer of all of the best ABBA songs – if you give it a chance to. Contrast the deliberate dryness of much popular music now, designed to punch through on a phone or into inadequate headphones. There's a scale in the Tretow ABBA productions that few aspire to now – a use of sound which is very close to the play of light, and which wraps even the ABBA songs you might think you can resist in a kind of grandeur.

Yet, perhaps if you want to be cured for good of your scepticism about 'Thank You for the Music', you need to hear it with all of that cut away.

In 2017, Benny released, under the impressive imprimatur of the Deutsche Grammophon label, the album *Piano*, a collection of ABBA pieces, songs from the musical *Chess* and some other compositions, played as solo instrumentals. There was also an accompanying book of transcriptions (a faithful rendering by Göran Arnberg of what's played on the record; we had come a long way from my scrappy piece of sheet music for 'SOS'), which untrained amateur pianists like me could stare at in puzzlement and generally stub our fingers on.

Good photos, though: Benny at nine with a crew cut and, around his neck, an accordion almost as big as he is; Benny at nineteen, holding a cigarette and leaning coolly against the back of a Ford Thunderbird in a Stockholm side street in 1965; Benny at the keyboard with one hand thrown up and his head tipped back in what looks like a state of quasi-religious ecstasy on stage with The Hep Cats in the same year . . .

Anyway, in a note at the beginning of the book, Benny writes: 'In endeavouring to reach for some core within them, I find that the more I strip away the clothing, i.e. treatments and arrangements from the "original" versions, the closer I feel to the music, regardless of whether it was created last year or forty years ago. In a strange way, I feel like I am playing my memoirs.'

Listen, then, to Benny playing 'Thank You for the Music' and appreciate the life in it. In his hands, alone at the piano, it's ragtime and music hall and cabaret and operetta all at once, and as it folds those things together, it becomes completely timeless. It feels like the crystallisation of every folk song that came Benny's way in his childhood and every piece of light-programming that filtered into his ears via Swedish radio in the 1950s. It's the answer to the voice in his head that must have told him that this song was in there somewhere, and that if he just kept playing, and trying things, and playing some more, he would eventually find it. It's the culmination of that ambition that he and Björn had from the beginning, which was to write – some way, somehow – the universal pop song. And some way, somehow, they ended up writing a whole batch of them, but perhaps none, you have to concede, quite so universal as this. It's the party piece to end all party pieces and with everything taken away from it, and just the piano left standing, you realise that what ABBA arrived at here is nothing short of a melodic miracle.

And that version of the song I would have no problem with in the 'failed Bluetooth in a crowded environment' test. In fact, I'd sit tight and proudly let it ring out across the café for a while, looking round the room and nodding slowly at anyone who engaged my eye.

Hell, I would happily strap large speakers to the roof of my car and drive slowly round the streets of my neighbourhood with Benny Andersson's version of 'Thank You for the Music' from the *Piano* album playing loud and clear. Because it is genius.

41

'Get with the beat, Baggy'

When *ABBA: The Movie* ended, the six of us attending Chiswick Cinema's special 'fan screening' stayed seated for a brief package of scenes that were cut from the film, and then watched a short documentary about the making of the Voyage show.

And then it was ABBA singalong time – our chance to get out in the aisles and, with the assistance of three special widescreen karaoke videos, let it all loose to 'Dancing Queen', 'Voulez-Vous' and 'Gimme! Gimme! Gimme! (A Man After Midnight)'.

So I jumped up, beckoned to the others to join me and we all ran down to the front, linked arms and tore absolute holes out of those vocal lines as they passed before our shining eyes.

All right, not really. One of our six-strong congregation walked out before the first number started, and another left midway through it. The rest of us sat loyally, but silently, in our seats.

Oh well. It was a chance to hear those songs again, played good and loud through the cinema's hefty system – another opportunity to indulge the core project of this book, really, which has been to make myself listen to things that now blow past me in their easy familiarity, and try to remember, or belatedly discover, what's actually there.

By the summer of 1978, ABBA had their own Stockholm recording studio – Polar Music Studio, with its name emblazoned across the blue carpet in its entrance and a large sculpture standing in reception, *The Music Machine* by Rune Söderqvist, the designer of the ABBA logo, an artwork hammered together from old instruments and capable of playing the melody of 'Thank You for the Music' in chime form. Planning for the studio had, according to Michael B. Tretow, basically involved 'making a list of everything we wanted to have'. So Polar Music Studio had five separate recording rooms, an eight-sided control room with giant glass windows, and walls decorated with a mural of blue sky and clouds in an attempt to defeat the traditional 'basement' feel of studios the world over. Where most studios at the time had one 24-track mixing desk, ABBA's had two. Where other studios relied on the engineer in the control room to create the mix that each of the musicians heard in their headphones while they were recording, here everybody had their own individual headphone-mixing unit to create their own preferred blend. It was a state-of-the-art facility and would soon have other bands (Led Zeppelin among them) queuing to borrow it. As Michael B. Tretow declared, 'the Polar Studios can supply you with almost everything except hiss, noise, distortion and a decent cup of coffee'.

Polar Music Studio closed in 2004 and the building now houses a gym. But, for four years, it was ABBA's creative hub and sanctuary. Their last three albums before the sabbatical – *Voulez-Vous*, *Super Trouper* and *The Visitors* – were all recorded here. And it was the place where ABBA could properly become what they perhaps longed to be all along: a studio band.

They would go out on the road again in the autumn of 1979, travelling through Canada and the US, and then across Europe, playing six consecutive nights at Wembley Arena in London that November, along with shows in Stafford and Glasgow, their second and last batch of live appearances in the UK. But if touring had been a chore and an expensive and inefficient grind before, it was now additionally complicated.

In her 1997 memoir, *As I Am*, Agnetha said of that 1979 tour, 'For me it was awful. Björn and I had separated and I had torn myself away from the children. I just wanted to be home, home, home. But I had no choice. Björn and I were agreed about doing this tour together, despite the divorce, so we had to form a new relationship with each other and work together in a new way . . . The whole time I ached inside for the children and from homesickness.'

No doubt working with an ex-partner in the enclosed and intense space of a studio had its challenges, too, no matter how nicely the walls were painted. But at least it was their studio. And at least they could go home afterwards. The first track recorded in this welcome retreat was 'Summer Night City', and ABBA's high-disco phase was underway.

I have to be honest: I had little purpose for this music at seventeen, nor in the immediate years beyond. My disco era seemed to start with the purchase of the *Saturday Night Fever* soundtrack album and pretty much end with the thrill of bunking successfully into the movie. The music called to me, but the lifestyle didn't. Dancing, again; I think I've already raised some of my difficulties around dancing. So I didn't go to discos. I went to gigs. And I went to gigs, not to dance, but to stand and stare at people on stages.

So did all my friends. While other people were going to discos to dance to 'Voulez-Vous', we were going to gigs at Essex University – Stiff Little Fingers, the Tom Robinson Band, Thin Lizzy, AC/DC. Sometimes at those gigs we jumped up and down in unison. But mostly we stood and stared. We once attended the John Peel Roadshow, which was technically a disco, in that it was a disc jockey playing records. But we stood and stared at that, as well.

Our loss, maybe. But, in those years, dawned an opinion that I seem to have carried with me ever since – that disco ABBA is good ABBA, but that disco ABBA is not the best ABBA. The slightly flat and featureless instrumental breakdowns at the end of 'Voulez-Vous' seem to me to indicate the point at which the demand for sustained dance performance and 12-inch remixes begins to erode some of the band's supremely high-minded principles about song construction. They were going with the flow here, which was great. But ABBA had never gone with the flow, which was, to my mind, greater.

But as Bagheera says to Baloo in *The Jungle Book*, 'Get with the beat, Baggy.' Four minutes and forty-nine seconds in the company of 'Gimme! Gimme! Gimme! (A Man After Midnight)' at volume in a practically empty cinema will amply refresh you, if you need it, on the matter of that song's ingenuity and its abiding ABBA-ness. There's the gratifyingly eccentric decision to open the track with sixteen seconds of solo guitar riff. There's the duel that takes place throughout between the bass synth and the bass guitar. There's, as usual, the absolute clarity and ringing power of the combined vocal parts, which are honed and firmed and seem to come hurtling through the air. And, best of all, there's the teasing, extended build to the chorus (0.56–1.08), with Agnetha's vocal note held for six seconds while the cinematic strings reach boiling-point underneath it.

And also notice the glorious possibility that Benny's opening whistly synth figure (0.17–0.33) could well be a gentle lift from – of all hardcore disco sources – the opera *Samson and Delilah* by the French composer Camille Saint-Saëns (1835–1921). See 'Bachanale' from that work, a light-classical radio staple, which also, incidentally, contains a source for the hopping marimba part in 'Mamma Mia'. (And Benny had possibly been there on another occasion, too: the aria 'Mon coeur s'ouvre á ta voix' has at the very least a dim echo of the melody of 'Thank You for the Music' about it.)

And then, again, there's that extraordinary timelessness about the production – its refusal, even while doing genre-music, to sound generic. How many disco records from the '70s instantly, and narrowly, evoke their period? Not this one.

And, accordingly, it survives. Indeed, it powers on. There's a tremendous moment in a video on YouTube of what seems to be a daytime set by the French DJ Folamour in slightly challenging circumstances at the 2019 FLY Open Air festival at Hopetoun House in Edinburgh. The link to all this was posted by someone called ABBAcats in the comments under a recent interview with Agnetha in the *Guardian*, along with helpful instructions to go to the point around the thirty-minute mark.

The gig is taking place in an unprepossessing open-sided marquee, on a grey, rainy day. You can practically feel the cold. Some of the crowd, in their late teens and twenties, are wearing kagoules or other bits of plastic against the weather, and although many of them are hopping about willingly enough with drinks in their hands, there's a lot of distractedness and a general feeling that some time-serving is going on.

And then, without warning, Folamour drops the build-up to the chorus from 'Gimme! Gimme! Gimme! (A Man After Midnight)', with the chorus itself to follow, and it's like a match on petrol. The place goes nuts, arms up everywhere, and suddenly this damp marquee appears to be hosting some kind of utterly joyous and entirely invigorated revivalist meeting.

When that record was made, the phrase 'absolute banger' would only have been employed to refer to a badly crocked car, and even now it's probably not an expression that should be coming unironically to the lips of anyone in their sixties.

But look at what that forty-year-old song does to that tent. Absolute banger.*

Not quite the same in the Chiswick Cinema, though, I concede. 'Gimme! Gimme! Gimme! (A Man After Midnight)' faded, the screen went black and the house lights came up. The four of us quietly picked up our coats, walked separately down the stairs and stepped out into the night.

But I think we'd all learned something.

---

* https://www.youtube.com/watch?v=wL-VMOGAhzE

42

Critical mass

The critics didn't much care for *ABBA: The Movie*. One film reviewer upbraided Lasse Hallström for failing to get under 'the silky skins of the quartet' any more than the news reporter in the film does.

'But then,' this writer concludes, 'that's the name of their particular game – look, listen, but don't touch. A bland band.'

Meanwhile, a music writer in the *Guardian* offered this: 'ABBA has two good-looking ladies (Agnetha Fältskog alone makes much of the film worth looking at) but they are no threat. You can look but not touch. If you did, the bodyguard in the film (the best realistic rock touch) would haul you off. She'd walk away still smiling, hair still perfectly in place.'

So, what's going on here? Who are the women in pop music that, by contrast with Agnetha Fältskog, it's OK for the generalised 'you' in that sentence to touch? And what kind of touching is the character of the bodyguard preventing the 'you' from doing, if the consequence of his intervention is that Agnetha walks away 'still smiling' and with her hair in place?

The women in ABBA are 'no threat', we're told. But what about the men who are frustrated about being unable to touch the women in ABBA in the way they seem to want to? Are they a threat?

So many questions.

It wasn't just the movie, though. The critics didn't really care for ABBA in general at this point in their life. On the evidence of one of the Royal Albert Hall shows, the *Guardian* suggested ABBA had 'not come a long way since their Eurovision win at Brighton', and accused them of having 'written and repeated formula-winning songs'. They had by now followed 'Waterloo' with, among others, 'Fernando', 'Money, Money, Money' and 'Dancing Queen'. What repeated themes actually link these records? What is the formula connecting a campfire folk ballad sung in the voice of an ageing war veteran, a Russian-flavoured Topol spoof, and a slow-disco track? There doesn't seem to be an obvious one. But it all washed over the *Guardian*, anyway. 'It sounded good without meaning much,' the paper concluded.

Even in Australia, where ABBA's stock seemed so high, they didn't get an easy ride from the press. There's a scene in *ABBA: The Movie* where the band are in a hotel room going through reviews of their performance and seizing on the headline 'AGNETHA'S BOTTOM TOPS SHOW'. A little archive work will reveal to you that Benny's carefully placed thumb is obscuring the word 'DULL' between the words 'TOPS' and 'SHOW'.

On their second tour of the UK, in 1979 – when Agnetha and Frida, with new, shorter hair and flicks, wore stripy Lycra, and where Benny and Björn, with hair entirely unaltered, came dressed for judo – their 5 November show in London drew the following despairing sigh-in-a-headline from the *Daily Express*: 'Oh, ABBA! What a damp squib for Bonfire Night.'

Another paper's verdict was 'Polish, but no passion', which was becoming the go-to accusation around ABBA.

It seemed that they couldn't cut it convincingly live, nor, for many critics, on record. Here, the challenge for writers was to concede how popular this stuff was without revealing quite how much you resented doing so, and it was a challenge which many failed. Did pop writing have a problem with popularity – and, by extension, with people? When you read some of the reactions to ABBA, you sometimes wonder. 'Clever, escapist, expertly tailored for the rock-MOR-disco cross-over market,' was one verdict. '[Their music] comes in bursts of two-and-a-half-minute perfection, if that's your idea of all pop music should be.'

'Expertly tailored' is another of those phrases in which praise for craft includes a dark seam of suspicion. And it must have been quite exhausting for the artists on the end of these appraisals to be commended for creating 'perfection' and then asked 'What else you got?'

'The one thing they can do unlike anyone else is make hit singles,' a critic wrote, 'highly impressive taken individually, but indigestible and vacuous taken in bulk.'

Again, this seems an odd thing to say about a band as mercurial as ABBA. But also, where on the label does it say that ABBA's songs are to be 'taken in bulk'? That's up to the listener, isn't it? Otherwise, it's like the argument that we should blame Gary Lineker for the UK's obesity crisis because he once advertised crisps. But he wasn't saying we should *only* eat crisps.

Whisper it, but perhaps the problem wasn't with ABBA so much as with the nature of rock criticism. In *Seasons in the Sun: The Battle for Britain, 1974–79*, Dominic Sandbrook notes how 1977 dawned with the release of Pink Floyd's *Animals* album, and quotes a review from the *NME* which instantly hymned it as 'one of the most extreme, relentless, harrowing and downright iconoclastic hunks of music to have been made available this side of the sun'.

'Perhaps it was not surprising, then,' Sandbrook continues, 'that although the album sold well, it never toppled ABBA's *Arrival*, The Shadows' *20 Golden Greats* or Frank Sinatra's *Portrait of Sinatra* from the top of the chart.'

One of the things about extreme, relentless and harrowing music is that it tends to get good reviews. I mean, if it's done well, obviously; I'm not saying that the extreme, relentless and harrowing *automatically* gets a tick. As I mentioned earlier, I was a reviewer of pop records for a while in the '90s, and I don't doubt that – now, as then – the extreme, the relentless and the harrowing has to prove itself on a case-by-case basis.

But I think we can say generally that the extreme, the relentless and the harrowing tend to be far more popular with people who are being paid to listen to music than with people who pay to listen to it. And, as a consequence, misunderstandings can potentially arise among critics about the extent to which listeners share their appetite for a damn good musical harrowing.

ABBA weren't harrowing – unless you found them too sugary or too rich, or too wan, even, each of which could be harrowing in their own way. But they certainly weren't harrowing in the ways that critics approved of and liked to write about and recommend, and that was an issue for them.

And neither, it seemed, did they have that other quality that critics like to run a diligent check for: roots. This absence was highlighted in detail by a critic in the *Guardian* who saw in

ABBA only 'a computerised retread of all that is commercial'. In that sense, he could at least detect a presence in their composing and in the scope of their productions of The Beach Boys and Phil Spector, which was all to the good.

'Yet ABBA have something lacking,' the critic went on. 'The Beach Boys evolved from a particular society and musical background which they reflected and were part of, while Spector fully understood the evolving black American musical scene in the Sixties when he created his spectacular musical backdrops. ABBA have no such roots, no such reference points. Their songs are performed with apparent high emotion – exhaustingly so, if listened [to] at length – but unlike great rock music it's not believable emotion . . . It's the shallowness behind those brilliantly catchy tunes and clever arrangements, and the lack of that intangible thing called feeling, that ultimately becomes depressing. All that effort, all that skill, for such banality, such weak lyrics . . . Ultimately, it seems they have nothing to say.'

Let's leave aside the detail that only one of the Beach Boys actually surfed. (Not Mike Love – Carl Wilson.) And let's not get into the argument about whether the glorious sun-drenched Californian beach culture with which we associate that band was as much created by their music as reflected in it. More interesting, perhaps, is the assumption that ABBA's roots in Swedish folk and northern European schlager, and in the communal music of the Swedish summer folkparks, don't count in any way as roots. So only certain kinds of root are proper roots? And ABBA have the wrong ones?

A big problem for ABBA, then. And a big problem for writers on the topic of ABBA. For a certain kind of rock criticism, it's an article of faith that authenticity is the prime ingredient –

that, without an authentic root, nothing worthwhile can be grown. But, as Don Breithaupt wrote, regarding the members of the jazz-rock band Steely Dan and their background at the liberal arts establishment Bard College in New York State, 'authenticity comes from the darndest places'.

Indeed. And then what if a song were a good story – and not a story about the writer at all, but about someone else that they entirely dreamed up? Whither authenticity then? What if the things that drive a person to a musical instrument include a sense of their own *inauthenticity,* or a desire to find roots which don't seem otherwise to be manifesting themselves? What, in fact, if there is nothing intrinsically authentic about picking up a guitar or sitting down at a piano in the first place? What if rawness has already necessarily been left behind by the artist on their way to the studio – indeed, on the way across the room to the keyboard?

And what if showbusiness plays a part, and what if Mick Jagger in fact *isn't* a street-fighting man after all (no, really!), but someone possessed of imagination and longing, neither of which human qualities connect directly to 'roots' as much as they represent a desire and a means to move beyond them.

What if the central motivation for a piece of pop music turns out to be a desire to *uproot*, in fact – to be anywhere but where the writer finds themself? In other words, what if the fire underneath a pop record is the yearning, not to reflect one's roots and culture, so much as to escape them and create a life in someone else's culture, with someone else's roots? Do those conditions render music invalid? Yet surely that's the story of Dartford's Rolling Stones in a nutshell. Mick and Keith were able to tap so deeply into their Dartford roots that they tunnelled all the way through to the American south where the blues were happening, and ultimately got themselves into a position where they never needed to go to Dartford again.

Perhaps the most authentic thing about some pop performers is their desire to escape what they authentically are – to live larger, more colourfully, to feel things more deeply, see things more brightly, to make something bigger and more legible out of the frequently unglamorous nature of their own emotions, something which then rings true. It doesn't always work, of course, but when it does there's room for that in pop, surely.

Actually, whisper it, but maybe that's the *story* of pop: authenticity in the darndest places. Yes, even Sweden.

43

'Good? Swedish, mate'

It has been claimed that 1978 was the year the UK reached peak Swedish. ABBA were everywhere in the charts. Björn Borg was taking off his red tracksuit top, carefully adjusting his headband and calmly thrashing everybody who came near him at Wimbledon, while simultaneously attracting swooning, Beatle-style worship for his largely sweat-free troubles. And Ronnie 'Super Swede' Peterson was tearing up Formula 1 in the company of his Lotus teammate Mario Andretti (and would be tragically killed in an accident in the first lap of the season-ending Italian Grand Prix that October).

Furthermore, SAAB, the extremely cool Swedish aircraft-turned-car company, had just launched the SAAB 900, which was destined to become both a design classic and the discerning yuppie's chariot of choice. Altogether, this was clearly a moment in the culture when it was possible to feel that if it was Swedish, it had it going on.

Including preserved vegetables. The design writer Jonathan Glancy recalled: 'That year I remember a south London greengrocer describing the virtues of a bottle of pickled beetroot to a dubious middle-aged gent. "Good? Swedish, mate!" Very nearly said it all. Sweden was the land of unmit-igated quality.'

Has any year since yielded cultural dominance for Sweden at such levels? Some might make a shout for 1987, when the first IKEA store opened in Warrington. But IKEA, though eventually ubiquitous and fantastically convenient if you needed a bookshelf, wasn't exactly Borg + ABBA + Pederson + SAAB.

Neither, really, was the Swede Sven-Göran Eriksson's period in charge of the England football team between 2001 and 2006. Indeed, upon Eriksson's appointment (he was the first non-national to be handed that sacred role), the *Daily Mail* notoriously declared: 'We've sold our birthright down the fjord to a nation of seven million skiers and hammer throwers who spend half their lives in darkness.' Five years later, when England's quarter-final-stage exit from the World Cup on penalties brought Eriksson's reign to an end, the *Mirror* ushered him out with the line, 'He banked, he bonked and he ballsed it up.' The *Sun* went with 'Goodbye Tosser'.

Not much 'Good? Swedish mate!' going on in that period.

In 2017, there were perhaps flickerings of a Swedish revival when *Vogue* magazine told its UK readers that they should 'forget hygge', the Danish lifestyle concept which had recently seen British people thinking unusually hard about cosy jumpers, wood-burning stoves and candles. '2017,' *Vogue* said, 'will be all about lagom.' They were predicting a big year ahead for the Swedish concept of 'just enough', as in the Swedish proverb, 'lagom ar bast', or 'there is virtue in moderation'. They could point to a book to back their hunch: Oliver Johansson's *Living Lagom: 250+ Simple Steps to a Balanced, Happier and More Sustainable Life*. But unless I missed it, lagom had a merely moderate year in 2017, as perhaps the spirit of moderation was always destined to.

So, 1978, we probably have to conclude, retains its crown. And were ABBA felt to be cool at this ragingly cool point to be Swedish? Hardly. That label would forever evade them. But *ABBA: The Movie* begat *ABBA: The Album*, released in January in the UK after a backlog at the pressing plant blew out the plans for a pre-Christmas release (Epic Records: still cocking it up, ABBA-wise, at every turn). Maybe the songs on that record, and also those who liked them, were free to move a little more easily in 1978's Swede-friendly air.

ABBA: The Album brought us 'Take a Chance on Me', its chk-a-chk rhythm inspired, Björn would reveal, by the slap of his trainers on the pavement while he was out for a run one day. Here was a piece of joyful, bouncing pop, rare in the ABBA catalogue in that its joy seemed so unalloyed. For something moodier in the same rhythm, you needed perhaps to turn to Blondie's 'Heart of Glass', recorded in June 1978, which was 'Take a Chance on Me' in a cloudier form. But there was no hard centre of melancholy here: not in the *a capella* plain-chant opening; not in the wriggly guitar figures between the verse lines; not in the starburst of sound launched by the word 'magic' at 1.08–1.11; and definitely not in the kick of renewed energy which the song gains on each of the stop-and-start entries to the chorus (1.22–1.24 in the first instance).

Even the return of Agnetha to a seductive speaking role at a couple of points has a tongue-in-cheek feel to it, as does the cartoon-soundtrack skitter down the keyboard that almost seems to be sniggering at her the second time (2.07–2.09). As for the cheerful ba-ba-ba's that replace the words as the chorus repeats at the end (from 3.34), they didn't seem to ask so much as to insist that you joined in with them.

Better still, and at another level of complexity, was 'The Name of the Game', which was released to trail the album at the end of 1977 and became another UK number one. Here, subtly enacted, is the tale of someone demanding to know where they stand, and yet confessing to every shade of vulnerability as they do so. If this had been the only song ABBA had ever released, then surely they *would* have been regarded as cool. It's certainly an amazing piece of song-building. The sultry minor verse, sung high and softly by Agnetha and Frida's twinned voices and decorated with anxious scribbles of electric guitar, gives way (at 0.38) to a more ringingly solo-voiced minor bridge, which then, amid trumpets, opens out at 0.55 into the chorus in a glorious shift from minor to major.

But that chorus then develops into its own second phase (at 1.14), closing down into the minor key again, before in turn standing aside (at 1.29) for yet another discrete section – just voices over a gently pulsing bass drum. And that, too, builds and takes off in its own direction (at 1.51) before the song finally resolves (as ABBA believed every good song should) with the singing of the title.

By this point, it has taken the track two whole minutes to run once through everything that it has to offer. Yet 'The Name of the Game' isn't some kind of bolted-together, 'Bohemian Rhapsody'-like, multi-part Frankenstein's monster, no three-act 'Band on the Run'. It's an entirely integrated, unpretentious, through-written pop song, and no pop composer at this time, one now realises, was anywhere near to operating in this league.

And I won't by any means be the first to point out that the repeatedly climbing bass over the syncopated keyboard in the introduction is Stevie Wonder's 'I Wish' slowed down. But 'spot the influence' is, of course, an easier game to play than 'use the influence'. Apparently, all the members of ABBA adored Wonder's *Songs in the Key of Life*. And so did I, badgering my parents to buy it for me for Christmas in 1976, and playing its four sides and the four-song bonus 7-inch that came with it until their grooves were pretty much planed smooth. But I didn't step away from it and, while it was still fresh in my head, write 'The Name of the Game'. And that, I would now have to acknowledge, is one of the essential differences between me and ABBA. And, I would hazard, between you and ABBA, too.

One other thing about 'The Name of the Game': it's four minutes and fifty-two seconds long. Contrast the 2.45 of 'Waterloo' and the between-three-and-three-and-a-half-minute durations of 'SOS', 'Mamma Mia' and 'Money, Money, Money'. The late '70s had long since shredded the notion of the 'perfect three-minute pop song', and many complained about it at the time, citing grave overindulgence and regrettable pomposity. Punk and new wave were certainly doing their best to speed things up and cut things short again.

But it's hard to argue that there was anything forced or over-long in the way ABBA were occupying those new, wider spaces. On the contrary, on 'The Name of the Game', they seemed to be expanding into them.

44

All together now

And here are ABBA in New York in January 1979. And here is the television presenter David Frost, stepping onto the stage at the United Nations General Assembly to introduce them as they open *The Music for UNICEF Concert: A Gift of Song*, a televised musical spectacular designed to publicise the start of the International Year of the Child and to raise money for UNICEF's world hunger programmes. This night of a thousand stars is going out to seventy countries and will be viewed by 300 million people.

And what we're seeing here, clearly, is the early stirrings of the elite-tier, rock-based charity fundraising boom that will reach its apotheosis six years later with Live Aid. Elton John is on the posters but he doesn't show up. However, the Bee Gees, Rod Stewart and Earth, Wind & Fire have made it, and so have John Denver and Olivia Newton-John.

And so have ABBA. ABBA do 'Chiquitita', having already pledged to donate to the UN Children's Fund half the royalties generated by sales of the single, a gift which will end up being worth about $4 million. The band are all in black and gathered very closely around Benny at a white grand piano on a circular plinth.

And 'Chiquitita' is full-scale, unrepentant schlager-ABBA, with its huge, arms-aloft, singalong, sway-along chorus in which the 'little girl' of the title is resoundingly reassured that everything will be OK, that the grieving and the sense of loss will pass and love will renew and all will be well. As a choice of number goes, on a night when Rod Stewart is turning out 'Da Ya Think I'm Sexy?' and Earth, Wind & Fire are offering 'September', it feels a touch incongruous and behind-the-times, but it seems to work as an anthem for the event and it comes off OK.

At the end of the show, there's one of those whole-cast sing-alongs, a medley which starts with ABBA's 'He Is Your Brother' and then segues into Jackie De Shannon's 'Put a Little Love in Your Heart', at which point it's 'pass the microphone' time. We get some lines from a cheerfully geeky-looking John Denver, and then a few more from Donna Summer. Then Barry Gibb of the Bee Gees, in full disco-god mode, steps to the fore and works the stage with a very blonde Olivia Newton-John. The members of Earth, Wind & Fire pass the baton to Andy Gibb, the rogue Bee Gee brother, who duets a little awkwardly with a kohl-eyed and leopard-printed Rod.

ABBA, off to one side, clap along and smile. There's something odd about seeing them hanging with the stars in this community of pop. It's not as though they haven't earned their place here. In fact, in terms of the mega-wattage of their fame and the scale of their record sales, they could comfortably lord it over most of the people here.

And yet we're so used to seeing them in isolation. All along they've been such a separate entity — musically, stylistically, temperamentally, linguistically — that watching them mix and mingle in chummy, shoulder-patting proximity to pop's glitterati somehow strikes an oddly muffled note; it makes them seem almost vulnerable, in fact. It's as if ABBA are part of this world – at its molten centre, indeed – and yet from somewhere else altogether.

45

Slippery slope

And now come forward a couple of months, to April 1979. To the accompaniment of a Ronnie Hazlehurst-arranged overture (orchestra-buffed glimpses of 'Dancing Queen', 'Mamma Mia', 'Honey, Honey', etc.), a Swissair DC-9 lands in Geneva, and the four members of ABBA de-plane in overcoats, apart from Björn, who is braving the wintry elements today in a green plastic bomber jacket. They cross the runway to a white helicopter, which bears them into the sky and away, eventually bearing down on skier-dotted slopes at the resort of Leysin.

This is *ABBA in Switzerland*, a BBC co-production and an Easter Monday treat for those of us with nothing better to do. It's impossible to overestimate the extent to which ABBA – who have been in our lives for five years at this point – still really only exist for us in Britain as figures from a TV-special netherworld, a place where life is frequently not quite as we know it, drenched in a particularly bleaching kind of electric light and obeying its own laws with regard to things like dress, conversation and facial expressions.

But this is pretty much the only access we get, so we tune in, and – one inexplicable twenty-person dance routine to a boogie-woogie medley later – the band skip out through the curtains in front of a live audience, some of whom are waving Swiss flags to remind us of our location. And, in fairness, television studios set for light entertainment do not readily declare their locations and, with the exception of the occasional Polish staircase, appear to vary little from country to country, so we can be grateful for the prod.

Tonight, we'll get the hits, like 'Take a Chance on Me', and a new song, 'The King Has Lost His Crown', and we'll also get some heavily scripted chatting between songs. The long winter nights of Sweden are referenced and how they leave plenty of time for doing the things the band enjoys (telegraphed joke on the way here) . . . like writing songs! Then Frida and Agnetha introduce one of their favourite groups, whom they say they are very glad to see back together again, and Roxy Music play 'Dance Away' and somehow it's no great surprise to find Bryan Ferry in a posh Alpine ski resort.

Then comes a video sequence shot on the slopes with ABBA very competently skiing while 'The Name of the Game' plays. Later, we will see Björn whipping at great speed around an ice rink. And then we get 'Eagle', with shots of the film star David Niven mysteriously taking part in some kind of hot-air balloon rally. Niven's presence is never explained, except that this is a plush ski resort in the '70s, and he is David Niven, so perhaps we are not even intended to be curious any more than we are about the presence of Bryan Ferry.

After this, Björn and Benny introduce another guest.

'Is it a bird, is it a plane? No, it's a bush . . . Kate Bush.'

Alan Partridge, you should have been living at this hour.

Bush appears in a purple gown, crouching and cowering and

wheeling her arms backwards while singing her latest single, 'Wow'. She is, very much as she tells us, all alone on the stage tonight, but she compensates by diving and churning, making pistol shapes with her fingers, slapping her haunches, widening her eyes, smiling, frowning, grimacing – covering more emotions than most of us will get to express this whole year, and all inside a busy three minutes. As the song says: unbelievable.

Then it's everybody into pink pyjamas for 'Chiquitita', whose opening line gets a burst of audience applause in recognition. Benny, hammering away at a white grand, is up out of his seat, Jerry Lee Lewis-style, for the coda.

And, before long, some children are on the stage, dressed as clowns and cowboys, and 'Thank You for the Music' is being sung and the credits are rolling.

We've been another hour in ABBA's company and I would say we're still none the wiser.

46

The partisans' party

Just before 4.00 p.m. on a Friday afternoon in May 2023, I join a winding queue outside the ABBA Museum in Stockholm and immediately feel a little underdressed. Near me is a woman in white platform boots and another in bright blue velvet trousers, *à la* Agnetha in Brighton in 1974. Someone has come dressed as the *ABBA Gold* sleeve – trim black suit and gold tie – while someone else is in a superb mock-snakeskin onesie.

There are also many satin tour jackets, some from the Voyage show but others marking ABBA's two-week trip round Japan in 1980, their final on-tour performances. These are the members of the International ABBA Fan Club, who generally convene annually in Roosendaal in the Netherlands, but who this year have amassed in the Swedish capital for a special 'ABBA Day' party in honour of the museum's tenth anniversary. My jumper and jeans aren't really cutting it here.

No matter, though. I am an interloper in this company, in any case – an observer, working on a book – and practically an ABBA agnostic by comparison with these true and through-it-all carriers of the ABBA flame. Also, as people around me in this queue happily hug, kiss and enthusiastically reunite, it occurs to me that I am possibly the only person here who doesn't know anybody else. Still, the atmosphere is warm and friendly, and once the doors have opened, we file in, deposit our coats, take one of the offered glasses of sparkling wine or water, and move through into the party room.

The biographer Philip Norman wrote an article for *The Times* not long ago in which he stated: 'I've noticed that the lighter and sweeter the music, the more grimly obsessive are its hardcore fans.'

So, Norman explained, while writing critically about The Beatles and Elton John had brought him reactions at a certain level, nothing had unleashed a deluge of opprobrium upon him quite as much as expressing his opinions and findings with regard to the benign, glasses-wearing, softly rock 'n' rolling Buddy Holly.

Well, maybe defenders of the fragile are just instinctively inclined to deploy extra muscle as they erect their cordons. Dangerous to generalise, of course. But certainly, from my own experience as a reviewer of pop music, fans of, say, Iron Maiden seem more inclined to roll with the punches than fans of, say, Cliff Richard.

And fans of ABBA? Well, I'm about to find out, I guess.

Once everyone's through the door, the ABBA The Museum Choir assemble on the stage and give us an immaculate ten-voice close-harmony medley of ABBA classics. Then Helga van der Kar, the fan club president, warmly welcomes us all along, followed by Ingmarie Halling, the museum's creative director, who also welcomes us and thanks us for our support for ABBA and the museum, and expresses how much she is looking forward to us all seeing the new exhibit on the theme of the ABBA Voyage show.

Then some paper plates of cheese and cut-up vegetables are circulated, and it's karaoke time. Frequently, karaoke seems sent to remind us that being able to sing is a rarer talent than many people imagine. Here, though, with fans taking it in turns to get up onto the stage and seize the mic, some genuinely reputable work gets done, amid some very assured stagecraft which, given that it's still only about 5.30 in the afternoon and nobody is even close to drunk yet, is impressive.

'Gimme! Gimme! Gimme! (A Man After Midnight)' gets some particularly heavy rotation, obviously enough, and 'The Winner Takes It All' is also to be heard multiple times. This is not surprising. Later this year, in the poll of these fans' Top 100 ABBA songs, 'The Winner Takes It All' will come out top. But the cognoscenti would hardly be alone in thinking that. According to a 1999 Channel 5 poll (and nobody has ever disputed the value of those), 'The Winner Takes It All' is Britain's favourite ABBA song and also, according to another poll by the same channel seven years later, Britain's favourite break-up song.

And yet, in terms of its basic underpinning, ABBA never wrote anything simpler. In stark contrast to the complicated plotting we've been noticing elsewhere, 'The Winner Takes It All' gets hold of a simple, standard four-chord progression and simply walks it round and round – through the verse, through the chorus, through the central breakdown, through the outro. It's unvarying. And, consequently, the song seems to end up building this almost hypnotic momentum and its pull becomes relentless. The plotting is left to Agnetha's extraordinary lead vocal. She doesn't want to talk, the song says. But she does want to cry out – long and loud. And her voice gradually climbs the mountain from talking to crying then eventually, as if overcome, she falls silent and, amid perhaps the finest outbreak of Benny's Rachmaninov-style piano pounding on record, lets the choir take it away. It doesn't really get more melodramatic than this in a just-under-five-minute pop song.

There's something mysterious going on with the pace of 'The Winner Takes It All', too. We think of it, probably, as a ballad. Yet after the drums come in, our old friends at songbpm.com measure the track at a positively disco-pulsing 126 beats per minute and rate it 'high energy' and 'somewhat danceable', which, you may remember, was where they placed 'Dancing Queen'.

But dancing is not really what 'The Winner Takes It All' is for, though, is it? The energy under this song seems to be driving something else – a wedge against sadness. It's a song that commands you to stand still, looking wrought but defiant and clutching at the air while the track blows around you.

Well, there's a lot of looking wrought and defiant, and even some clutching at the air, going on at this ABBA Museum karaoke session, and that's for sure. Nevertheless, after perhaps the third or possibly the fourth rendition of 'The Winner Takes It All', I glance at my phone and realise, with a small sinking of the spirit, that more than two hours of further ABBA karaoke stand between me and our promised private access to the exhibits in the museum, which is mostly what I'm here for.

Still, I pass some of the time by circulating. I get to shake hands with Brian Harrifield from Nebraska, who is a legend in ABBA fan circles for having attended eighteen consecutive concerts on ABBA's 1979 North American tour, and for having, at one of those shows, caught a towel thrown from the stage by Frida. This item he selflessly donated to the museum where it continues to reside.

And I talk to a British woman who remembers listening to ABBA songs on Radio Luxembourg and seeing the 'Knowing Me, Knowing You' video and wanting to experience snow like that because it didn't look like the kind of snow you ever got in Britain, and who recalls going to a boy's house because he had a copy of 'The Winner Takes It All' on 12-inch single with a *pop-up sleeve* and how could you not want to be close to someone with one of those? And she tells me that ABBA are about her childhood, first and foremost, and that these ABBA events are like a bridge which takes her straight back there and away from (and these are her words) 'the crap of now'.

And I talk to a woman who grew up in communist East Berlin during the days of the Berlin Wall, and who became an ABBA fan when she heard 'Ring Ring' on the radio. 'I thought – *Wow! What IS this?*' Soon after, she caught what she remembers as the band's solitary East German television appearance and was hooked. You could get Bulgarian or Polish pressings of some of the records, but what you really needed was a retired person. Retired people had easier access to West Berlin than most, so she would send a retired relative through the Wall with a shopping list and her scant pocket money and her complicated instructions: check the B-side of the single and if it's a track that hasn't already appeared on an album, please buy it. If it's an album track, please don't.

In 1989, on the night the wall came down, she knew nothing about it. She was preparing a presentation for her university students and had the radio and the television off in order to concentrate. The next day, a friend took her through a gap in the wall to the West. What struck her was the smell: they used a different kind of petrol there. She changed some money to

West German marks and bought a Walkman with a microphone and built-in speakers.

And I explain to someone from Denmark that I'm going to write a book about ABBA and they shrug and say they can't really see the point because ABBA books are all the same, re-cycling the same old stuff, and none of them tell them anything they don't already know. I try to rally and say that maybe I'm going to try to write a book which isn't for the die-hard ABBA fans first and foremost – those who have long since made their peace with being interested in the band, or more likely never had to make peace with it in the first place – but is more for people who find they have had the members of ABBA and their music in their heads, on and off, practically all their lives without really trying, and might be curious about how that's come to happen.

They shrug again.

Ah, well. I'm keen to know how these fans see these four people who they know so intimately, but don't actually know – these four people who are so present in their lives, without actually being in their lives. So I ask about the characters of these ABBA members, as the fan club members perceive them.

What about Benny, for instance?

Loveable, people seem to think. Easy-going. A little distant, maybe – lost in music. Still out there doing it, with Benny Andersson's Orkester, a Swedish roots band. Benny, whose grandfather and father both played the accordion, who got his own accordion at six, and whose grandfather taught him the song 'Där Näckrosen Blommar' ('Where the Water-Lily Blooms'), which was pretty hard for little hands unless you took it slowly. Benny, whose summer highlight without fail was sitting on the porch and playing with those two grown-ups.

Benny, the global pop star who was moved by nothing as greatly as he was moved by the kind of Swedish folk music you could play on a porch.

And Björn?

Funny. Clever. The brains of the operation, the one looking after the ABBA brand. Also remote and a little hard to read, it's true. But would have got more credit for being the kind of pop star he was, maybe, if the band had happened a decade later, in the '80s, when the image of the elite recording artist as a savvy businessperson in control of their own destiny enjoyed some kind of vogue. Amazing lyricist, of course. Amazing composer.

And Frida? The survivor. Frida, who lost her husband, Prince Heinrich Russo, to pancreatic cancer in 1999 after seven years of marriage. Frida, whose thirty-year-old daughter was killed in a car accident in 1998. Yet still standing strong – a great woman. Tough for her, of course, having been, ridiculously, 'the other one' in the partnership with Agnetha; tough for her being five years older than her band-partner at a stage in their lives when five years really amounted to a proper age difference. But look how she came through it, look how she always stood tall, look how often, in the clips and photos, she seems to be the one having the most fun.

And what about Agnetha?

One woman tells me that she used to go with some other ABBA fans and stand on the road at the end of the drive to Agnetha's house in the country outside Stockholm in the hope of catching a glimpse of her. And one day Agnetha drove up, pulled over, wound down her window and spoke to them.

'She was nice,' this fan says. 'No photos. But nice.'

Then she quickly adds, 'This was in 1995, before the stalker. We stopped after that.'

Ah, yes: the stalker. In 2000, a Dutch forklift truck operator was convicted on ten counts of harassment, served with a restraining order and deported from Sweden. In 2003, having violated the restraining order, he was given a suspended prison sentence and deported again. He had bought a property near Agnetha's and bombarded her with letters and gifts. She responded to his attentions but then asked him to stop and leave her alone, at which point (according to reports of the case) he continued to follow her, appeared outside her window at night, sent her a newspaper clipping about a saga of jealousy that had led to bloodshed, and at one point drove in circles around her car outside a supermarket.

Agnetha, then: a little fragile, a little vulnerable, in need of protection. But a truly great pop star who always wanted to put the important things first: children, home. Painted by the press now as a recluse, but that's the press. Not a recluse, just very private. Agnetha, who was married and divorced a second time, whose mother took her own life in 1994 and who lost her father just a year later. Agnetha, also emphatically a survivor.

And all of these impressions, as I gather them, seem rich and humane and perfectly plausible to me, although, of course, they're based on a glimpse here, a photo grabbed there, and so much of it is conjecture, really, and projection, and we could be talking about characters in a TV show.

Here's one thing, though: the story of these ABBA fans, at least, is a story with an uncomplicatedly happy ending. There must have been times down the years when these fan club gatherings felt like a rare safe space for a love that dared not speak its name. But these people weathered all that and watched the rest of the world come round to a position closer to their own – a position in which ABBA were international treasures, indispensable music-makers, highly reputable craftspeople. And then, on top of that, they got the reunion that even the most wildly optimistic among them had learned to stop dreaming about.

Moreover, the reunion didn't let them down. Two songs from the 2021 *Voyage* album are in the top ten in that members' poll of ABBA songs: the bouncy comeback single 'Don't Shut Me Down', which is at number four, and the theatrical ballad, 'I Still Have Faith in You', which is at number eight. And, yes, there might be a little recent-uptake bias going on in those results, but I could be persuaded to agree with those voters about the value of the second of those songs. 'I Still Have Faith in You' would slide effortlessly onto *ABBA Gold*.

These fans would have imagined themselves gathering to mark the accumulating anniversaries of receding events, toasting ever dimmer memories, blowing on the weakening embers of their increasingly antique obsession. And then, entirely out of nowhere, forty years on, the band regroups, brings them a whole new album of material and a remarkable concert to go to. It's a story out of ABBA fanfic.

Well, OK, not quite, because most of the ABBA fanfic that I've seen (and there's a lot of it out there) tends to feature plots in which Björn and Agnetha tearfully rekindle their love in the vicinity of an open fire, while, nearby, and often in the same room, Frida and Benny exchange a forgiving look, glide into each other's arms and begin to dance. (The longing for an ABBA reunion takes on a slightly more thorough-going form in the world of ABBA fanfic.)

But even so, it's quite the most satisfying conclusion. In this case, the winners really have taken it all and what's not to enjoy about being a fully-paid-up, card-carrying ABBA fan in 2024?

When I leave, midway through the evening, after a nice long look around the museum, the karaoke is still raging.

47

Ears of cloth

'Super Trouper' came out in November 1980. The band had the title for the album and they had an unfinished track in the stockpile and they found that quite by chance the proposed title metrically fitted the song. Bingo. It was another huge hit all around the world, and a number one single in the UK – the band's last one of those.

And I thought it was ridiculous. Or, at least, *Not the Nine O'Clock News* thought it was ridiculous. And as a consequence, I, too, thought it was ridiculous, because this was a time in my life when it seemed important to be on the same side as *Not the Nine O'Clock News*.

Attracting adamantine support across the nation's sixth forms, BBC2's weekly satirical sketch show was one of those rare comedy programmes with its own bible: *Not!*, a spin-off book designed to look like a parody of the short-lived news magazine *Now!*, and seeming to hold the same mesmerising and potentially cult-inducing qualities that *The Brand New Monty Python Bok* had held for those who came to it in 1973.

So, one Monday night in December 1980, when an episode of the show closed with the ABBA parody 'Supa Dupa' (composed by Howard Goodall and Richard Curtis), complete with thoroughly gross Vaseline-lensed video, I duly fell in line. There was Pamela Stephenson pretending to be Agnetha (and picking her nose in close-up); there was Rowan Atkinson, the future Mr Bean, pretending to be Björn; there was a bearded Mel Smith doubling really rather easily as Benny; and there was Griff Rhys-Jones pretending to be Frida. Such images could affect a teenage mind. I was eighteen and it seemed to me that ABBA had just been irreparably run over by a satirical juggernaut. And, in a really quite appallingly disloyal severance with my own not-so-distant past, I also seemed to be entirely OK with that.

'One of us is ugly, one of us is cute,' they sang. 'One of us you'd like to see in her birthday suit.'

Also: 'We believe that if you have three tunes in a song / And a showbiz cliché, nothing can go wrong.'

ABBA, of course, I would eventually come back round to. And obviously that three-tunes-plus-cliché formula is WILDLY INADEQUATE. But 'Super Trouper' still hasn't recovered. Or not for me, anyway.

I was obviously dissuaded from listening to it properly, too. I mean, it was everywhere at the time, and you can hardly say it has been completely out of sight in the intervening years. Yet right until I started doing this book, I thought the chorus of this song went: 'And like a Super Trouper, dreams are going to find me.'

It doesn't. And why would it? That doesn't mean anything.

No, it's about the Super Trouper's *beams*, and how, tonight, they're going to find you, Super Trouper being the name of a theatrical spotlight, such as might pick out a singer on a stage. And the song, of course, being about feeling worn down by life on the road, but then finding energy again in the knowledge that that special person is out there in the audience, watching you.

Well, *obviously*.

Another cloth-eared admission, though. They're mounting up here.

But it's not only me. I've just asked my wife if she knows what a Super Trouper is. She knows the song – of course she knows the song; who *doesn't* know the song? – and could sing along with it, if challenged to. But did she actually know what the song was on about?

'Is it something to do with space?' she said.

'What, like a supernova, you mean?'

'No, like in *Star Wars*.'

'Stormtroopers?'

'Maybe.'

Sometimes in that place in your head where you think pop songs are, there's just nonsense. You carry these songs around with you your whole life, and then it turns out you've barely even heard them.

48

Grief and artificial sunsets

On 26 May 2023, one year to the night after it opened, I go with my wife to see ABBA Voyage. I want to see the show again because I'm writing this book, but I'm also keen to know if it was as good as I remember it from the opening night. I'm wondering how much the emotions it stirred up in 2022 were coloured by the experience of watching it in the presence of the actual ABBA, and whether the generally glitzy 'Oooh, look there's Kylie!' nature of the evening turned my head.

In order to create scrupulously neutral conditions for this important experiment, I've booked the same pair of seats I was given for the opening. And although the live band present some potential variables, the ABBA-tars, as I understand it, will be delivering exactly the same show, word-for-word. So, all in all, I'm banking on being able to form a conclusion that stands up lastingly to scientific scrutiny.

(Good job, by the way, that I didn't book for the day after this. Frida, Benny and Björn turned up and waved from their seats in a special appearance to mark the show's first anniversary. This was entirely their right, of course, and no doubt thrilling for everyone in the audience, but I'm glad they butted out on the night I was there. They would have completely ruined my experiment.)

As we head for our places, I spot in the distance one of the ABBA superfans I saw in Stockholm just a few weeks earlier, the guy in the tremendous faux snakeskin onesie. And it would by no means be going out on a limb to suggest that he's been to ABBA Voyage before. All of the fans I spoke to in Stockholm had seen the show more than once. Some had clocked up five or six visits and were planning more.

But, in this particular guy's case, I think you would know anyway, because he's walking towards the auditorium with a kind of forward-leaning purposefulness, and with a speed and manner very different from everyone else's slightly hesitant shuffles. It's the kind of walk you might adopt while heading directly to the milk aisle in a familiar supermarket, or on the way back into the office after lunch. He's clocking on, ready to sling his jacket over the back of his seat, log on to his terminal and get back at it – another day at the ABBA coalface.

We, too, take our seats, and Round Two (for me) begins. And, yes, I enjoy the glimmering lights behind the snowy forest backdrop again, experience another nostalgic surge at the sight of the band's four figures in silhouette, re-spend the first couple of songs feeling slightly weirded out and perplexed by questions about what, exactly, we're watching, only for those questions somehow to re-evaporate and the pleasure to re-kick in. And yes, I'm obliged to conclude that the show does indeed go to work on your emotions, even in the absence of Frida, Benny, Kylie, etc.

Indeed, one moment hits me even harder than it did the first time. And it happens during, of all things, 'Chiquitita'.

Let it lie for a decade or four, and 'Chiquitita' can easily file itself away in your memory under F for 'flim-flam: '70s, piece thereof.' We'd been here before with ABBA and the flamenco guitar and the Spanish flavourings, had we not? It's famously the case that practically nothing in the ABBA catalogue after 1975 sounds like anything else in the ABBA catalogue. So that made this song a rare instance – possibly even the only instance – of ABBA opening themselves to the accusation of self-plagiarism by those who felt that 'Chiquitita' was basically 'Fernando 2' – the little sister, if you will, of 'Fernando'.

And I don't know: maybe you need to have some grief under your belt before a song about grief and trying to get beyond grief can really have its way with you. But returning to this track after all those years of casually dismissive neglect, it was revelatory to me just how *passionate* it is, how much it lacks, in fact, any trace of either flim *or* flam. And as so often, it's about those voices most of all. As Björn once said, regarding the effect of Frida's mezzo stretching after Agnetha's soprano: 'There's a metal in the sound and you can hear it from far away.' Indeed, and it was startling to me, listening anew, how much of that metal is in 'Chiquitita', how hard the voices push in the chorus, the force with which they do their consoling, swollen with defiance.

Try convincing me of any of this when 'Chiquitita' came out, though, back at the beginning of 1979. By that point, punk rock had blown through and new wave had arrived right behind it, and I was listening on repeat to XTC's *Go 2*, their second album, which I'd acquired, just as I had their first, from Parrot Records, a tiny, grimy-windowed independent store in Colchester's Balkerne Passage with informed and deeply scornful staff. Just entering in a school blazer, let alone carrying a sleeve to the counter to buy it, took courage at elite-mountaineering levels.

But I was bracing myself and buying, in the same shop, singles like 'Milk and Alcohol' by Dr Feelgood, who I went to see at Essex University, and 'Sound of the Suburbs' by The Members, and 'Hit Me With Your Rhythm Stick' by Ian Dury & the Blockheads, and 'Hong Kong Garden' by Siouxsie and the Banshees, and, in the latter case, getting intrigued by the idea that you could write a song about a Chinese takeaway in Chislehurst High Street, because somehow, at that point in time, that seemed a nobler and more urgent calling than writing a song with flamenco guitar in it about someone who might have been as far away as South America and who was enchained by her own sorrow, of all the dull things.

And would Siouxsie, Agnetha and Frida get along if you put the three of them in a room together? Well, maybe they would, but there would be certain stylistic differences, for sure – in the hair department for one, and the eye make-up department for another, and the wardrobe for a third. And heard in the shadow of Siouxsie and the Banshees . . . well, I'm sorry, but ABBA's 'Chiquitita' sounded like the kind of music you might buy in Woolworth or WH Smith and I was busily conditioning myself to sneer richly at the very idea of such proletarian shopping.

I had moved on, in short. New pastures, new sounds. New knitwear, too, now I mention it: mohair things, anything a bit straggly or a bit wiry. And black drainpipe jeans. And baseball boots.

Yes, I had moved on. And if you had asked me, I would have told you firmly that, no: I couldn't see myself going back.

And now here I am, forty-four years later, at ABBA Voyage, for the second time, watching not even ABBA but a *simulation* of ABBA sing this song about heartache, scars, grieving and the longed-for release from grieving. I'm also watching a very artfully realised total eclipse of the sun, which is the backdrop for this number, the room glowing orange and then slowly falling dark as the song plays, which is quite something.

And, you see, the thing is, everyone at ABBA Voyage sings along to the chorus of 'Chiquitita'. That's the point of it – they all just pile in. They pile in on it like you wouldn't believe, raising their arms and swaying.

And here's something else to which my attitude has clearly changed with age: people singing along at concerts. I used to hate that. Audience participation! 'I haven't come here to hear *us* sing, I've come here to hear *you* sing. Get on with it!' But now – and I can't really tell you why – I just find it moving. I mean, properly moving.

I went to see the French band Phoenix not long ago at the Brixton Academy. They opened with 'Lisztomania' and immediately turned the first chorus over to the audience, who needed no invitation and sang it for them, word-perfect. I was in bits. Went to see Jacob Collier at the same venue. He came out and straight away converted the audience into a choir. Same thing: bits.

So I'm slightly vulnerable in advance, I guess. But then there's 'Chiquitita' itself, and all the things I mentioned above about 'Chiquitita' – the power of the singing, the defiance of grief in it, the iron nature of its consolation, the stuff in that song that I wouldn't and couldn't have got to with any amount of effort in 1979.

·   And it is just so extraordinary how this manifestly artificial, openly fake show ends up evoking so much in the way of *feelings*. In an interview, Ludvig Andersson, the show's co-producer, attributed that ostensibly unlikely outcome to the blurring of 'the borderline between real and fantasy worlds', and how the show's peculiar position between those borders 'triggers feelings about youth and ageing, mortality and immortality'.

And there seems to me to be a lot of truth in that, and especially at this exact point in the show, when the sun is disappearing before our eyes and the audience has got hold of that chorus, and I mean, *really* got hold of it, and the whole place is a sea of arms in this gradually darkening room, and two of my brothers are dead and, oh, for god's sake, now I'm crying in the middle of ABBA's bloody 'Chiquitita'.

49

Portrait of the artists

The morning after the ABBA Museum's tenth anniversary party, I head to Skansen, Stockholm's expansive open-air museum and family playground, pick up a map and make my way to a yellow-painted clapboard hut tucked under the trees down a side path. This building was once the studio of the Swedish painter Julius Kronberg (1850–1921), but is probably more famous for being the setting for the shadowy group portrait on the sleeve of ABBA's final album, 1981's *The Visitors*. That's certainly what will be bringing ABBA fans to the site throughout today, in groups of twenty, some of them looking a little worse for karaoke, but all of them keen to take part in this ABBA weekend's final act of homage.

Our chaperone here will be Osva who, in common with all the public-facing staff at Skansen, wears a traditional Swedish costume – in her case, a floor-length pale green smock dress and a straw boater with a green ribbon tied around it. My group gathers in a loose horseshoe-shape on the uneven grass. At our feet, a sleeping duck briefly untucks its head from its wing, decides it has seen and heard it all before, and tucks its head back under again.

Osva gestures to the bust of Kronberg mounted beside the building. 'Here he is in person,' she says. 'The one you came to see – or maybe not, I suppose.'

I'm pretty sure at first that this is a joke, but it's delivered so dryly that it could equally well be a chastisement – like, you philistines are here for *the wrong thing*. Moreover, as Osva continues with her deftly etched outline of Kronberg's life and times, his marriage and his children, his death in 1921 and his gift to the city of this two-room atelier . . . well, I begin to wonder whether she has entirely missed her audience, despite the clues being offered by the usual hats and satin tour jackets.

But then we go inside, and I realise that I have got Osva completely wrong. There are two rooms here, and Kronberg's actual skylit studio with an easel in it is visible through an open door. But that's going to get about as much attention from this particular group as the floor of the Sistine Chapel or whatever is hanging opposite the *Mona Lisa* in the Louvre. So Osva walks us right past it into the adjacent sitting room, hung with Kronberg's giant painting of Eros wreathed in fiery clouds, and taps on an iPad. While we all stand silently, the strains of ABBA's 'Like an Angel Passing Through My Room', from *The Visitors*, plays thinly into the curtained gloom. Osva lets it drift away and, with the appropriate mood firmly set, tells the story we've come to hear: about how it was a late November afternoon, cold and dark in Stockholm; about how cameras and lights were set up in the Kronberg studio; about how the Skansen staff had been told that someone important was about to descend on the park, but weren't told who.

Finally, a black car swept in and drove along the path to the atelier and Björn Ulvaeus climbed out. After a short interval, two further black cars arrived, bearing Frida Lyngstad and Agnetha Fältskog. Last to arrive was Benny Andersson, significantly late.

The room remained cold. As instructed by the photographer, the four took their separate positions under the painting. The camera clicked and almost as soon as ABBA had arrived, ABBA had left again in their separate cars, leaving behind one of the oddest and most remote-looking album portraits ever to be published by a pop group on the eve of its disintegration.

50

Transmission ends

And here are ABBA a year after that, in 1982, with Noel Edmonds in a camel-coloured sports jacket, on *The Late Late Breakfast Show*. Here they are, compliantly taking their seats together on the studio sofa to promote an ABBA singles compilation, Benny and Björn in suits and ties, Agnetha and Frida in knee-length knitted dresses and long black boots: Björn at thirty-seven; Benny at thirty-five, nearing thirty-six; Frida, her hair tinted purple now, a week short of her thirty-seventh birthday; Agnetha at thirty-two.

And is this excruciating because of the tensions that seem so clearly to be crackling between them across the cushions, or just because these semi-rehearsed conversations in primetime promo-land are *always* excruciating?

'I find it really difficult to believe that it's ten years that you're celebrating now,' says Edmonds. 'And the papers, recently, there have been stories that you're going to split – eventually.'

Björn waves a dismissive hand. Benny sits with his arms folded. Frida concentrates on a distant point across the studio. Agnetha smiles wanly.

'It would be more of a feeling, I think,' says Björn, 'because when we were recording an album, we would feel that it's not fun anymore, we haven't got anything more to give. And that would be the time to split.'

'We should have done that a long time ago,' says Benny. Everybody on the sofa laughs a little.

Edmonds asks them to 'play us out'. Benny gets up and moves a few feet to a Fender Rhodes piano, Björn picks up an acoustic guitar and sits on the arm of the sofa. A competition-winner called Kevin materialises next to Edmonds, ready to clap along. They play 'Thank You for the Music'. Agnetha seems merely casually involved until she hits the line about everyone listening when she starts to sing, at which point she opens up loud and shows that she can inhabit it even now. Frida encourages the audience to join in.

But they've run out of time and the credits are already rolling and even before they reach the chorus, the transmission ends and the programme cuts.

And that's ABBA all but gone, and this is pop music in the '80s and everybody knows that, in that game, when you're gone there's no coming back.

ACKNOWLEDGEMENTS

Thank you to Gill, Joanna and Paul, my hot dates at the opening night of ABBA Voyage, where this book got going. And thank you to Paddy for encouragement, thoughtfulness and the soupçon of Saint-Saëns.

It's a privilege to be commissioned and edited by Holly Harris. And thank you to everyone else at Simon & Schuster who has worked on this book, most particularly Alex Eccles, Jess Barratt, Sarah Jeffcoate, Alison Macdonald, Zoe Maple, Hannah Paget, Nige Tassell, Clare Wallis, Pip Watkins and Suzanne Baboneau.

Thank you, constantly, to my friend and agent, Georgia Garrett.

And thank you most of all to Sabine, Barney, Joe and Mabel, who have heard more ABBA emanating from my devices these past months than they might have hoped to, but who never once complained about it.

A NOTE ON SOURCES

Anybody who attempts a telling of the ABBA story ends up accruing a massive debt to Carl Magnus Palm, ABBA's Boswell, whose exemplary books, articles and sleeve notes about the band are the primary sources for all ABBA scholarship, not least my own stab at it here, particularly his biography *Bright Lights, Dark Shadows* and the immensely clear-sighted piece of work that is *ABBA: The Complete Recording Sessions*. I have also very much enjoyed and been inspired by Christopher Patrick's unique *ABBA: Let the Music Speak*, and I was grateful to the author for conversation by email during the writing of this book. I took great pleasure seeking clarification and memory jogs in *ABBA: The Official Photo Book, ABBA The Museum: The Souvenir Book* and, of course, all over the place on YouTube. The sole work of autobiography by an ABBA member thus far is *As I Am: ABBA Before & Beyond* by Agnetha Fältskog with Brita Åhman, and naturally I feasted on that.

The official International ABBA Fan Club publishes an excellent quarterly magazine which I love for many reasons, not least its adoption of the format of the old *Beatles Book* fan periodical; I drew extensively on its back issues here, and I am grateful to the club's president, Helga van der Kar, for answering my queries. My research trip to Sweden wouldn't have been half as much fun without my copy of Sara Russell's *The ABBA Guide to Stockholm*. ABBA's TV appearances are superbly curated online by Russell on the website abbaontv.com, and their concerts are similarly registered in style by the website abba-theconcerts.de. I shopped for ABBA vinyl where all good people satisfy their second-hand record needs: The Record Album in Terminus Road, Brighton.

IMAGE CREDITS

1. TT News Agency/Alamy Stock Photo; Archive PL/Alamy Stock Photo; TT News Agency/Alamy Stock Photo; Classic Picture Library/Alamy Stock Photo

2. TT News Agency/Alamy Stock Photo; K & K Ulf Kruger OHG/Getty

3. TT News Agency/Alamy Stock Photo; Roger Tillberg/Alamy Stock Photo; Jan Persson/Getty

4. Gems/Getty; courtesy of the author; Rolls Press/Popperfoto/Getty; John Downing/Stringer/Getty

5. Bengt H. Malmqvist © Premium Rockshot; courtesy of the author; Keystone Press/Alamy Stock Photo; TT News Agency/Alamy Stock Photo

6. Jan Persson/Getty; courtesy of the author; David Redfern/Staff/Getty

7. ullstein bild Dtl./Getty; TT News Agency/Alamy Stock Photo

8. PA Images/Alamy Stock Photo; Stephen Chung/Alamy Stock Photo